# ESCAPE

### *from the* LAND

## OF SNOWS

# ESCAPE

## *from the* LAND

## OF SNOWS

THE YOUNG DALAI LAMA'S

HARROWING FLIGHT TO FREEDOM

AND THE MAKING OF A SPIRITUAL HERO

Stephan Talty

CROWN PUBLISHERS
NEW YORK

Library of Congress Cataloging-in-Publication Data
Talty, Stephan.
Escape from the land of snows: the young Dalai Lama's harrowing flight
to freedom and the making of a spiritual hero / Stephan Talty.—1st ed.
1. Bstan-'dzin-rgya-mtsho, Dalai Lama XIV, 1935– —Childhood and
youth.   2. Escapes—China—Tibet.   I. Title.
BQ7935.B777T36 2010
294.3'923092—dc22                    2010019827
[B]

ISBN 978-0-307-46095-0
eISBN 978-0-307-46097-4

Printed in the United States of America

*Design by Maria Elias*
*Maps by Jeffrey L. Ward*
*Cover design: Jennifer O'Connor*
*Cover photographs: Superstock (mountains); Matthieu Ricard/Getty Images*

10  9  8  7  6  5  4  3  2  1

First Edition

For Karen and Suraiya

At the bottom of patience is Heaven.

—Tibetan proverb

# CONTENTS

# KEY PERSONS

Here is a list of the people who are featured in the following pages. A handful of Tibetan words and phrases are also used in the book. If at any time you're unclear about these terms, please consult the glossary on page 263.

**Athar:** Athar Norbu (also known as Lithang Athar), a Khampa guerrilla trained by the CIA and reinserted into Tibet as a conduit to the resistance.

**Noel Barber:** The foreign correspondent for London's *Daily Mail* in 1959.

**Barshi:** Barshi Ngawang Tenkyong, a junior official at the Norbulingka who on March 9, 1959, spread rumors of threats to the Dalai Lama.

**Choegyal:** Tendzin Choegyal, the Dalai Lama's younger brother, recognized as the high lama Ngari Rimpoche.

**Choekyong Tsering:** The Dalai Lama's father.

**Diki Tsering:** The Dalai Lama's mother.

**Gadong:** The second-most important oracle in Tibet, after the Nechung.

**John Greaney:** The deputy head of the CIA's Tibetan Task Force in 1959.

**Gyalo:** Gyalo Thondup, the Dalai Lama's second-oldest brother, who escaped from Tibet in 1952 and later acted as a conduit to the American government.

**Heinrich Harrer:** Austrian SS member and soldier in the German army during World War II who escaped a British colonial prison camp in India and fled to Tibet. Author of *Seven Years in Tibet*.

**Ken Knaus:** A member of the CIA's Tibetan Task Force. Later, author of *Orphans of the Cold War: America and the Tibetan Struggle for Survival*.

**Ketsing Rimpoche:** Abbott and leader of the Amdo search party for the Fourteenth Dalai Lama.

**Lhamo Thondup:** The first given name of the Fourteenth Dalai Lama.

**Lhotse:** A Khampa guerrilla trained by the CIA. Athar's partner in their surveillance and reporting on the resistance.

**Lobsang Samden:** One of the Dalai Lama's older brothers.

**Mao Zedong:** The chairman of the Chinese Communist Party and leader of the People's Republic of China, 1949–76.

**Narkyid:** Ngawang Thondup Narkyid, monk official on the Council of Lhasa. Later, the Tibetan language biographer of the Thirteenth Dalai Lama.

**Nechung:** The state oracle of Tibet.

**Ngabö:** Ngawang Jigme, a progressive *kalön* who served as Tibet's governor-general during the Chinese invasion of 1950 and later served within the post-1959 government.

**Norbu:** Thubten Jigme Norbu, the Dalai Lama's eldest brother.

**George Patterson:** Scottish doctor, religious seeker, and Tibetan activist who worked as a correspondent for London's *Daily Telegraph*.

**Panchen Lama:** The second-highest-ranking lama, or religious authority, in Tibet, after the Dalai Lama. In 1959, the Panchen Lama was the former Lobsang Trinley (1938–89).

**Phala:** The Dalai Lama's Lord Chamberlain, who controlled all access to His Holiness.

**Reting Rimpoche:** The Dalai Lama's first regent, 1933–41. He died in prison under mysterious circumstances after unsuccessfully attempting to regain power in 1944–45.

**Shan Chao:** A Chinese diarist in Lhasa in 1959 who kept a record of the uprising.

**Soepa:** Tenpa Soepa, a junior official at the Norbulingka in 1959.

**Yonten:** Lobsang Yonten, scion of a prominent nationalist family and a protester during the 1959 rebellion. Later, a member of the security staff of the Tibetan government-in-exile.

**Zhou Enlai:** The first premier of the People's Republic of China, serving from 1949 to 1976.

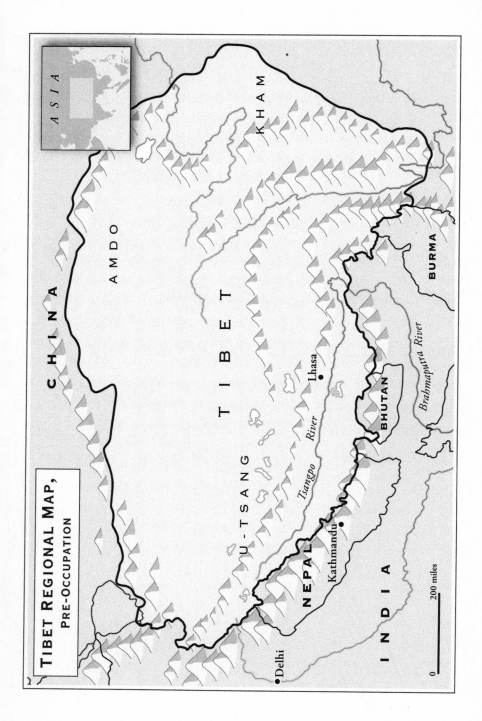

TIBET REGIONAL MAP,
PRE-OCCUPATION

ASIA

CHINA

AMDO

KHAM

TIBET

U-TSANG

Lhasa

Tsangpo River

BHUTAN

Brahmaputra River

BURMA

NEPAL

Kathmandu

INDIA

Delhi

0        200 miles

# INTRODUCTION

Early one morning in March 1959, His Holiness the Fourteenth Dalai Lama walked slowly along a gravel path that led away from his small home at the Norbulingka, his beloved summer palace. The air just after first light still carried a snap of cold that reached from the Himalayas, and the sun was only now beginning to warm the breeze. This was his favorite time to walk the grounds, after rising for prayers and breakfast at 5:00 a.m., when everything was still. Against a sky beginning to lighten, the leaves of the palace trees—poplar and willow, mostly—fairly pulsed green. It was the Dalai Lama's lucky color.

He was deep in thought, and then deep in the effort to avoid thinking. When he lifted his head he could spot thrushes and willow warblers and even an English kingfisher as they swung through the branches and then out over the two thick walls that surrounded the palace's 160 acres. The Norbulingka, three miles outside the capital city, Lhasa, was the place the Dalai Lama felt most at home.

As the Dalai Lama walked, he could hear the calls of his pet monkey, which was tethered to a stick in another part of the Jewel Park. If he was lucky, he would spot the musk deer that roamed the grounds, along with cranes, a Mongolian camel, and high-stepping peacocks. He could also hear the occasional burst of gunfire that echoed outside the walls. Out there, thousands of his fellow Tibetans were camped, guarding against what they thought were conspiracies to kill or abduct him. There were, the Dalai Lama was convinced, no conspiracies, but that didn't change the power or the direction of the uprising that was gathering in the streets of Lhasa. The crowds would not let him leave, and their very presence was inciting the Chinese, who had occupied the country, or retaken it from a corrupt, intriguing elite, if you asked them, nine years earlier.

The past few days, since the uprising had begun, had run together in a "dizzying, frightening blur." The Norbulingka couldn't have appeared more serene as it took on its new greenery, but it seemed that the future of Tibet was spinning out of control just outside its walls. The Dalai Lama felt that he was caught "between two volcanoes." But there were actually more than two sides; the Tibetans themselves were divided. As was his own mind, particularly on the question of what to do now: stay in Lhasa, or flee to a safe haven in the south, or even on to India itself?

As the thin monk, just twenty-three years old, usually luminous with energy, paced slowly along the path, he was successfully avoiding returning to his small whitewashed palace, especially the Audience Hall, where he held his meetings. (It was even furnished with chairs and tables instead of Tibetan cushions, as an optimistic nod to the foreign diplomats he'd hoped to welcome, but the Chinese allowed few visitors.) Bad news was all that arrived there these days. The Chinese official Tan Guansan, one of the leading officials on the influential Tibet Work Commission, had made a point of coming to see him over the past few months, and the confrontations had become increasingly ugly. And for months the Dalai Lama had been receiving messengers arriving from Lhasa and beyond with stories of Chinese atrocities against his people—beheadings, disembowelments, accounts of monasteries burned with monks inside them—that were so outlandishly brutal that he had to admit he himself didn't believe them all. "They were almost beyond the capacity of my imagination," the Dalai Lama remembered. It simply wasn't possible for human beings to treat one another that way. Now new reports were coming in daily through the gates of the Norbulingka, watched not only by his bodyguards and Tibetan army troops but also by representatives of "the people's committee," a bewildering concept in Tibet, which had been ruled for centuries by aristocrats and abbots, under the authority of the Dalai Lama himself. These bulletins told him that the Chinese were bringing artillery and reinforcements into Lhasa and installing snipers on the rooftops of his restive city. He could sometimes feel the rumble of tanks' diesel engines as the vehicles negotiated the narrow streets.

What he was trying to avoid thinking of as he walked was the dream he'd had last year. He'd seen massacres in his mind, Tibetan men, women, and children being shot and killed by Chinese troops and his lovely Norbulingka turned into a "killing ground." This he kept to himself. (But some of his subjects would later report they had had the same dream at the very same time.) He knew that such scenes, if they were allowed to unfold in Lhasa, would be the prelude to something much larger. "I feared a massive, violent reprisal which could end up destroying the whole nation," the Dalai Lama said.

Lhasa (whose name means "place of the gods") had first appeared to him as a city of wonders. Almost twenty years before, he'd entered the capital on a golden palanquin constructed of a curtained box set on poles carried by teams of young men, with massive crowds cheering his approach and bowing to him with the ceremonial *katas*, or white scarves, in their hands. "There was an unforgettable scent of wildflowers," recalled the Dalai Lama. "I could hear [the people] crying, 'The day of our happiness has come.'" But it hadn't. In fact, during his reign, disaster had followed disaster. Men in the east of the country were now being "driven into barbarism," forced to fight the Chinese and dying in the battles, ensuring themselves a rebirth as lower animals and demons. And Lhasa too was growing unstable.

The sun was climbing over the small mountains to the east. Soon he would have to return to the palace.

Perhaps what was most shocking about what had happened in the past few days was that the idea of escape wasn't entirely repugnant to him. It would be devastating to his people, for whom he was Kundun, the Presence, the spirit of Tibet itself. It would be equally devastating for the nation, for the idea of an independent Tibet, and it cut at his heart to contemplate what it would mean for the future. But it wouldn't necessarily be devastating to *him*. The notion of escape had always appealed to the Dalai Lama, ever since he was a boy in the Amdo hills, before the search party seeking the next incarnation of Chenrizi—the deity that manifested itself in each successive Dalai Lama—had knocked on his parents' door. When he was only two, he would pack a small bag, tie it to a stick, and tell his mother he was leaving for Lhasa. He had always been an unusual boy, but those moments astonished her. And twenty years later, the idea of leaving still intrigued him. He knew that freedom of the kind he had tasted only briefly in his life was impossible in Tibet. Even without the occupation, Lhasa for a young Dalai Lama was often a dark and suffocating passageway.

He didn't wish to leave, nor was it even clear that he could if he wanted to. Some 40,000 Chinese troops were stationed in and around Lhasa, and he'd have to be spirited past their patrols. And if he did flee, Tibet, in a way, vanished from Tibet. He was central to every Tibetan's sense of his or her own life in a way that no other leader, not even Mao in China—Mao, who was finally revealing himself in these horrible days—could equal. He was the storehouse of the Buddhist Dharma, a subject that had once bored him profoundly but that now quickened his every thought. Was it possible that that too could disappear from his country, from the earth itself?

The Dalai Lama took the path that turned and wound back toward his home on the Norbulingka grounds. He could hear the crowds stirring outside. The chants would begin soon. He didn't hurry.

*One*

# AN EXAMINATION OF
# PRIOR MEMORIES

little more than twenty-five years earlier, on the morning of December 12, 1933, hundreds of excited monks had milled around one of the open, stone-floored courtyards of the enormous winter palace, the Potala, their breath visible in the thin air of 12,000 feet. They were there for their annual audience with the Thirteenth Dalai Lama, the Fourteenth's tough, visionary predecessor.

But when the maroon-robed monks entered the meeting room, instead of the holy person of the Thirteenth, his compact body and steely gaze, they saw propped on the golden throne an empty robe. His Holiness, it turned out, was too ill to attend the audience, and his followers would be granted only a chance to commune with his garments, a ceremony the Tibetans call "inviting the clothes." One monk began to weep. Rumors about the Thirteenth's bout with a flu-like illness had been sweeping through Lhasa for days. The monk felt instinctively that His Holiness was not going to live long.

Five days later, his fears came true, and the Dalai Lama passed away from natural causes. The announcement was made by dancers on the roof of the Potala, beating out a somber rhythm on traditional *damaru* drums, and by the sight of butter lamps being placed outside, which in Tibet is a symbol of death. The population was grief-stricken, openly crying on the streets of Lhasa. Each Dalai Lama creates an impression of what the institution could be, and the Thirteenth, who'd held the throne for fifty-four years, had set a high bar. He had been a handsome man with a shaved head, an intense, transfixing gaze, and the flourish of a thin mustache. Far from emitting a Buddha-like serenity, his official portraits reveal a Tibetan prince, one well versed in the politics of fear and retribution. But he had presided over the nation's entry into at least a sort of independence, and he was beloved.

An old saying decrees that whenever two Tibetans get together, there will soon be two political parties. Tibetans are notoriously fond of political intrigue, and at the Potala there were competing loyalties, power struggles, and infighting that sometimes turned lethal. But the Thirteenth had expertly negotiated the dark waters of political life. On his ascension to the throne in 1879, the Dalai Lama's jealous regent had attempted to use occult magic to get rid of him, placing a "black mantra" in a finely crafted pair of shoes that were then given to a powerful lama, boosting the mantra's killing power. Having escaped the assassination attempt, the Thirteenth had ordered the ambitious regent drowned in an enormous copper vat. It was an example of his frequently ruthless nature, but it was also a fact that one often needed to be very tough to survive in the Potala Palace.

The Thirteenth's great mission in his lifetime had been to modernize the country and usher Tibet into the company of independent nations. He believed that the age-old threat from Tibet's ancient adversary, China, would return, more powerful than ever, and that his nation, backward and isolationist in the extreme, would prove to be easy prey for its huge neighbor. But by the time of his death, it was clear that he'd utterly failed in this mission. The leaders of Tibet's great monasteries thought that opening the country to the world would spell the end of their domination and the end of Tibet's role as the keeper of the Dharma. They equated modernity with atheism. Westerners were seen as *Tendra*, enemies of the faith, and enemies of the men and institutions that supported the faith. One monk remembered that, growing up, he was taught that India was the holiest place on earth but that "everywhere else is to be feared." It was even permitted to kill intruders rather than let them contaminate Tibet.

The Thirteenth dreaded what lay ahead for his country. As part of his last will and testament, he left to the Tibetan elite, and to his eventual successor, what some called a divine prophecy. But when one reads it, it turns out to be a hard-nosed political analysis of Tibet's position in Asia and a stern warning about the future. It reveals what a steel-trap political mind the Fourteenth's predecessor possessed, and how clearly he saw disaster's approach:

> In particular we must guard ourselves against the barbaric Red communists, who carry terror and destruction with them wherever they go. They are the worst of the worst.

Already they have consumed much of Mongolia. . . . They have robbed and destroyed the monasteries, forcing the monks to join their armies, or else killing them. . . . It will not be long before we find the Red onslaught at our own front door . . . and when it happens we must be ready to defend ourselves. Otherwise our spiritual and cultural traditions will be completely eradicated. . . . Even the names of the Dalai and Panchen Lamas will be erased. . . . The monasteries will be looted and destroyed, and the monks and nuns killed or chased away. . . . We will become like slaves to our conquerors . . . and the days and nights will pass slowly and with great suffering and terror. . . .

Use peaceful means where they are appropriate, but where they are not appropriate do not hesitate to resort to more forceful means. . . . Think carefully about what I have said, for the future is in your hands.

It was a remarkable document. Dog-eared copies of it were passed around in Tibetan villages for years, and the young Fourteenth Dalai Lama would study it nightly to learn the intricacies of Tibetan grammar.

The death of a Dalai Lama has always been a deeply traumatic event for Tibetans. The state is always most vulnerable in the time— traditionally ranging between nine and twenty-four months—that the search for the new incarnation is carried out and a successor named. (The spirit of the former Dalai Lama does not immediately incorporate itself into a new body; indeed, the Fourteenth Dalai Lama was not even born when his predecessor passed away.) The nervous anticipation that all Tibetans feel on the death of their

Precious Protector flows partly from the fatal and scarred history of the Dalai Lamas. The Ninth through the Twelfth (from 1807 to 1875) had all died young, believed poisoned either by their regents, who wished to hold on to power, or by the representatives of the Chinese throne, the *ambans*, who wished to keep a pliable regent in power and prevent the rise of a great lama. Others had died in their prime under suspicious circumstances, among them the rebellious Tsangyang Gyatso, the tragic Sixth. He was a carouser, a poet, a bisexual hedonist who had written some of the most beautiful lyrics in all of Tibetan literature. The loveliest, so often quoted that they now serve as his epitaph, cry out with something the Fourteenth Dalai Lama would come to know intimately—the desire for escape:

> *White crane!*
> *Lend me your wings,*
> *I will not go far, only to Lithang,*
> *And then I shall return.*

In the summer of 1935, nearly two years after the death of the Thirteenth, the search for his successor began in earnest. The corpse of the Thirteenth had provided the first clues. Monks had prepared the body to lie in state in a coffin lined with salt, dressed in his finest gold brocade robes, with the head facing southward, the direction of long life. The next morning, they found the head had turned toward the east. They returned it to its original position, but the next day the same thing happened again. It was a sign that the Fourteenth Dalai Lama would be found in the provinces bordering on China.

Village leaders and authorities all over Tibet looked for telltale signs that the spirit of Chenrizi had been reincarnated, that the new *bodhisattva*—a being who has attained complete enlightenment but postpones Nirvana to help others obtain liberation—was among them. Finally, Reting Rimpoche, the regent who was the political head of Tibet until the next Dalai Lama could be found, traveled ninety miles southeast of Lhasa to the mystical lake known as Lhamo Latso. Along with a search party, he climbed to the top of a nearby mountain, set up camp, completed his prayers as ritual music played, then gazed down on the clear alpine waters below. Some of Reting Rimpoche's fellow searchers saw nothing but the turquoise surface of the lake rippling in the breeze. But the regent witnessed a succession of images rising from and then disappearing in the deep waters: the Tibetan letters *Ah, Ka,* and *Ma,* a three-storied monastery with a gold and green jade roof, a white road leading to the east, a small country house with unusual blue-green eaves, and, finally, a white-and-brown dog standing in a yard. When the regent reported the vision to the National Assembly the following year, the members consulted the Nechung Oracle, the state's chief medium, then decreed that three large search parties would head to the east to conduct a thorough search for the child Fourteenth. In September 1937, the Year of the Fire Rat, the search parties set out from Lhasa: one party headed northeast toward Amdo (which began with *Ah,* the first letter the regent had seen in the lake), the second party traveled due east to Kham, and the third southeast toward the regions known as Takpo and Kongpo. They were heading into territory as desolate, in places, as the surface of the moon.

Tibet is awash in superlatives. It is the highest country on earth and the most mountainous, with three-quarters of the country's territory lying at 16,000 feet or higher, a full three miles above sea level. It's ringed by world-class mountain ranges on three sides. In the north, the Altyn Tagh range separates Tibet from China's Xinjiang province and the Gobi desert. To the west is the Karakoram system, across which lie Kashmir and Pakistan. In the south are the almost impenetrable Himalayas, which cut Tibet off from India, Nepal, and the kingdom of Bhutan. Mount Everest, on the border with Nepal, is the crown in a line of mountains that top out at more than 25,000 feet. The mountain ranges are so high that they even dictate Tibet's weather, intercepting storm fronts before they can shower the plains beyond with water, leading to the "rain shadow effect" that has made Tibet so arid. The country receives only eighteen inches of rain and snow a year.

From this ring of summits, the land drops down to a huge plateau that is hardly any more conducive to human or animal life. Most of Tibet is so high and cold that trees and vegetation—beyond a few native bushes—will not survive. The north is marked by glaciers, marshes, and quicksand pits. The central province of U-Tsäng is so wind-blasted that it's called "the land of no man and no dog" by Tibetans themselves. The *changthang*, or northern plains, present an alien landscape that across thousands of miles alternates between flat lengths of earth covered in yellow borax, beautiful deep lakes, and miles of soda and salt deposits that are so bright they can cause snow blindness in travelers. This entire area once lay under the Tethys Sea, which left behind only vast mineral deposits and the occasional river churning white with rapids.

The landscape gives Tibet a physically intoxicating air. Things happen here that happen in very few places on earth. It's possible to get frostbite and an intense sunburn at the same time. You can safely dip your hand in a pot of boiling water, as water boils at a much lower temperature. You can spot a man walking toward you from ten miles away because the land is so flat and the air so clear. It's one of the sunniest places on earth, but frost covers the ground over three hundred days a year. For centuries, the *misers*—bonded servants who worked for aristocrats or monasteries for their entire lives—slept crouched on their hands and knees, with every stitch of clothing they owned piled on their backs, looking like they were bowed in prayer. Any more contact with the frigid earth and they'd have frozen to death.

The land limits the number of people who can live on it. Cold, altitude, and alkaline soil conspire to give the country a small population stretched over 500,000 square miles, the size of Western Europe. In 1950, only about 2.5 million people inhabited the nation (this includes ethnic Tibetans living in the country's border areas), fewer than 5 per square mile, while the rest of Asia averaged above 200 per square mile. Tibet, the most sparsely populated country on earth, fairly echoes with emptiness.


The Amdo search party experienced the harsh landscape firsthand as they went in search of the child reincarnation. Led by Ketsing Rimpoche, the thin, bookish abbot of Lhasa's influential Sera Monastery, the group took two full months to travel the thousand miles to Amdo, battling almost continuous snowstorms and temperatures that plunged well past −10 degrees. They carried with them items that had belonged to the Thirteenth as well as a list of potential candidates, boys who'd distinguished themselves by certain signs (especially touching or asking for holy relics that belonged to high lamas) or by a maturity beyond their years, or, as the process was not completely apolitical, children who had powerful sponsors backing them. In March 1937 they arrived at the storied Kumbum Monastery, founded 350 years before by the Third Dalai Lama on the grounds where a great Buddhist leader, Tsongkhapa, had been born. On first seeing the buildings, constructed in a Chinese pagoda style, the members stopped and exchanged glances. The monastery's main structure, known as the Temple of the Golden

Tree, was three stories high, and its roof was tiled in gold and green jade, exactly as Reting Rimpoche had seen at the sacred lake. The Lhasa dignitaries tried to contain their excitement.

The team had spent weeks drawing together a list of candidates, finally compiling fourteen names. But one by one, the early candidates failed the ancient tests, designed to coax out of the boys irrefutable signs that the reincarnated spirit of Chenrizi dwelt within them. The Panchen Lama, second only to the Dalai Lama in status as a religious leader, had suggested three of the boys, one of whom had died before the search team arrived. Now two remained. A team of search party members visited the first boy's house and quietly sipped tea as the child's mother presented the candidate, freshly scrubbed and dressed in brand-new clothes (although the search party's mission was supposed to be secret, word often leaked out that an important reincarnation was being sought). At the first test, recognizing a rosary that had belonged to the Great Thirteenth, the boy proved painfully shy and didn't reach out to grab the relic. Soon, he burst into tears and ran out of the room.

The episode points up a hidden aspect of the search for a Dalai Lama. Though it proceeds according to a mystic protocol, deep in its workings there rests a certain psychological agenda, a second-order intent. Boys who were thought to be possible candidates were questioned; if the child ran off or hid behind his mother's skirts, he was immediately eliminated as a candidate. A child who was the reincarnation of the Dalai Lamas, divine-like beings who had ruled Tibet for hundreds of years, couldn't be a milquetoast. Without quite stating it, the search favored the bold.

The next boy on the list, Lhamo Thondup (or "wish-fulfilling goddess"—the Tibetans often gave androgynous names to their young children), was destined to be the Fourteenth Dalai Lama, and he certainly qualified as a bold spirit. Lhamo had been born on July 6, 1935, into a peasant family in the village of Takster in northeastern Tibet near the Chinese border. He was the fifth child of sixteen, only seven of whom lived past infancy. His father was a farmer and horse trader named Choekyong Tsering and his mother was Diki Tsering. (Tibetans do not take their names from either their fathers or their mothers, and they often take on new names after auspicious events.) Diki Tsering had given birth to the boy as dawn approached in a rough-hewn cowshed behind the main house, among the family's yaks and calves, while a single mustard lamp threw shadows on the wall. Lhamo Thondup's arrival was marked by unusual signs: his eyes were wide open at birth, and his father, who'd been ill for many weeks as his wife's pregnancy advanced, jumped out of bed after the boy arrived, so fully recovered that his wife accused him of faking his illness. (It was an early indication of strains in the marriage, as Diki Tsering believed her husband often avoided work, while she bent over in the fields with her latest infant strapped to her back.) Told he'd had a son, his father was pleased. "Good," he said. "I'd like to make him a monk."

Lhamo Thondup had grown up like any other boy in the rugged eastern territories. He lived in the family's flat-roofed house with its unusual turquoise eaves, and he played in the fields of wheat and barley (after being warned about the wolves that sometimes snatched children away), making little houses in the haystacks and wrestling with his brothers. His tiny village sat on a plateau, surrounded by bright green hills, a typical Tibetan landscape. "Clear springs of water fell in cascades," he remembered, "and the birds and the wild animals—deer, wild asses, monkeys, and a few leopards, bears, and foxes—all wandered unafraid of man." With his mother, he would tend the family shrine, placing offerings of butter or dried fruit to the Buddha. In the evening, the family might receive visitors, neighbors or merchants whose yaks snorted outside, the men dressed in fur caps, thick *chubas* (long sheepskin coats), and square-toed leather boots, while the women wore long sleeveless dresses over bright cotton blouses. The young Lhamo Thondup would often jump on the windowsill and pretend to be riding away toward the capital, Lhasa, or pack a bag for parts unknown. But so did his older brother, and so must have thousands of other Amdo boys. It was only in retrospect that his games attained a kind of prophecy.

As a boy, Lhamo Thondup was closer to his mother, a deeply loving woman whom all the children sought out when they needed to be comforted. But his personality had flashes of his father's dark moods. His father was strong-minded, prone to bursts of intense anger, sometimes cruel. He would kick or slap his sons when unhappy with them, and once, when the nervous Lobsang, Lhamo's elder brother, failed to ride a horse properly, his father had swatted the animal and sent it off like a shot. Lobsang tumbled from its back and slammed to the ground, suffering a severe concussion. The future Dalai Lama was prone to the same kind of outbursts. "I used to torture my mother," he admits. "When she would carry me on her shoulders, I would pull her ears to steer her this way or that." But it was an anger with a difference: he fought the local bullies and jumped into fights on the side of the underdog. "I have memories of running after those I perceived to be the tormentor in any fight," the Dalai Lama said. "I just could not take the sight of the weak being harassed."

This impetuous boy was the last candidate recommended by the Panchen Lama. The abbot from Lhasa, Ketsing Rimpoche, went to see the boy himself, disguised as the servant of a religious pilgrim, a tattered sheepskin robe thrown over his shoulders. Around his neck he placed one of the Thirteenth's rosaries. With two attendants and a government official in tow, the abbot set off for the boy's village, home to about thirty families. When they reached the outskirts of Takster, they spotted the house immediately, a standard Tibetan rural home distinguished only by its turquoise roofing tiles. In its yard was a tall wooden pole on which hundreds of prayer flags had been tied, each flap of wind sending the devotion written on it skyward. A brown-and-white Tibetan mastiff was chained near the front door, and it began to bark furiously as Ketsing Rimpoche and the three others made their way down to the house. The door opened and the woman of the house came out. Ketsing Rimpoche's servant, disguised as an aristocratic pilgrim, asked if they could use the woman's kitchen to brew some tea. She immediately agreed and invited them in. It was the three others' job to keep the parents and any siblings busy while Ketsing Rimpoche talked to the young Lhamo Thondup.

As the travelers filled their kettle and chatted with the unsuspecting mother, a young boy emerged from another room and spotted the scholarly abbot, who was sitting on a small platform inside the kitchen. Lhamo Thondup was two and a half years old, with penetrating brown eyes and a confident expression. He walked up to the abbot, took the rosary in his tiny hands, and said, "I want that."

The words seemed to echo in the room. The attendants turned to look at the boy. Ketsing Rimpoche smiled and said, "If you guess who I am, you can definitely have it."

"You are a lama of Sera," said the boy.

Ketsing Rimpoche nodded. "And who is this?" He pointed to the government official with him.

The boy turned to look. "That is Lobsang Tsewang," the boy said. Then he remarked that the other two visitors were from Sera Monastery. Each answer was correct. Packed into the tiny room, the men who'd come a thousand miles to find the next Dalai Lama shot glances at one another. They felt themselves to be on the verge of one of the central miracles of their faith, the return of Chenrizi to earth, a thing of almost inexpressible joyfulness.

The party stayed the night at the young boy's house. Ketsing Rimpoche played with him but asked him no further questions. The next morning, when the party was leaving, Lhamo Thondup burst from the front door and ran after the group from Lhasa, crying that he wanted to go with them. The search party could console the weeping boy only by telling him they would return soon.

Back at the monastery, Ketsing Rimpoche sent a messenger off with a telegram to the authorities in Lhasa, telling them (in prearranged code) of their discovery of a promising candidate. The messenger set off for Sining, where the message would be relayed through India and China and finally back to Lhasa, along Tibet's only telegraph line. Four weeks later, the reply arrived: "The young Takster boy sounds very interesting," it read. "We have high hopes for him." Ketsing Rimpoche was instructed to continue the examination.

As the abbot departed for Takster for the second time, the entire search party of forty men went with him. The monks blew on their conch shells, the sound of the Dharma's constant victory over ignorance, always a favorable omen. Along the way, the party met a young Chinese man ferrying wood to his home by donkey and asked him the way to the boy's house. The man told them to take the lower of two possible paths to their destination, and soon they came to a clearing that they recognized as the spot where the Thirteenth Dalai Lama had stopped briefly while traveling through the area decades before. It was a minor landmark in the spiritual map of Tibet, but the excitement of the search party increased. It was as if a string of portents were leading them onward to Lhamo Thondup.

When the forty dignitaries tramped down into their enclosed yard, Diki Tsering and her husband knew that their youngest boy was destined for something greater than a life as an Amdo farmer. They suspected he'd been marked as a high lama. Already, one of Lhamo Thondup's older brothers had been recognized as the reincarnation of another holy man. And the search party's appearance came as a relief: their little boy had been tormenting them ever since Ketsing Rimpoche had left, wanting to know when the abbot would return and asking his mother to brew her best tea and cook a special meal so that the abbot and his companions would be happy when they arrived. The boy had even piled some of his possessions on the kitchen table and told his bewildered mother, "I'm packing to go to Lhasa." But they didn't dream that the dignitaries were there to find the next Dalai Lama.

Ketsing Rimpoche, now dressed in his abbot's robes, presented the boy's father and mother with presents and requested to see Lhamo Thondup alone. The pair showed the abbot and his attendants to their bedroom, and the search party placed a long wooden table across the bed. On it, Ketsing Rimpoche laid the items he'd brought from Lhasa for just such an occasion: two black rosaries, two yellow rosaries, two *damaru* hand drums, and two walking sticks. One item of each pair had belonged to the Thirteenth. The other hadn't.

The bright-eyed Lhamo Thondup entered the room, crowded with strange men, and calmly walked over to Ketsing Rimpoche. The abbot greeted him and held up the two black rosaries. He asked the boy which one he wanted. Lhamo Thondup immediately pointed to the Thirteenth's and placed it around his neck. The same thing happened with the yellow rosaries. The tension in the room, a mix of anticipation and nerves frayed over months of searching, mounted. Ketsing Rimpoche pointed to the walking sticks. Lhamo Thondup considered, then reached for the wrong stick—it belonged to Ketsing Rimpoche himself. The members of the search party froze. One mistake would disqualify the boy. But then Lhamo Thondup gently let go of the stick and grabbed the Thirteenth's cane, holding it up in front of him. The officials in the room let go of a collective breath. Later they would realize that the first walking stick had actually belonged to the Dalai Lama briefly before he gave it away to a monk. It was as if the boy had felt the spiritual traces of the Thirteenth, like fading fingerprints.

They came to the drums. The lamas had purposefully matched the Thirteenth's plain old drum with a luxurious model done up in gold, ivory, and turquoise, its ball attached with a beautifully brocaded tassel. The boy instantly grabbed the right one and turned it quickly in his hand, tapping out a rapid little beat. "Now that we had witnessed these miraculous performances," wrote a member of the search party, "our minds were filled with deep devotion, joy, and gaiety."

The final step was a physical examination. There are eight marks associated with the discovery of a Dalai Lama, including curling eyebrows, wide eyes, large ears, tiger stripes on the legs, and a curling imprint resembling a conch shell on the palm. The members of the search party found three on the person of the young boy, enough to confirm their find. Some of the men in the room bowed their heads, their eyes filling with tears. In that moment, they recognized not only their old master, their beloved Thirteenth, but the spirit of Chenrizi, the *bodhisattva* of Infinite Compassion, which was with them again here in this crowded, airless room in an obscure corner of Tibet. The boy staring at them with his bold brown eyes also reassured the men that one day they too would be reincarnated into another life, that the faith they'd followed their entire lives was alive and true.

## TO LHASA

*I*n the heat of mid-July, a week after his fourth birthday, the newly christened Dalai Lama set out on his journey to Lhasa. He was attended by fifty travelers, including his older brother Lobsang (at six years old, closest to him in age), his parents, and an uncle, as well as bodyguards, the entire search party who had discovered him, and a group of Muslim merchants who had been called on to make a loan toward the $300,000 ransom demanded by the region's governor and warlord, General Ma Pu-feng, for letting the child incarnate leave. There were also mule drivers and scouts necessary to command the 350 horses, mules, yaks, and camels that would carry the pilgrims' belongings for the three and a half months it would take to reach Lhasa. It was raining lightly as the expedition set off.

Lhamo Thondup had been elevated beyond his family's wildest imaginings, but he was still a mischievous, generous boy who'd inherited his father's temper. On the road, Lhamo fought ferociously with his brother Lobsang, forcing the driver to call his mother, who always found the older brother in tears and the Dalai Lama sitting in the golden litter, smiling, with a look of triumph on his face.

As feisty as he was, the boy often became overwhelmed by the attention. When the caravan arrived at a village along the route, hundreds or thousands of Tibetans often waited, thronging the road and asking for his blessing, causing the four-year-old to break into tears. What the Dalai Lama especially remembered from the trip was the wildlife, the *drong* (wild yaks), *kyang* (wild asses), and *nawa* (Himalayan blue sheep), "so light and fast they might have been ghosts." He was also struck, as a young child uprooted from his familiar landscape, by the forbidding remoteness of the territory they were passing through, "gargantuan mountains flanking immense flat plains which we struggled over like insects."

Still days away from the capital, the boy shed his peasant clothes for the last time and was dressed in the maroon-and-gold robes of a Buddhist monk. Then the *Mendel Tensum* was performed, in which the boy was presented with a reliquary, a scripture, and a statuette of the Buddha of Long Life, gifts appropriate to a high lama. His head was shaved, and he was given a new name as well, Tenzin Gyatso. By these modest steps, the boy from Amdo prepared himself to become the Precious Protector of Tibet.

It is one of the more charming traditions of Tibetan life that no one is allowed to leave on or return from a trip unattended. A young boy who is being sent off from Lhasa to a remote monastery will find dozens of friends and family taking the first part of the trip with him, sending their loved one off with tears and assurances that they will be waiting for his return. And on his arrival back, he will again find a party of friends and neighbors waiting for him on the road, ready to escort him back. To set off alone on a journey would be seen as deeply uncivilized. For the next Dalai Lama, the tradition was filled by battalions of Tibetan soldiers, officials, and the heads of the capital's three great monasteries, who journeyed out from Lhasa to meet the caravan. When the Amdo party approached Lhasa, the dignitaries met them on the plain two miles outside the capital. They brought with them "the Great Peacock," a special wooden throne used only for greeting the new incarnation on his arrival in Lhasa. Among the officials was a humble monk named Ponpo ("the boss"), who would be in charge of the Dalai Lama's kitchen. This self-effacing man would become the Dalai Lama's surrogate mother in the lonely and alienating days to come.

A daylong ceremony followed, which to the young boy's eyes consisted of enormous swarms of people, more than he thought even existed in the world, coming to greet him and receive his blessing. What seemed like the entire population of Lhasa waited for him in the capital, a sea of shining faces flooding around his litter. The boy felt "as if I were in a great park covered with beautiful flowers while a soft breeze blew across it and peacocks elegantly danced before me."

To understand the Fourteenth and his role in Tibetan life, one must understand the nature of Tibetan Buddhism and its place within the nation. Tibet pursued the building of monasteries and the pledging of huge numbers of monks as state ends. One out of every four young men was placed in a monastery, often when he was six or seven years old. The monasteries sought these extraordinary num-bers of monks for both theological and political reasons: not only to advance the Dharma, the way of the Buddha, but also to draw as many Tibetan families as possible into the monastic economy and to build up their political base. As anywhere, numbers translated into power. The monasteries also doubled as universities, offering the only real education that peasant children could hope for, while at the same time owning huge tracts of land and collecting revenues that dwarfed the government budget. Buddhism was much more than a state religion; it was the sole reason for Tibet's existence. The faith became the institution around which all other things in the society were molded: the economy, the military (or lack thereof), foreign policy, domestic policy. One explorer described Tibet as one "huge monastery inhabited by a nation of monks." Stealing from a monastery's funds was considered a graver offense than kill-ing one's own parents.

This single-minded pursuit also meant that these institutions were far from the tranquil places of meditation that one thinks of when one hears the words "Tibetan Buddhist monastery." The enor-mous complexes were roiling, highly political outposts in which not every initiate was dedicated to the pursuit of the Dharma. The Dalai Lama, in later years, spoke of a monastery where only one in five of the thousands of monks was actually a serious student of Buddhism, while the others spent their time distracting themselves or fighting off boredom ("organized gold-bricking," *Life* magazine would call it). And one young monk painted a rather harrowing portrait of elderly monks' pursuit of him and other young boys whom they wanted as *drombos*, or homosexual partners. Neither Tibet nor its premier institutions, the monasteries, was free from the vices of the world.

The heroes of this formerly martial society were no lon-ger warriors and chieftains but monks who walled themselves up in mountain caves to meditate, with a small hole cut in the wall through which food was passed to them once a day. Or the *lung-pa* ("wind men"), who were said to have achieved such a high degree of concentration that they could overcome the laws of physics and fly through the air for hours at a time. The promise of Mahayana Buddhism, the school that had taken root in Tibet, is that a human being, through sustained and devout effort, can rise through his life cycles to become a *bodhisattva*, an "enlightenment-being" who has achieved complete wisdom and compassion for others. And it is selfless empathy for others that leads to Buddha-dom. The lotus, the symbol of Tibetan Buddhism and the subject of its central mantra *Om Mani Padme Hum!* ("Oh! The Jewel in the Lotus!"), is born in the dank mud of a swamp, but it rises above the clammy muck to unfurl its beautiful clean flower. One could in the same way free oneself of the base hatreds of human existence and come to embody enlightenment and the "jewel" in the mantra, pure compassion.

The fact that the most revered *bodhisattva* in the land, Chenrizi, was resident in the person of the Dalai Lama made him not only a spiritual leader and the political head of state but the example of what every Tibetan Buddhist strove for, a perfect model of what a human being should and could become. Chenrizi was "the Lord who looks down," a being who, constantly on the verge of attaining Nirvana, postpones his final transformation in order to help others end their suffering. He was therefore, in a sense, the final aim of the nation, the end product of its special mission in the world.

The Tibetans do not even have a word for "religion." It isn't something apart. It abides in life always.

After his entry into Lhasa, the Amdo boy was installed in the summer palace, the Norbulingka, as he awaited his enthronement, "the last temporal liberty I was ever to know." On the cold morning of February 22, 1940, he was taken to the Potala, the winter residence that loomed over Lhasa, its height accentuated by an architect's trick: the walls angled inward from their base, as did the windows, making the building seem to soar even higher than it did. The boy was led to the Lion Throne, which had been vacant for six years but kept supplied with fresh food, holy water, and new flowers, as this was the seat of a spirit on its way back from distant parts. The British delegate to the ceremony, Sir Basil Gould, walked into the Hall of All Good Deeds of the Spiritual and Temporal Worlds and saw the new incarnation for the first time: "The Dalai Lama," he wrote, "a solid, solemn but very wide-awake boy, red-cheeked and closely shorn, wrapped warm in the maroon-red robes of a monk and in outer coverings, was seated high on his simple throne, cross-legged in the attitude of Buddha." The boy was surrounded by five abbots, and Gould was struck by the "devotion and love" they showed the Fourteenth as well as the "extraordinary steadiness of his gaze." The ceremony that followed seemed to go on forever: two mime performances were followed by dance, song, readings of national history, blessings and counter-blessings. It was the boy's introduction to the marathon Tibetan rituals he would come to know so well (and loathe so thoroughly). The Dalai Lama remained composed throughout, and many people remarked that he seemed to recognize the officials who had served his predecessor.

The new Dalai Lama took his place at the Potala Palace and began his apprenticeship to the political and spiritual leadership of Tibet. Sitting atop Marbori, "the Red Hill," the Potala was a seventeenth-century masterpiece, but it wasn't an easy place to live in. To go anywhere in it you were forever stepping over thick wooden transoms, climbing up stairs or ladders, the sight lines constantly broken by wooden pillars, by doors to hidden chapels, by corridors that spun off to another of the thousand rooms. It was freezing cold during the winter. And the Dalai Lama soon learned that his living quarters were placed so high above his people that he could see them only through a telescope. He would often study the criminals, who were closest to view (the Potala even contained a prison), men who when they saw the sun flashing off His Holiness's telescope lens would bow their heads and look away out of reverence. The palace's attic was rumored to be haunted by giant child-snatching owls and ghosts, ghosts that terrified the young Dalai Lama when he first stayed there, and its many chapels were filled with the remains of his predecessors in gargantuan *stupas*, or golden burial vessels. When he wasn't studying or playing, the boy would wander among the *stupas*, the emeralds and rose-gold facets on the tombs occasionally catching a ray of light from the butter lamps and sparkling in the cold gloom. The Potala was too big to truly know, a Buddhist metropolis with offices, meeting rooms for the National Assembly, two treasuries and a large armory, a dungeon hard by the national library, and uncountable chapels. Its interior barely lit by the sun but only by candles and the glimpse of open courtyards, it was as dark and fragrant as a cave inhabited for centuries.

The Fourteenth was often intensely lonely at first. His nervous and rather meek brother Lobsang went to live with him, but his parents were installed in their own home in Lhasa and were allowed only periodic visits. In their absence, the boy latched on to his beloved Ponpo, his caretaker, forming an attachment that would last for decades. "So strong was [our relationship]," the Dalai Lama said, "that he had to be in my sight at all times, even if it was only the bottom of his robe visible through a doorway or under the curtains which served as doors inside Tibetan houses." Like the Dalai Lama's mother, Ponpo was a forbearing, kindhearted person who fed and soothed the boy. But the memory of his mother lingered. The Dalai Lama's younger brother, Choegyal, was installed at Drepung Monastery, a few miles from Lhasa, having been recognized as the reincarnation of a high lama. There Choegyal grew desperate for any hint of his old life, especially the warm presence of Diki Tsering. "I missed my mother terribly," he remembers. "She used to send me homemade cookies, lollipops, chewing gum . . . all wrapped up in a scarf. I would sniff the scarf, desperately trying to recapture the smell of her." The Dalai Lama suffered similar pangs.

As a boy in the freezing Potala on long afternoons, the young Fourteenth Dalai Lama would sit for hours on the shiny *arga* floors, made of chipped stone and waxed with butter, and gaze up at intricate murals hundreds of years old. These became his history lessons. Extending from floor to ceiling, they told the story of Tibet in flowing allegories and luridly colored portraits.

The Dalai Lama learned about Songtsen Gampo, the Tibetan king who, beginning around AD 629, transformed Tibet into a relentless military power. His armies pushed into Nepal and Burma, into Tang-dynasty China, the border areas of India, and the neighboring kingdom of Zhang Zhung. But he also established Lhasa as a cosmopolitan mecca, sending scholars to northern India to create a written Tibetan language and bringing astrological systems from China, laws and civil administration from the Uighurs, and art from Nepal. The king, in his most lasting legacy, then imported Buddhism to Lhasa and declared it the official state faith. Before Songtsen Gampo, the Tibetans had practiced Bön, "the nameless religion," a shamanistic belief system populated by demons, vengeful ghosts, snake-gods, and devils who called for human sacrifice and who could only be controlled by a priest known as a "bön," or invoker of spirits.

Gampo's successor, Trisong Detsen, summoned the legendary guru Padmasambhava from India and encouraged him to journey to every corner of Tibet, teaching the Four Noble Truths: *to live is to suffer; suffering is caused by desire; desire can be overcome; and the path to that overcoming is embodied in the Noble Eightfold Path— right view, right intention, right speech, right action, right livelihood, right effort, right mindfulness, right concentration.* Sin is not the great villain in Buddhist philosophy; ignorance is. We sin because, in our ignorance, we fail to see how lying and stealing and committing violence harms our own karma and leads only to more suffering. Tibetan Buddhism has often been called a science of the mind, and with some justification. It's a struggle to understand life and overcome its illusions so that one may gradually attain a sublime equanimity. Padmasambhava was the first to expound its principles in the Land of Snows.

The guru didn't attack Bön so much as cannibalize it, incorporating the faith's demons and legends into the Buddhist pantheon and thereby giving even the simplest peasant a clear way of comprehending the new religion. It was said he faced down the Bön deities by causing massive avalanches, stopping the wind, and bringing the waters of frigid lakes to a boil, all through a mind honed by constant meditation. By the twelfth century, Buddhism had conquered the country, this time not by imperial decree but by capturing the hearts of ordinary citizens.

The young Dalai Lama slept in the Great Fifth's bedroom, on the seventh—and uppermost—story of the Potala. "It was pitifully cold and ill-lit," he remembered. "Everything in it was ancient and decrepit and behind the drapes that hung across each of the four walls lay deposits of centuries-old dust." He made friends with the mice who came to steal the food left as offerings for the Buddha. In the morning, after his 7:00 a.m. breakfast, the Dalai

Lama and his brother Lobsang were given their lessons together, beginning with reading and memorization of Buddhist texts. The Dalai Lama was trained through the traditional Tibetan methods. First, he was taught to read and then to write (including a very exacting course in penmanship, divided into training in one script for writing manuscripts and in another for official communications and private letters). Then he began to memorize the classic scriptures, both to sharpen his memory and to give him a basic understanding of Buddhist principles. This was followed by *nyam tee*, "teaching from experience." Here a lama would be invited to the Potala to give a lecture on a specific virtue, illustrating the point with real-life stories and quotations from Lord Buddha and the classic Indian authorities. Next came perhaps the most important step of all, the practice of meditation, where the student was left alone in complete silence to contemplate the lessons of the day and to begin the internal explorations that are the grist of the monk's life. Finally, that development was tested in debates with tutors and teachers, accompanied by a series of stylized gestures—the questioner, for example, would try to distract his adversary by slowly raising his right hand above his head and then slapping it into his left palm.

At 10:00 a.m., every day, His Holiness and his brother would be separated, and the Fourteenth would be escorted to a meeting with the members of his government, who ascended the steep stairs from their offices on the second and third floors. He was not allowed to speak. His regent, a flamboyantly corrupt monk named Reting Rimpoche, directed the nation's business.

When the Dalai Lama was a child, political affairs and religious studies were sheer drudgery. His tutors found the boy to be bright, with an impressive memory, and deeply concerned with underdogs, the friendless and abused. But he didn't work at his lessons. "My only interest was in playing," the Dalai Lama admitted. He was a strong-willed boy more interested in concocting elaborate war games than anything else. He was almost worryingly obsessed with gadgets, war machines (challenging his keepers to make tanks and airplanes out of balls of *tsampa* dough), military drills, and dangerous stunts, such as running off a ramp and jumping, to see who could leap the highest. Because the Dalai Lama was forbidden to have friends his own age, his adult attendants were shanghaied into mock battles. The young boy would toss missiles made of dough at their heads, and they would fire back.

He hadn't yet overcome his legendary temper, either. After losing a game to his sweepers (who swept the gleaming floors of the palace clean), His Holiness would sometimes stand and glower at them, literally shaking with rage. The ancient myths held that the Tibetan people had descended from a ravenous she-beast, and Tibetans believed Chenrizi had come to watch over them because of their wild nature. But at times it was the Dalai Lama who seemed ungovernable, a spirit of fury unleashed in the echoing rooms of the Potala.

It was only with the sweepers that His Holiness had what could be called a normal relationship; the others used formal language when speaking to him, addressing the institution, the superior being, instead of the young boy. Protocol gave his ministers strict rules for what they could and couldn't do in the Dalai Lama's presence: sitting, for example, was sacrilege. In fact, the Dalai Lama often saw only the tops of his subjects' heads, as they bowed low at the first sight of him and he, by tradition, looked up in the air. Nor could he be punished: when the Fourteenth did something bad, it was his timid brother Lobsang who was lashed with a whip hanging on their tutor's wall. The Dalai Lama had the curious fate of being neglected and spoiled at the same time.

When His Holiness was just eight, Lobsang, the last daily link to his old life, left for private school. Now the two brothers would see each other only on the occasional school holidays. "When he left after each visit," the Dalai Lama said, "I remember, standing at the window watching, my heart full of sorrow, as he disappeared into the distance." His estrangement from a normal childhood was complete. "Those children wrested from their families," wrote the Tibet scholar Giuseppe Tucci, about the young Dalai Lamas,

> subjected to the strict supervision of elderly wardens . . . led through the endless maze of lamaistic liturgy and dogmatics and plunged forcibly into the ponderous works of their former embodiments, certainly do not know the blissful astonishment of childhood. Such strict discipline, such statue-like immobility as the dignity of that office imposes, the daily intercourse with gloomy, elderly people, look to me like a violent, ruthless suppression of childhood.

As he entered his teens, the Fourteenth was barely treading water with his studies. At thirteen, he was introduced to Buddhist metaphysics, and his mind shut down completely. "They unnerved me so that I had the feeling of being dazed, as though I were hit on the head by a stone." The only things that moved him were the stories of the Buddhist martyrs and the passages about suffering and forbearance that the scriptures abound with. At times, he would shed tears when reading them. But for the rest, he only let the verses play on his lips, not even trying to memorize them. He would edit the stories in his head to make them more exciting, or conjure up cliff-hanging adventure stories to avoid boredom.

. . .

Summer brought the move to the Norbulingka, and the young Dalai Lama quickly grew to love the rambling green place. He would take his younger brother, Choegyal, out on the pond in a tiny boat that could fit only the two of them. They would stare down over the gunwales of the boat and drop food to the fish that they could see flitting in the green water. His attendants would walk along the shore, tracking the progress of the vessel. The Fourteenth proved to be a daredevil, falling into the pond one time while trying to retrieve a stick and being rescued by a janitor who happened to hear his calls.

When, at fourteen, he first met the Austrian soldier Heinrich Harrer (who would go on to write the memoir *Seven Years in Tibet*), the two worked a film projector together. At one point, the Dalai Lama convinced Harrer to speak through a microphone and announce the next film to his tutors sitting in the theater, which Harrer did in the casual way of a Westerner. "He laughed enthusiastically at the surprised and shocked faces of the monks when they heard my cheerful, disrespectful tones," Harrer remembered. Harrer found the Dalai Lama to be an ebullient, confident teenager who felt the suffocating traditions of his office keenly. "From the first day of the year until the last, it was nothing but a long round of ceremonies," the Dalai Lama wrote. "This formalism regulated every detail of our everyday life. You had to observe it even while talking, even while walking." He preferred gossiping to politics—and the intrigues that swirled around Lhasa were as complex as any Tudor plot. When his father died in 1947, allegations circulated that he'd been poisoned as part of a complex conspiracy. (There was even one rumor that said the Fourteenth was not the real Dalai Lama but an imposter.)

Harrer described the young man he met: "His complexion was much lighter than that of the average Tibetan. His eyes, hardly narrower than those of most Europeans, were full of expression, charm and vivacity. His cheeks glowed with excitement, and as he sat he kept sliding from side to side. . . ." The Dalai Lama wore his hair long (probably, Harrer thought, as protection against the freezing cold of the Potala Palace), suffered from bad posture as a result of many hours spent bent over books in his badly lit study, and had beautiful hands, which he kept folded. "He beamed all over his face and poured out a flood of questions," Harrer remembered. "He seemed to me like a person who had for years brooded in solitude over different problems, and now that he had at last someone to talk to, wanted to know all the answers at once."

His Holiness was interested in the world outside Tibet but had few ways of learning about it. He had a seven-volume account of World War II, which he'd had translated into Tibetan, but there were large patches of world history that were a mystery to him. World War II had reshaped societies outside the Himalayas' ranges and set in motion the forces that would threaten to overwhelm his country, but the Dalai Lama learned about the battles by paging through back issues of *Life* magazine, which arrived in Lhasa months after their issue date, already musty with age.

All he had for an insight into power was the Tibetan myths and the murals that looped and spiraled across the walls of his palace. They told him how the great imperial era of Tibetan history, a time of conquest and national consolidation, drew to an end in the ninth century. The line of religious kings was terminated, and Tibet spun off into regional fiefdoms ruled by warlords and local chieftains. By the thirteenth century, when Genghis Khan marched on Tibet, he found waiting for him not a formidable opponent arrayed in battle formation but a few chieftains waiting with gifts.

The skirmishes between China and Tibet would continue for centuries, but China was now the dominant power. And for the Han, nomads such as the Tibetans were more than outsiders or enemies. They were alien, a people "not yet human, because they pursued a lifestyle similar to wandering beasts." Tibetans were destined to be seen by the Han as primitive hunter-gatherers who'd never joined the human fold. Barbarians.

The murals the Dalai Lama gazed at were also a family tree. In the mid-seventeenth century, the line of politically dominant Dalai Lamas began with the political genius of the Great Fifth. Before him, the Dalai Lamas were simple monks and abbots who were recognized as reincarnations of Chenrizi, the *bodhisattva* of Infinite Compassion. But the Great Fifth, as the leader of a relatively new sect of Tibetan Buddhism still seeking its place among competing schools, cannily reached out to Gusri Khan, founder of China's great Qing dynasty. Gusri Khan sent his soldiers to Tibet and, in a series of withering battles, defeated the Fifth's rivals and installed the Dalai Lama as ruler of a newly unified Tibet. Tibet's Buddhist rulers had struck a grand bargain with Peking, allying themselves with a more powerful neighbor. Having traded the sword for the prayer wheel, they would now depend on foreign protectors for their security. It was a compromise that would come to haunt the Fourteenth.

For hundreds of years after the Fifth's death in 1682, the curious relationship between Tibet and China waxed and waned according to the strength of the dynasty in Peking, ranging from periods of direct political control (as during the reign of Lha-bzan Khan from 1706 to 1717) to spans when the head Chinese representative in Lhasa was no more than "a mere puppet whose strings were pulled by the Dalai Lama." Successive Dalai Lamas sought alliances with the emperors of the Qing dynasty and were allowed to carry out domestic policy under their protection, watched over by a succession of *ambans*, or representatives of the emperor, who were given varying degrees of control over Tibetan affairs. Peking's representatives still had the ability to have disobedient Tibetan officials flogged (sometimes to death), but their supposed inferiors often found ways to outwit or outlast them. One *amban* complained that the Tibetans "very often . . . left orders unattended to for months on the pretext of waiting for the Dalai Lama's return or for decisions yet to be made, simply ignoring urgent requests for answers." Most often, true power lay in the hands of the Dalai Lama and his cabinet.

The Qing dynasty began to dramatically weaken in the mid-nineteenth century when rising imperialist powers such as England and Russia started to impinge on its territories. By 1911, China had descended into a patchwork of warring chieftains and provinces, and after 1913, Tibet began to consider itself a fully independent nation. But it failed to grasp its best chance at autonomy, even declining to petition the United Nations for recognition as a sovereign state. Tibet, the keeper of the Dharma, remained locked behind its wind-whipped summits.

Until a resurgent China, under Mao Zedong, returned.


Despite the company of old men and what could have been a soul-crushing separation from his family, the Dalai Lama was somehow able to retain the sympathies and qualities of a child. While locked up in the Potala, he would watch the prisoners held in the yard below. "Many of them were sort of my friends," he recalled. "I watched their lives every day. Many were common criminals, but still I could see their pain as a boy. . . . So when I first came to power, I released all [of them]." His previous self, the Thirteenth, would have frowned at the gesture. But it was very much in keeping with the new incarnation.

This is really the Dalai Lama's first great triumph. He didn't become a wild and rebellious hedonist, like the Sixth. He didn't retreat into religious isolation, like the Eighth. He didn't attempt to mold himself into a political mastermind, like the Fifth, or a sharp-elbowed strongman, like the Thirteenth. The teenaged Dalai Lama somehow found the strength to remain himself, a charismatic and simple-hearted young man in a dangerous time.

*Three*

# ACROSS THE GHOST RIVER

*I*n 1950, when the Dalai Lama was fifteen, the twentieth century arrived in Tibet in the form of the People's Liberation Army. Some 80,000 battle-trained Chinese soldiers crossed the "Ghost River" that separates China from the Tibetan province of Chamdo. The Tibetan army that faced them was badly trained, badly equipped, and, at 8,500 soldiers and officers, almost ludicrously undermanned, a legacy of the monasteries' distrust of the military. In Tibet, soldiers were thought of as social outcasts because they killed living things, against the Buddha's strict prohibition. "[They] were held to be like butchers," remembered the Dalai Lama, and, like butchers, they were called "impure bones" by other Tibetans and forbidden to marry outside their group. Centuries after conquering large swaths of Asia, Tibetan soldiers had to import their techniques and their marching songs and even their vocabulary from the British army, as there were no words in Tibetan for things such as "fix arms." The memory of military aggression had faded so thoroughly, even the words had disappeared.

Warriors from eastern Tibet, the Khampas, put up a spirited resistance to the invasion, but the Tibetan army collapsed and resistance was quickly extinguished. During the onslaught, a frantic Tibetan official telegraphed the *Kashag*, the Tibetan cabinet, for instructions and was told the members could not respond because they were on a picnic. "Shit on the picnic!" (*"Skyag pa'I gling kha!"*), he famously wired back.

Tibet reacted to the threat from China with a kind of spiritual rearmament. Buddhist monks were ordered to read the Tibetan Bible at public ceremonies attended by throngs of praying villagers and farmers. Smoke appeared on the summits of holy mountains as monks took turns stoking fires that burned fragrant incense. New prayer wheels sprang up in remote corners of the country, holy relics were brought out from dusty vaults, and believers implored the spirits to protect the Dharma and the Tibetan people. But nothing stopped Mao's battalions.

Mao turned his eyes to Tibet after winning his brutal war with Chiang Kai-shek's army, the Kuomintang. "China has stood up" were the Communist leader's famous words when he declared the People's Republic in Tiananmen Square. The Communists had come to power as fierce nationalists, and restoring Tibet to the fold was high on their list of priorities. One of Mao's first objectives after the takeover was the reunification of the motherland, the recovery of lands that, in the Chinese mind, had been lost to "splittists" or imperialists in the decades and centuries before. On January 7, 1950, a Communist general announced that the People's Liberation Army had wiped out the last of the Kuomintang resistance in southwest China; he added that the army's next mission would be to "liberate our compatriots in Tibet."

Occupying the country offered Mao a foreign policy victory as well as a domestic one: It would move China's border from the Yangtze River to the Himalayas, giving Peking an almost impregnable buffer against land armies sweeping across from India eastward or from Pakistan and eastern Turkistan northeastward. And it would eliminate the possibility of a free Tibet becoming a staging ground for imperialists in London, Washington, or Tokyo. "What is meant by independence here," wrote one Chinese official from Lhasa, "is in fact to turn Tibet into a colony or protectorate of a foreign country." Steeped in the powerful tradition of Chinese victimhood, Mao and his followers sincerely believed that Tibet belonged within the new China. Every move toward independence was regarded by the Chinese as the first crack in a dam that would result in national disintegration. Traditionally known as "the treasure house of the west," Tibet also held vast quantities of copper, lead, gold, and zinc, along with million of acres of forests and—unknown to Mao at the time—reserves of oil, uranium, and borax. It had resources that China could use to grow.

For Mao, it was essential that the Tibetans be reunited with the homeland, along with the Mongolians, the Uighurs, and the rest of China's far-flung minorities. "The relationship between Tibet and China would be like brothers," he said. "The oppression of one nationality by another would be eliminated. All nationalities would work for the benefit of the Motherland." The Communists acknowledged the deep cultural differences between the two nations—they were hard to ignore—but they insisted that the two societies had grown together over centuries. The Tibetans, on the other hand, believed that the relationship had been one of equals, and that Tibet had kept control of its own internal affairs, its cultural institutions, and its political independence.

Each side hid uncomfortable truths behind their interpretations of history: The Chinese failed to acknowledge that they'd forced a civilized Tibet to accept their protection at the point of a spear and that their control over their neighbor often slipped into a ceremonial façade as the dynasties in Peking faltered. And when the Tibetans painted the relationship as a primarily spiritual bond, they ignored China's military and political influence. But the Tibetans carried the deeper point: over centuries of intense contact, their nation had never willingly assimilated into Han society.

In 1950, none of that mattered. China had taken Tibet. After the invasion, *Life* magazine asked the question that was on the minds of Tibet-watchers everywhere: would the Dalai Lama now become "one more in the succession of Moscow-pulled puppets?"

The Dalai Lama, and the world at large, knew little about Mao in 1950. The Chinese leader was unquestionably a political genius, a supremely magnetic personality who was unmatched in his ability to get his followers to do the unthinkable for him. Mao promised the Chinese people deliverance from the chaos that had racked the nation since the breakup of the Qing dynasty in the mid-nineteenth century. Mao reversed a century of Chinese history and unified the country. And he promised to end the intrusions by foreign powers that were regarded by the average citizen as a deep and lingering humiliation.

But the Great Leader, as he came to be known, also conducted one of the most ruthless campaigns in history, not only against the armies of Chiang Kai-shek but against his own cadres. He believed himself to be one of history's great upsetters, the men who shatter existing societies and remake them through terror. "When Great Heroes give full play to their impulses," he wrote, "they are magnificently powerful, stormy and invincible." Thousands of his own followers were killed or driven mad in campaigns carefully planned by the Communist leader himself. His cadres used new techniques to get confessions from "rightists," such as "angel plucking zither," where a wire was run through a man's penis and then up around his ears, and his interrogators strummed the line, causing intense anguish. Mao even composed the posters for rallies in which rich peasants were executed after torture sessions in front of baying crowds:

> *Watch us kill the landlords today.*
> *Aren't you afraid?*
> *It's knife slicing upon knife.*

Once in control, Mao remade China with a diabolical completeness, using mass terror and raw intimidation. The campaign was literally dehumanizing: at one point, the Chairman even considered replacing citizens' names with numbers. In coming to power, Mao had lived up to his childhood nickname, *shisan yazi*, "boy of stone."

When the Chinese invaded, the Dalai Lama was three years short of the traditional age for ascending the throne. But posters began to appear on Lhasa streets condemning the government and demanding that the Dalai Lama take up the leadership of Tibet. Street songs—one of the only forms of protest that the average Tibetan had access to—carried the same message. The aristocratic ministers were often seen as crooked and self-serving; they eagerly cooperated with the occupiers in return for vast sums of money. "The noblemen were getting truckloads of silver," says Professor Gray Tuttle of Columbia University. Even the young Panchen Lama, the second most powerful figure in Tibet and traditionally a rival to the Dalai Lama for power in the country, came out in favor of the occupation and traveled to China to accept cash payments for his support.

Only the teenaged Dalai Lama, who'd barely begun to make his mark on the society, was seen as incorruptible. Tibetans believed, above all, that he would protect them and the Dharma.

As the nation turned to him, the Dalai Lama felt only a rising panic. He knew he wasn't ready to lead. "The challenge filled me with anxiety," he said. "I knew nothing of the outside world, and had no political experience." But the decision wasn't his. After debating the issue, government ministers decided to leave the matter in the hands of the two state oracles, the Nechung and the Gadong. The Nechung Oracle was evasive, saying only, "If you don't make good offerings, I cannot protect the welfare of religion and of the people." The Gadong, too, was unresponsive. Only after a government official chastised the oracle did the Gadong come alive. He spun into a monk's dance and ended up directly in front of the Dalai Lama. The oracle prostrated himself three times and laid a *kata*, the white offering scarf, at His Holiness's feet, saying, "His time has come." The Nechung Oracle was brought back into the room and seconded the decision.

The Dalai Lama ascended the throne on November 17, 1950, a date chosen by the state astrologers. "I had to leave my adolescence behind and prepare myself as best I could to lead the country," he said. "I was faced with the immediate prospect of leading my country as it prepared for war."

The young monk had no training in politics, no leadership

philosophy, and no close advisers he could trust implicitly. Even among the sweepers, his favorite—a man who'd become his playmate and his guardian—was gone by this time. "I realized that in a way his death symbolized the end of my childhood," the Dalai Lama wrote. He was as alone, as unmoored, as he'd ever been.

Then a remarkable thing happened. The Buddhist scriptures that had seemed so dull and lifeless for so many years began to sing to him. In his midteens, he began delving into the huge body of Buddhist literature and finding in it inspiration and guidance. Part of the change came in regard to his famous outbursts that verged on physical violence. The young monk "began to realize what a destructive thing anger was," he remembered, "and I was making a big effort to control my terrible temper." But Tibet's darkening fate also urged him on.

Faith transformed the Dalai Lama's life just as Tibet entered a fatal crisis. And one can surmise that anxiety over what lay before him, and the fact that he was essentially alone in facing it, sent the Dalai Lama searching for a true compass. What is beyond question is that he found that direction, at long last, in the Dharma.

A year later, in the southern Tibetan city of Dromo, the sixteen-year-old Dalai Lama sat listening to a news broadcast from Radio Peking on an old Bush radio hooked up to a car battery. He and his ministers had retreated here, to a region that the PLA had not yet penetrated to, when word of the Chinese invasion reached Lhasa. Now His Holiness was forced to listen as the Chinese announced that their armies had ended Tibet's "enslavement and suffering" under foreign imperialists. "I could not believe my ears," the Dalai Lama remembered. "I felt physically ill as I listened to this unbelievable mixture of lies and fanciful clichés."

The Chinese occupation was codified in the "Seventeen Point Agreement for the Peaceful Liberation of Tibet," signed by Chinese and Tibetan negotiators on May 23, 1951, without the approval of the Dalai Lama or his government. The agreement had, on the face of it, several clauses that reassured the Tibetans about their sovereignty over domestic issues. Clause 3 gave them "national regional autonomy." Clause 7 guaranteed protection for Tibet's Buddhists, decreeing that "the religious beliefs, customs and habits of the Tibetan people shall be respected." But other points made it clear that the Chinese Central People's Government would control the external affairs of the country, national defense, and even domestic policy. In effect, all the levers of power would be in the hands of the Chinese. The Tibetans would have to rely on Mao's goodwill to ensure that their political rights were respected and their culture survived.

Hoping to recruit the necessary allies, Tibetans turned to the wider world. They were bitterly disappointed. The Dalai Lama's oldest brother, Norbu, opened a channel of communication with the U.S. State Department—and the CIA—asking them to assist the beleaguered Tibetans. The Americans were eager to come to an agreement but needed assurances the Dalai Lama would publicly resist the Communist regime. Nehru's India, worried about offending the Chinese and angered that its neighbor had sought assistance from Washington instead of from New Delhi, offered nothing. (Indian officials were also sensitive on the issue of annexing land, having themselves recently taken over the disputed regions of Hyderabad and Kashmir.) The British regarded the occupation as a fait accompli and felt that the Anglo-American reaction should follow the lead of India. Their diplomats also believed that opposing China would complicate "peace moves" to end the Korean conflict. In short, the British concluded that supporting Tibet offered no advantages—diplomatic, military, or commercial—but only risks that could complicate the Cold War in Asia. Only tiny El Salvador offered to sponsor a resolution at the United Nations condemning the invasion. The Americans became the Tibetans' last, slim hope.

In July 1951, the U.S. government sent the Dalai Lama an unsigned letter laying out its conditions for helping the Tibetans. It began paternally by warning His Holiness that the Communists were a new phenomenon: "Some of your advisors probably think that they understand the Chinese Communists and can make a bargain with them. We do not think that they understand Communism or the record of its leaders." The document went on to call the Dalai Lama the "chief hope of Tibet" and argued he would be most effective outside its borders "to symbolize the hopes of the Tibetans for the recovery of Tibet's freedom." If His Holiness disavowed the Seventeen Point Agreement, the United States was prepared to "issue a public statement of our own supporting your stand." Washington would back the Dalai Lama's cause in the United Nations, and it would supply his government with loans and light arms. But only if he formed a serious resistance to the occupation.

The letter's first lines address a common perception of the Dalai Lama: that he had no faith in his own advisers. American officials couldn't even be sure their messages were getting through to His Holiness. One State Department cable complained that the "God-king is almost inaccessible except to certain traditional advisers and certain family members." His Holiness was the nominal head of government, but, at just sixteen, he hadn't even begun to install his own trusted advisers, a process that could take years. "He was isolated in Lhasa," notes American Buddhist scholar Robert Thurman. "He would hear gossip from the janitors in the Potala."

And at this crucial moment, the Tibetans were bitterly divided among themselves. The Dalai Lama's older brothers Norbu and Gyalo, along with some lay officials in the Tibetan government, favored rejecting the Seventeen Point Agreement and seeking asylum in another country (India was the leading candidate, with Thailand and Ceylon also mentioned). The Americans agreed and pressed the religious issue to make their point: "If Tibet is to be saved from the enemy of all religions, Communism," wrote Robert Linn, an American consular official in India, "it will be necessary for you to show the highest courage and act at once."

Lobbying for the Dalai Lama's return to Lhasa were high government officials and the entire religious establishment. The abbots strongly favored ratification of the Seventeen Point Agreement, believing Buddhism would be protected, along with their own powerful and exalted positions. Many government ministers, aristocrats, and merchants also encouraged the Dalai Lama to make peace with Mao and return to Lhasa. They argued that the meager help offered by the Americans (and the complete lack of support from India) would doom any fight against the Communists. Besides, the Tibetan experience in regard to Chinese power was that it always faded over time. "Everything turns like a wheel," said the editor of the *Tibet Mirror*. "Tibet will once again enjoy its original freedom and independence, free of all Chinese control."

At this critical point, in exile from his capital and his throne, His Holiness decided to ask for divine guidance. His ministers chose an old divination method, putting two bits of paper, one decreeing the Dalai Lama should return to Lhasa and the other advising exile, inside two small balls of *tsampa*. The balls were dropped in a bowl and rolled around under a painting of the Palden Lhamo, the wrathful protectress of Tibet. When one of the balls dropped from the bowl, it was opened. The message? The Dalai Lama must return to Lhasa.

As the Tibetans prepared for the journey, a Chinese delegation arrived in Dromo on July 16, 1951. The apprehensive Dalai Lama, who was "half convinced they would all have horns on their heads," met with a general, who handed him a copy of the Seventeen Point Agreement. His Holiness signed it. By doing so, he was effectively declaring Tibet a region of China. But His Holiness declined to see it in strictly political terms. Instead, he sought out the Buddhist meaning of the encounter. When he was meeting with the first Chinese Communists he'd ever seen, he was encouraged, simply, to find them to be human. "Regardless of all the suspicion and anxiety I felt beforehand," he said, "during our meeting it became clear that this man, although supposedly my enemy, was in fact just a human being, an ordinary person like myself. This realization had a lasting impact on me."

For to be human, the Dalai Lama believed, was finally to be good. It was, given the situation, an almost perversely optimistic view of the world and of the Chinese Communist Party. But it illustrated His Holiness's political philosophy. "What comes naturally, I do that," he said. "It is spontaneous. I never sort of calculate." Previous Dalai Lamas had used force, alliances, violence, and cunning to advance the cause of Tibet. As much as they sought to embody compassion, they'd been necessarily ruthless when dealing with Tibetans who betrayed them or their Mongol overlords.

But the Fourteenth turned to religion as his guiding philosophy. "I had still had no theoretical training in the intricacies of international politics," he recalled. "I could only apply my religious training to these problems, aided, I trust, by common sense." While Mao had grown up internalizing Sun Tzu and *The Art of War*, the Dalai Lama sought out the loving Buddha.

Not everyone agreed with the Fourteenth's approach. He was simply too soft, it was felt in certain circles, too much the representative of Chenrizi, the compassionate one. "His Holiness is very humble and has a bit of a child nature," one senior Tibetan official told him during a conversation about the Chinese intent. "Chinese are brazen and will not hesitate to exploit this." The Dalai Lama often behaved like a lama trying to redeem his people, not a politician trying to lead them. "He thought people were so good," admits Choegyal, his younger brother. "But what the Chinese were saying and doing were not the same thing. They wanted to destroy Tibet."

His Holiness was facing, in Mao Zedong, a leader who seemingly had strayed as far from his mother's devout Buddhism as it was possible to. "Absolute selfishness and irresponsibility lay at the heart of Mao's outlook," write his biographers Jung Chang and Jon Halliday. The Chairman himself knew Buddhism; he'd been raised in the religion. But he lived by a different moral code. "Of course there are people and objects in the world," he wrote, "but they are all there only for me. . . . They have nothing to do with the reality of my own self." And when it came to violence, the Chairman was enthusiastic: "We must kill. . . . And we say it is good to kill."

One of the Dalai Lama's daily contemplations was the Buddha's teaching that enemies make the finest teachers. But how to balance the word of Buddha with what was happening around him, to face evil and call it evil? In his first encounter with the Chinese, the Dalai Lama came away as a naïve boy. He had a great deal to learn.


After the first shock of invasion, the Chinese entered Tibet on cat's feet. Chinese officials and soldiers were told to avoid "big nationality chauvinism," to speak to the Tibetans gently, to pay for everything they requisitioned, and to strive to make the natives happy. An order published in the *People's Daily* on May 26, 1951, told those traveling to Lhasa and beyond to "truly respect the Tibetan people and serve them in order to get rid of the huge gap left by history between Hans and Tibetans and to win trust." Mao's takeover of Tibet displayed an almost infinitely delicate touch and a sense of what individuals in a distant land would accept in an occupying force. The Chinese Communists didn't yet have a sympathetic base in Tibet and the PLA didn't have the infrastructure or the troop strength to dominate the country, so Mao persuaded, instead of terrorized, his new subjects.

Every effort was to be taken to mollify the Tibetans. "When the Chinese first came, they spoke very sweetly," said one monk from Kham. "They said, 'We have come to bring development. We are the same . . . same race, same color. We are brothers. We have come to help you. After we have done that, we will go back.'" The Chinese also spent lavishly on everything from barley to houses to labor. "We had a saying," commented a Tibetan government official. "Communist Chinese are grateful parents—incessant rain of cash." Marxism was barely mentioned; the silver coin, not the hammer and sickle, was the emblem of those first years of occupation.

The Chinese's strategy in Lhasa was to draw His Holiness into their camp. "Make every possible effort to use all suitable means to win over the Dalai Lama and a majority of the upper strata," Mao instructed his officials in Tibet, "and isolate the minority of bad elements in order to achieve long-term goals of transforming Tibetan economy and polity gradually without spilling blood." Above all, the Chinese left the monasteries and the religious authorities alone, knowing that to be seen as enemies of the faith would be to guarantee fierce resistance.

For the first stages of the occupation, the strategy in large part worked. The Dalai Lama had been distraught and enraged by the invasion (and his own government's abject failure to stop it), but the reports of a disciplined PLA and Tibet's need for modernization gave him hope. A key moment in the relationship came in the summer of 1954, when the Dalai Lama visited China for a nearly year-long tour. China's material progress under the Communists awed the Dalai Lama: hydroelectric dams, tractor factories, the sheer dynamism of a state-controlled economy in its first flush of production was a vision of what Tibet could become. And the ideas behind what he saw thrilled him as well. He thought Marx's beliefs were deeply attuned to his own, perhaps the closest match to the tenets of Buddhism he'd ever encountered. The emphasis on justice and equality made these beliefs far more attractive to the young leader than American-style capitalism. "The more I looked at Marxism," he said, "the more I liked it." His main objection, of course, was to the system's atheism, but he felt a synthesis between Buddhism and communism could be worked out.

"If you've ever been to where the Dalai Lama grew up, even today it's quite a poor area," notes Professor Gray Tuttle of Columbia University, who visited His Holiness's hometown. "I imagine in the 1930s when he lived there, it was much like Appalachia at that time: dirt poor. Coming from there, he probably thought, 'With communism, things could be a lot better for a lot more Tibetans.'"

Indeed, back in Lhasa, all things Chinese were fast becoming the subject of a minor fad. "There is everywhere a keenness to imitate the Chinese," wrote one observer, "to dress, to talk, behave and sing as the Chinese do." Portraits of Mao were placed next to the Dalai Lama's in the domestic shrines of smart Lhasa homes. Tibet's aristocrats, who'd always looked to England or America for direction, now saw Peking as the new ideal.

When he finally met him, the Dalai Lama found Mao impressive in ways he hadn't expected. He was physically strange: The Chairman's dark skin was flawlessly smooth and covered with a perfect sheen, and his hands were doll-like, as if carved from fine cherrywood. He wore ratty clothes, "old and ruined," shirts fraying at the cuff matched with scruffy jackets, so different from the Dalai Lama's beautiful silk robes. And he had odd mannerisms. Mao spoke in slow, short sentences, and when he turned his head, it took him several seconds to complete the gesture, which gave the fifty-four-year-old leader an air of gravity. "I felt as if I was in the presence of a strong magnetic force," the Dalai Lama said. For His Holiness, coming from a court dominated by endless ritual, Mao's off-the-cuff naturalness was electrifying.

Mao seemed remarkably flexible, announcing at one point that "the pace of reform was dictated by the wishes of the Tibetan people themselves." The Chinese leader flattered the Dalai Lama by declaring that Tibet had been great in past centuries and could be great again, with China's help. The Dalai Lama chose to trust his own heart and believe in Mao's good intentions. The robotic obedience, the weirdly mechanical nature of daily life in China unnerved him, but he felt it was a passing phase in a great human project.

But there was a jarring moment during the official visit. During one conversation, Mao leaned over to the Dalai Lama and said conversationally, "Of course, religion is poison." The statement took the young Tibetan leader completely by surprise. "How could he have misjudged me so?" he wondered. "How could he have thought that I was not religious to the core of my being?" And on the way back to Lhasa, the Dalai Lama was struck by the unreality of what he saw. Every Tibetan peasant and nomad told the Dalai Lama that the people were thriving under Mao's rule, but their faces were twisted with grief and misery. Some cried as they told His Holiness how happy they were now. He sensed "a heavy air of foreboding" as he traveled home.

## Four

# EASTERN FIRES

In 1954, everything began to change. In eastern Tibet, Mao began to implement the same "democratic reforms" he had forced on Chinese towns and villages: collectivization, forced reeducation along Communist lines, the de-emphasizing of religious faith, and the persecution of public enemies, meaning in this case the rich, the Buddhist clergy, and "rightists." Large estates and farms were confiscated. Monks were forced to leave their monasteries and build roads or join the army. Children were taken away from their families and sent to China for schooling and Communist indoctrination.

Farmers were forced to attend meetings called *thamzins,* where enemies of the people—mostly the *Ngatsap,* wealthy traders, and *Ngadhak,* the rich and government officials—were paraded onto hastily built platforms in the center of town and beaten and spit upon until they confessed to their crimes. "We could not even look up at the other people," said Dorji Damdul (an alias), whose father was a village leader before the Communists came, "and we had to avoid passing by other people on the road, too. It was like we were not among the humans." Wages were slashed, and workers were even encouraged to donate their labor "for the good of the Motherland." The rhetoric of the early years changed. "They would say, 'We must bring development and become one,'" said one Kham monk. "'We must unite. We have one enemy. That enemy is the United States of America. They are different from us. Their hair is yellow. Their eyes are white. Their noses are pointed. We have to unite and face them.'" The villagers who were hearing these speeches had never seen an American.

The eastern regions of Kham and Amdo were the first to feel the new, suffocating regime. Beginning in 1956, Khampa men and women began appearing in Lhasa with unsettling stories: The Chinese were implementing forced labor. The People's Liberation Army had arrested a number of high lamas. And then: Monks were being tossed into pits and villagers were ordered to urinate on them, or doused in kerosene and set on fire, while the PLA soldiers mockingly called for them to ask Lord Buddha to intervene. "The Chinese captured and took away many monks," said one Buddhist initiate from the Ba region. "While they were being led away, the Chinese plucked dry *bolo* plants [a thorny bush] and slapped the monks with them. Many died." The bodies of seventy monks killed at a place called Dhungku Pang "were brought on yaks and piled at the monastery's cemetery."

The Khampas found few city residents willing to listen. Lhasans were traditionally dismissive of their countrymen: Khampas were widely seen as the most ruthless bandits in Asia. Even the Dalai Lama had to admit that their "most precious possession is a gun." The pistols and swords threaded through the Khampas' wide leather belts told you everything you needed to know about how they approached the world. "You never heard the name mentioned without an undertone of fear and warning," remembered Heinrich Harrer. Ironically, Lhasans looked on Khampas the way the Chinese looked on *them*: as barbarians.

One Khampa refugee recalled coming to the capital and telling people there that he'd witnessed the destruction of an important Kham monastery and the gruesome deaths of those inside. His listeners accused him of lying. They were his own relatives.


The Dalai Lama watched his eastern provinces rise up against the Chinese. Golok tribes and Khampa warriors attacked Chinese installations, emptied PLA arsenals of their weapons, and ambushed convoys and patrols. Charging into the mechanized Chinese ranks on horseback, bandoliers of bullets and grenades across their chests, they looked like throwbacks to another century. But they often prevailed in gruesome, all-out assaults. One leader, Gompo Tashi, remembered the Battle at the Nyimo River, in which an outnumbered force of Tibetans fought against thousands of PLA soldiers:

> As the buglers in our camp sounded the signal to attack, I led seventy horses on to the field. Galloping at full speed, we charged the enemy like wild animals, fighting them hand to hand. The Chinese were unable to resist the onslaught and withdrew to a nearby village. . . . We shot down every

door and window in [the] houses and eventually had to burn them, as this was the only way to destroy the Chinese who were hiding inside.

Escalation followed escalation. In southern Kham, a local revolt centered on Samphe-Lang, an important monastery in Changtreng. The grounds of the monastery were packed with 3,000 monks and families who'd been targeted by the PLA or displaced by the land reforms. A standoff ensued: the Khampas blocked up the river supplying the Chinese camp with fresh water, and the PLA dropped leaflets warning the rebels to surrender. And then one day out of a clear blue sky, a single plane emerged and dropped a ragged line of bombs on the monastery. Hundreds, perhaps thousands, died.

One of the men who silently carried these stories with him was named Lithang Athar Norbu, a calm, peaceful-looking young Khampa, just twenty-eight years old, who'd already passed through more personas than most Tibetan men would see in a lifetime: peasant boy, novice monk, assistant to a *shusor* (a businessman in monk's robes who traveled the country buying supplies for his Buddhist clients), and rebel. The Khampas were stoics by temperament and circumstance; they led harsh lives where a bullet from an enemy clan or amebic dysentery might kill them at any moment. Many people from Amdo didn't like to be seen crying even at the death of a child. But Athar had seen Tibetans slain by the Chinese; he'd heard the accounts of slaughtered monks, dying while PLA officers screamed that they'd been trying to civilize the Tibetans for five years but they were still animals. These stories were told over campfires on pitch-black Himalayan slopes, and the images of death and desecration had affected the young man deeply.

"Many of our loved ones we had seen die," Athar said. "Many in great agony. These are things you don't forget."

The CIA had taken notice of the rebels as early as 1952, and as the resistance gathered force, the agency formed the Tibetan Task Force to harass and degrade the Chinese occupation. Back in Washington, a small team—often just five or six agents—was involved full-time in planning operations, supplying the rebels, and training Khampas in the latest insurgency tactics and weapons. As the uprising in Kham and Amdo intensified during 1957, an order arrived in the CIA's Far East Bureau telling the agents there to find a small group of Tibetans for "external training as a pilot team that would infiltrate their homeland and assess the state of resistance." Athar and five other Khampas were smuggled out of Tibet by the CIA, with help from Gyalo, the Dalai Lama's brother. The operation was cloaked in secrecy. "Gyalo said, 'You cannot tell even your parents, relatives, or friends where you are going,'" Athar remembered. They'd never seen an American before, or an airplane, or an ocean. They were jerked from a medieval countryside into the Cold War.

After honing the recruits' skills on Saipan, often called the "Island of the Dead" because of all the Japanese skeletons left there during World War II, the CIA secretly brought the insurgents to Camp Hale in Colorado, which, at 9,200 feet, was the closest thing to Tibet's high plateau the U.S. Army could find. There the young rebels were given an accelerated course in the agency's many specialties: radio signal plans, hand-to-hand combat, first aid, sabotage, and night maneuvers. They practiced encoding and decoding with the agency's one-time pads, destroying the pages once a message was sent. They were handed compasses (they'd never seen one before) and told how to read a map. "At one point, we had to take our radio sets on our backs and go into the forest," Athar recalled. "Every day we had to practice sending telegrams about how Tibetans were fighting against the Chinese and the movements of PLA troops, until we could do it without making a single mistake." And they were introduced to the arsenal of the Cold War: 60mm and 57mm recoilless rifles, fragmentation explosives, incendiary grenades. They built booby traps and tossed Molotov cocktails at imaginary targets. They jumped out of planes. And, crucially, they learned to send Morse code messages via the rugged and waterproof RS-1 spy radio, used by agents from Prague to Saigon.

On October 20, 1957, after nine months away from their homeland, Athar and his compatriots prepared to reenter Tibet. Chanting the Buddhist mantra of purification, *Om Badzar Satwa Hung*, the Khampas boarded a black B-17 Flying Fortress in East Pakistan, all its markings carefully removed and its crew changed out for Czech and Polish expats. If the plane crashed or was shot down, there'd be nothing to trace it back to the CIA. The plane flew toward Tibet, the Khampas not even donning their oxygen masks until the altimeter read 18,000 feet, when their CIA trainer barked at them to put them on. When it was their turn, Athar and his part-ner, Lhotse, dropped into the moonlit night, above a spot chosen by the CIA's cartographer from hand-drawn maps dating back to a 1904 British expedition. "I could see the Tsangpo River gleaming in the dark beneath us," Athar remembered. "I was so excited to be back in Tibet." The pair landed close to the walls of Samye, the first Buddhist monastery in Tibet, a good omen. Each carried a British Lee-Enfield .303 rifle, a 9mm Sten machine gun, signal books, and "the L Tablet," a lethal cyanide ampoule tucked into a box filled with sawdust. If the Chinese captured them, they were to clamp the tablet between their teeth so that they couldn't betray the other guerrillas fanning out across Tibet.

"We pulled out our radio sets and sent a message saying we'd landed safely," Athar said. Soon a reply came from the CIA's

Tibetan Task Force. "Very happy to hear safely arrived. We are throwing a party to celebrate."

Athar and Lhotse's instructions from their CIA handlers were extensive. They were to meet with leaders of the resistance, who'd formed into a group called the Chushi Gangdrug ("Four Rivers, Six Ranges"—a reference to the land of Kham). The CIA wanted to assess the rebels' strengths, their needs, and their popular support, and Athar and Lhotse were given the job of providing hard numbers. The CIA also asked them to relay back as much information on the PLA as they could find: on airfields, troop strengths, available infrastructure, and the occupation's effect on the Tibetan economy. But most important, they were to meet with the Dalai Lama, draw out his true feelings on the resistance, and evaluate the threat to his life.

For centuries, Kham and Amdo had been estranged from Lhasa, the seat of Tibetan power. A Khampa army had even marched toward the capital in 1934, to sack it and free themselves of its pernicious influence once and for all, but the leaders had been betrayed before they got close to the city. Often, it seemed the only thing that bonded Tibetan to Tibetan was *tsampa*—the barley meal that everyone ate, regardless of class or region—and the presence of the Dalai Lama himself.

The blessing of His Holiness was absolutely necessary for any legitimate national resistance. "A word from the Dalai Lama," wrote the French explorer Michel Peissel, "one single proclamation, and all Tibet would undoubtedly have stood up and faced the Chinese." The Khampas couldn't help but suspect that the Dalai Lama himself had gone over to the Chinese side, while the Chinese suspected the opposite, that he was a secret supporter of the resistance. The leading Chinese official, Tan Guansan, dropped unsubtle hints about how they would address this. "When you have a piece of fly-blown meat," he said as the tension between the PLA and the Tibetans grew, "you have to get rid of the meat before you exterminate the flies." The Dalai Lama took it to mean that if he were killed, the rebellion would disappear.

Athar and Lhotse spent two days in hiding before venturing out to begin their mission. They disguised themselves as religious pilgrims, who could be seen in every town and hamlet throughout Tibet with their rosaries, their lips reciting a mantra, and their faces lined with exhaustion after months of traveling. The pair developed a technique: Lhotse would observe PLA locations through binoculars while Athar slipped a gun beneath his robe and walked into a local town to buy food. Athar's instructions were clear: "If I was recognized by the Chinese army, then I was supposed to begin shooting, while Lhotse would hit the main road and escape." They scouted the countryside, reporting on Chinese troop strengths and radar systems—and guiding CIA planes to their drop zones. "We'd send a message ahead saying there was going to be twenty-six bundles, or whatever, and how many mules they'd need to move the stuff," explains John Greaney, the deputy head of the Tibetan Task Force at the agency. Athar and Lhotse hiked to the target, built bonfires with dried yak dung, and watched as parachutes bloomed and the boxes of 2.36-inch bazookas, British Lee-Enfield rifles, grenades, and .30-caliber light machine guns came drifting down from 30,000 feet.

Finally, a year after he was dropped back into Tibet, Athar was able to arrange a meeting with Phala, the Dalai Lama's Lord Chamberlain, a tall aristocrat nicknamed "the keeper of the secrets." Athar was unaware that he was the latest in a line of rebels who'd come to Lhasa on the same mission. Emissary after emissary had made his way to the Norbulingka to ask the Dalai Lama for his blessing. But the Lord Chamberlain had turned them down, one by one.

Athar and the aristocratic minister met in the fragrant grounds of the Norbulingka, accompanied by a guerrilla leader named Gompo Tashi. But as soon as Athar revealed that he was working with the CIA, the mood changed. The Lord Chamberlain nervously remarked that they shouldn't be meeting at the summer palace, that Lhasa was filled with spies and Chinese sympathizers who would love nothing more than to connect the Dalai Lama with the rebels. "The Chinese were watching my every move," the Lord Chamberlain later said. The cabinet members were "terrified" of the Chinese, and it was well known that Mao and his lieutenants were obsessed with the idea of foreign imperialists working to split Tibet from the motherland. If word got out that the Dalai Lama was talking to the Americans, the consequences would be dire. Athar was astonished to hear that he couldn't even meet with the Dalai Lama to relay his request.

(Phala remembered the meeting differently. In his version, he told the two guerrillas the Dalai Lama knew all about the rebels and their links to America's spy agency. Not only that, His Holiness asked Athar and Lhotse to report to the Lord Chamberlain about their future operations. If Phala's account is correct, the Dalai Lama knew about the guerrillas' plans almost from the beginning.)

Deeply disappointed, Athar had to send a message back to Washington saying he'd been unable to gauge His Holiness's true feelings about the rebellion. A second meeting with the Lord Chamberlain was equally frustrating. The veil that had separated His Holiness from the rest of the world for centuries remained impenetrable. Meanwhile, the *Indian Express* in Bombay, which, unlike newspapers in New York and London, kept a watchful eye on developments in Lhasa, wrote in December 1958 about rumors that Peking was even thinking of deposing His Holiness

. . .

and replacing him with the second-most-powerful incarnate, the pro-Communist Panchen Lama. "As things stand," it said, "the Dalai Lama has no hope. Behind him stands his red shadow, the puppet Panchen Lama, whom the Communists will put in his place at the slightest sign of trouble."

It was an excellent prediction.


Even schoolboys knew that Tibet had arrived at a critical moment. Choegyal, His Holiness's younger brother, was a thirteen-year-old novice monk at the august Drepung Monastery (whose name means, literally, "pile of rice," for its white buildings piled at the foot of Mount Gephel). The Dalai Lama's family boasted sons of every temperament: Gyalo was remarkably tough and single-minded. The CIA agent Ken Knaus would later describe him as "an unguided missile," thrusting his arm straight out to denote the force of Gyalo's personality. Norbu was a religious-minded former abbot who'd been driven into exile by the Chinese, and Lobsang was so "nervous and insecure" that he would later suffer catatonic spells. But Choegyal, at thirteen, was mischief personified. At his monastery, where he was a less than willing initiate, he would carry needle and thread in his pocket to sew together the robes of monks sitting in front of him. The Dalai Lama called him "a constant source of delight and terror."

At Drepung, before the New Year came, the gossip had been of rebellion. "My classmates were all talking about resisting the Chinese," said Choegyal. "We knew there was going to be a fight, and we were sure we'd win." The tension was remarked on by everyone. During one of her weekly lunches with the isolated Dalai

Lama, his mother asked him one day about the rumors that the Chinese wished to do him harm. His Holiness laughed out loud.

"What could happen?" he answered.

"They will kill you," his mother replied.

"What good would that do them?" the Dalai Lama said to her. "And if they try to take me to China against my will, I won't go."

The answer didn't comfort Diki Tsering. If the Chinese tried to take her son away, he wouldn't have any choice in the matter.

At luncheon, she told her son, who couldn't travel freely outside the gates of the Norbulingka, that Lhasa was slowly being transformed. Khampa warriors were flooding the city, confrontations between Tibetans and PLA troops were increasing, and the frustration of the crowds was growing palpable. Lhasa looked "more and more like a military camp" than the festive city they'd known when they first arrived there twenty years before.

Perhaps remembering the Thirteenth's famous warning, the Dalai Lama responded disconsolately this time. One day, he said, the Chinese would take away everything that Tibetans held dear.

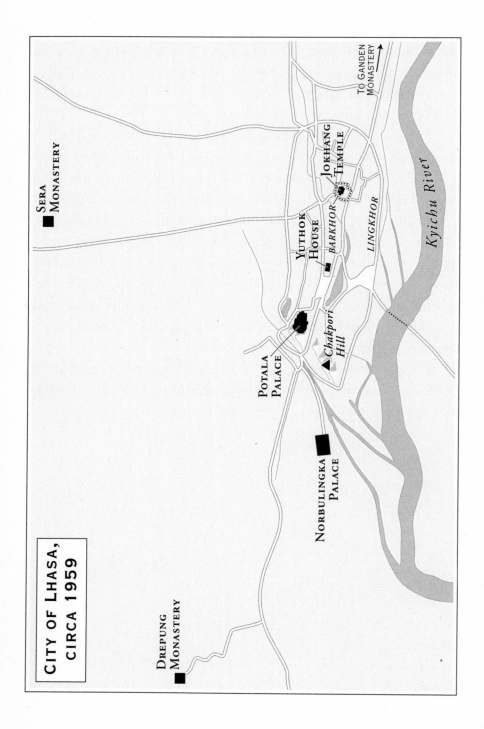

CITY OF LHASA,
CIRCA 1959

DREPUNG
MONASTERY

SERA
MONASTERY

NORBULINGKA
PALACE

POTALA
PALACE

YUTHOK
HOUSE

BARKHOR

JOKHANG
TEMPLE

LINGKHOR

*Chakpori
Hill*

*Kyichu River*

TO GANDEN
MONASTERY

*Five*

# A RUMOR

*I*n March 1959, the Dalai Lama sat studying in the Norbulingka. Mönlam, the Great Prayer Festival, was under way, during which thousands of monks came to the capital for meditation and to engage in the byzantine politics of the monasteries. This year the festival would see the young Dalai Lama take his examinations, called the *Geshe Lharampa*, to become a Master of Metaphysics, the highest attainment for a Buddhist monk, a grueling all-day affair in which His Holiness would have to face three panels of scholars in *Pramana* (Logic), *Madhyamika* (the Middle Path), and *Prajraparamita* (the

Perfection of Wisdom), followed by an evening session in which the country's most renowned teachers would test him in *Vinaya* (the canon of monastic discipline) and *Abhidharma* (Metaphysics). The nervous Dalai Lama was focused on only one thing: passing the test. To fail in any subject would be a humiliation.

Three miles away from the summer palace, Lhasa awaited. It was a dense, smoky city that quickly gave way to wild greenery and the odd, stunning palace. The English writer Perceval Landon caught its peculiar qualities at the turn of the twentieth century:

> This city of gigantic palace and golden roof, these wild stretches of woodland, these acres of close-cropped grazing land and marshy grass, ringed and delimited by high trees or lazy streamlets of brown transparent water over which the branches almost meet. . . . Between and over the glades and woodlands of the city of Lhasa itself peeps an adobe stretch of narrow streets and flat-topped houses crowned here and there with a blaze of golden roofs or gilded cupolas.

The city was meant to be in a lighthearted mood. Losar, the fifteen days of celebration marking the arrival of the Tibetan New Year, was approaching, and they were days that every Tibetan looked forward to all year. For weeks, monks had been shining the floors of their rooms by sweeping back and forth on rags tied to their feet. They'd hung newly laundered white curtains on their windows and cleaned every inch of their tiny quarters. In the city below, Tibetan mothers had been preparing special dough balls to be given out to friends and relatives. Inside were special ingredients that carried a message for the recipient: salt or rice was a good omen, chiles meant one talked too much, and bits of coal signified a black heart. Anything old, useless, or broken was gathered to be tossed out at certain crossroads in the city; it was considered bad luck to carry such items into the New Year. Silver butter lamps were polished and placed before Buddhist shrines, one in each home, and these were themselves cleaned and restocked with bowls of fresh nuts and dates. Hearths were dashed with scalding hot water, brooms brought out. All the rituals of renewal dreaded by lazy children were carried out in households across Lhasa.

The city was overflowing with people, jammed with perhaps three times its usual population of 30,000. Merchants in tiny dark stalls sold Chinese jade, yak meat marbled with fat, American galoshes, hand grenades, wireless radios, kimonos from Tokyo, sewing machines, and prayer wheels whose every turn sent a mantra upward to the heavens, along with copies of Bing Crosby's not-quite-latest records (it took up to two years for 78s such as "White Christmas" to make it to Tibet). Wild-looking nomads whose hair had never been combed and whose faces were blasted tones of red and brown from the winds of the eastern provinces made their circuit of the holiest site in Tibetan Buddhism, the fortresslike Jokhang Temple in the center of Lhasa. Away from the public squares, pregnant women lay outside stark naked even in the chilly air, their bellies oiled to catch the spring sunlight, which it was believed would give them an easy birth.

And then there were the green trucks of the People's Liberation Army. The soldiers, dressed in green drab, held rifles close to their chests as they looked down from the truck beds. The PLA soldiers were young, their faces expressionless. They were the phenomenally disciplined products of Mao's revolution, so different from the corrupt, drunken troops of previous eras. The soldiers of the PLA had been a common sight in Lhasa for years, but that March, hatred of them had suddenly spiked. Tibetans shouted insults to them or called for them to leave Lhasa, and there had been several stabbings of Chinese soldiers. Loudspeakers crackled to life with news of the country's deliverance: "Hail to the liberation of the Tibetans! You are people who are lagging behind in the world. We are the people who will help you. Our relationship dates back thousands of years. We have come to bring progress."

The PLA soldiers were often as miserable as the Lhasans themselves, though for different reasons. Tibet was a hardship post, in many cases thousands of miles from the soldiers' homes and among people known to be hostile to the Han—"the barbarians," as the common soldiers called them. The PLA troops called their mission "being buried," because the Chinese words for "bury" (*xia zang*) and "Tibet" (*Xi zang*) are so close, and because going to Lhasa was like a death.

If Lhasans had, at first, cooperated with the PLA, the troops' presence had now become stifling. "No one could speak their mind because someone might be listening," said Diki Tsering, the Dalai Lama's mother. She heard rumors of Tibetans who spoke out against the Chinese disappearing, their deaths blamed on Khampa bandits. "Gradually, life in Lhasa became unbearable," she remembered. "For months my daughter and I had been talking late into the night about means of escape."

But it was the resplendent, martial Khampas, the Golok men wearing yak-hide boots and bowler hats, and the others from outside the Vale of Lhasa whose presence signaled the greatest disruption in the balance of things. With their guns slung through wide leather belts, their dark eyes often appearing like slits in an agate mask, they were the physical reminders of a dissipated empire. Twelve hundred years ago, Tibet had been the premier Asian power, an empire that sprawled from Turkistan in the north, Changan in the east, Afghanistan in the west, and the Ganges River in the southwest. But now these men and their families were refugees in their own capital, having pitched their tents on the banks of the slow-moving Kyichu River to the southeast of the city.

It was as if a previous incarnation of Tibet were squatting in the city, waiting for events to unfold.

The spark that lit the thousand-year-old kindling came very early on March 10, 1959. That morning, what seemed an entirely innocuous rumor spread through the streets of Lhasa: the Dalai Lama was planning to go to a dance performance at the Chinese military headquarters. Minute by minute, the news seemed to accelerate along the cobblestoned streets and dark, narrow alleyways that ring the city. It was the kind of gossip that people found almost physically painful to keep to themselves. Women dropped the bowls they'd been kneading barley dough in and men let the cups of butter tea fall soundlessly from their hands as they got up and ran to the streets. Sixteen-year-old Lobsang Yonten, the son of an aristocratic family with deep ties to Tibetan nationalists, was off for the New Year's holidays and at that moment playing board games in one of the alley tea-stalls that dotted the city. He heard someone shout out the news of the Dalai Lama's visit to the Chinese camp, and the first thing that sprung into his mind was the thought, "I would sacrifice my life for His Holiness." Yonten instantly began running. He ran toward the Norbulingka, where the Dalai Lama was staying, as if the Chinese were lining up to shoot him at that very moment, because that is what the rumor meant to most Tibetans: that the Chinese were about to kill or kidnap their Precious Jewel.

As he emerged from the alley, Yonten could see others running flat out, east toward the Dalai Lama's palace. Although he couldn't see her, his sister, hair still wet, was flying toward the Jewel Park from another direction. She'd been in the midst of washing her hair when she'd heard the rumor and had begun running without remembering to grab a towel. Doors banged as houses emptied of people and merchants hurriedly shut their shops to join the crowd. The shouting grew louder as they ran. It was as if a small cyclone were sweeping Yonten and the others along the streets, pushing them the three miles to the Norbulingka.

To an outsider, the news would have meant nothing. The dance performance was one in an endless parade of visits and duties that the Dalai Lama spent his life carrying out, much to his own disappointment. The invitation stemmed from a near-forgotten conversation weeks before in which the Chinese official Tan Guansan had mentioned to the Dalai Lama that a new dance troupe had arrived in Lhasa and the Tibetan leader, out of politeness more than anything, had replied he'd like to see them. "It had been our painful experience under the Chinese regime that I did not have the option even to decline a social invitation," he remembered. But the visit hadn't been coordinated through the usual channels, and when the Dalai Lama's staff had found out about it the night before, one of them in particular—a young official named Barshi Ngawang Tenkyong—panicked.

A junior bureaucrat in the Tibetan government, Barshi had been on edge for any signs of Chinese intrigue. Tibetans believed that the Chinese often targeted high lamas. "By 1959, the people were experienced in the Chinese methods," says Narkyid, a Lhasa government official. "In Kham and Amdo, they would invite the top monk and sometimes shoot him and sometimes kidnap him. So everybody was thinking of this." Rumors had swirled through Lhasa for weeks about Chinese soldiers dressed in civilian clothes carrying bombs to the Potala Palace, or about three planes at a nearby airport waiting to take the Dalai Lama to Peking. "The Tibetans were out of their minds with worry about threats to His Holiness," remembers one Tibetan.

On hearing about the Dalai Lama's visit to the Chinese military HQ, Barshi decided to consult the Nechung Oracle. For hundreds of years, the Nechung had been the vessel for the spirit known as Dorje Drak-den, the personal protector of the Dalai Lama and the government of Tibet. Every major decision was brought before him.

As Barshi waited for his audience, cymbals clashed, the oracle's assistants began chanting, and the Nechung himself emerged, dressed in golden silk brocade, his tunic covered in ancient symbols, a mirror around his neck surrounded by amethyst and turquoise flashing in the darkened room as the spell took hold. The man sat on a cushion and soon his eyes bulged as the spirit of Dorje Drak-den began to enter his body. His breaths came in short, choppy bursts. A massive, ornate helmet was placed on his head, and it was now understood that the spirit was present in the room.

Barshi had asked the oracle what was the best course to protect the Dalai Lama. In his guttural voice, the Nechung replied that a ritual of Buddhist prayers should be performed in a specific order. With that, he abruptly stood up, indicating the session was over.

There is a saying in Tibet, "When the gods get desperate, they tell lies." Barshi sat openmouthed, astonished by the evasive answer, and as the Nechung turned to leave, the young official demanded clear instructions. They were talking about the life of the Dalai Lama, after all. The Nechung, clearly annoyed, hesitated and then sat down again. "It is time," he said, after a moment, "to tell the all-knowing Guru not to venture outside." It was an unmistakable sign that His Holiness was in danger.

The Chinese, inadvertently, had contributed to the aura of threat surrounding His Holiness. Days before the dance performance, Chinese emissaries had told the Dalai Lama's chief bodyguard (who was also his brother-in-law) that his traditional contingent of twenty-five bodyguards, strapping Khampas in burgundy robes with padded shoulders, were to halt at the Stone Bridge two miles from the military headquarters on the day of the recital. The PLA would take over security after that point. The Dalai Lama's advisers were shocked. Such a request had never been heard before; it was like asking the king of England to arrive at Peking airport alone and unescorted, like a common traveler. It was both an insult, the officials felt, and a warning. When the chief bodyguard protested, the Chinese messenger snapped, "Will you be responsible if someone pulls the trigger?"

On the night of March 9, the Lord Chamberlain and other government officials approached the Dalai Lama and told him that, in light of the highly unusual requests from the Chinese, he should stay away from the HQ. But the Dalai Lama, who hated the elaborate protocol of bodyguards and official retinues anyway, said he would attend. The Norbulingka was electric with tension. The Dalai Lama was, many believed, walking into a trap from which he and Tibet would never emerge.

That night, Barshi decided to take action. He sent an anonymous letter to the abbots of two nearby monasteries, alerting them to the Dalai Lama's visit, knowing the news would set off alarm bells among the monks in the hills above Lhasa. Barshi then bicycled to the Potala and to other points in the city, telling people to gather in front of the Norbulingka the next morning to keep His Holiness safe. Another junior official set off on a horse with the same mission, a Tibetan Paul Revere.

By seven o'clock the next morning, it was clear they'd touched off something they couldn't control.

As sixteen-year-old Yonten was running toward the Norbulingka, the Dalai Lama's mother was in her well-appointed Lhasa home, supervising the dyeing and embroidering of clothes, when a neighbor flung the door open and shouted to her, "What are you doing?!" Diki Tsering looked up, astonished. Although she'd been born a humble peasant woman, Diki Tsering had been raised to the exalted position of the Dalai Lama's mother. Few people spoke to her like the messenger just had.

The intruder didn't wait for an answer. "Everyone in Lhasa is going to the Norbulingka with sticks, clubs, knives, and whatever else they can lay their hands on," the man said, talking fast in the Amdo dialect. "Even if we have to die, we will stop Him from going!"

Her first thought wasn't about the Dalai Lama. She knew he was safe in the Norbulingka, surrounded by towering bodyguards and the Tibetan army. But her youngest boy, the impish Choegyal, had gone to the dance performance, and now he would be a hostage to the Chinese. Diki Tsering stood and went to the window.

As she stood listening to the bellowing of the crowd, Diki Tsering thought she could hear in it her youngest son, crying, "*Amala, Amala*" ("Mother, Mother").

At that moment, Choegyal was sitting wide-eyed in the Chinese camp watching a swirl of activity rotate around an absence—that of his older brother. At 7:00 a.m. a Chinese military truck had come to Drepung Monastery to pick Choegyal up for the dance performance. It was a beautiful spring morning, and he'd happily climbed aboard along with aristocrats, cabinet ministers, and abbots. But as the truck lurched toward the camp, the people inside heard a rumbling. "I didn't know what was happening," Choegyal remembers. "We looked out of the truck and we could see all these people running toward the Norbulingka."

Choegyal stepped down from the truck and found Tibetan schoolchildren waiting on either side of the path, looking at each vehicle expectantly as they held in their hands *katas* and bunches of flowers. Clearly, the Chinese authorities had no idea that Lhasa had risen up. Choegyal and the rest of the notables were ushered past the gate and then left to wait. The stage where the performance was to take place stood empty.

At the same time, a young monk was walking toward the Norbulingka with a group of his friends. They were startled to see a man come speeding down the road toward them on a bicycle, "puffs of vapor blowing from his mouth." The junior government official hurriedly explained that all monks were being summoned to the summer palace. His voice trembling, the man said that the PLA was preparing to take His Holiness to China.

The monks rushed to the Norbulingka, their wool robes flapping as they ran. There in front of the gates they found a huge crowd, perhaps 30,000 people, almost a third of the present population of Lhasa. More were arriving by the moment, streaming by and bowing in supplication toward the summer palace. Some were shouting; others prostrated themselves on the ground, weeping, calling out, "The wish-fulfilling Jewel is Tibet's only savior. Don't let the nobles exchange him for Chinese silver!" As he got closer to the Norbulingka, the young monk sensed that the mood of his fellow Tibetans was darker than he had first imagined. "The crowd was out of control," he said. Chants rippled through the mass of people, starting at one corner and spreading quickly to the opposite: "China out of Tibet!" people yelled. "Tibet for Tibetans!" In the middle of that roiling mass, sixteen-year-old Yonten felt the anger of the crowd radiate through him. "All the people seemed so furious," he remembers. "Some were crying and others became frenzied and senseless. It was so sad and thrilling at the same time."

Officials inside the Norbulingka rushed to the gates to see what was happening. Barshi and the others, who'd hoped to call a modest crowd to prevent the Dalai Lama from leaving, couldn't believe what they were seeing. "I was surprised they were coming out," says one. "I'd never seen anything like it." A junior attendant, Tenpa Soepa, was given the task of locking all the palace gates and telling the guards to let no one in. He hurried to the south gate, where the protest seemed to be focused, and walked through the small opening with heavy red doors, overhung with a white cloth fringe.

Moments before, a government official had arrived at the south gate in a jeep, driven by a Chinese chauffeur. A torrent of rocks and stones descended on the jeep, and the bloodied official had barely escaped with his life. Now, as Soepa emerged, he saw a man lying sprawled on the ground. It was Chamdo, a Tibetan government official who was a member of the hated PCART, the puppet committee through which China controlled Tibet. (The acronym stood for Preparatory Committee for the Autonomous Region of Tibet.) Chamdo was wearing a white shirt, black pants, dark sunglasses, and the Peking-style cap with a white dust mask favored by the Chinese, who weren't used to Lhasa's famous dust storms. The protesters had erupted at the sight of a Tibetan official seemingly dressed in the clothes of the occupier, and they'd knocked him off his feet. "That man looks like a Chinese!" a woman had cried out, and now, as Soepa watched, Chamdo lay on the ground, bleeding from his head, a circle of protesters looking at him in a thrilled hush at what they had done. Then the crowd shouted and leapt at him again, and Chamdo was lifted up and his body disappeared under a blur of arms and sticks and downward-swinging knives. "Chamdo had disappeared as though swallowed up," said one of the young monks from Drepung. The crowd howled his name and cried, "Kill him!" as it beat the man to death. Later, the body would be glimpsed at various spots around Lhasa, tied to a horse by its feet and being dragged at the front of a chanting crowd.

He was the morning's first casualty.

Bewildered, Soepa stared at the seething masses of his almost unrecognizable countrymen. There were small children with rocks in their hands, monks with old rifles and Molotov cocktails. There were blind men being led along to the protest, and women with butcher knives, and men with sticks torn from trees and sharpened into makeshift spears. *Where had these people come from?* he thought. Soepa saw the abandoned jeep left by the official who'd barely escaped with his life. "Some in the crowd had thrown knives which stuck in the car," he remembered.

The Tibetans were in a kind of ecstasy of rage, screaming at the top of their voices. But their wrath wasn't directed only at the Chinese, who'd already retreated behind the walls of their compounds. The Tibetans were furious at their own government officials, who'd greased the wheels of the Chinese occupation and grown rich off of it. Some in the Norbulingka thought they might be witnessing something else: the beginning of a civil war. The Khampas already nurtured a long-standing hatred of Lhasa bureaucrats; if they were joined by ordinary Tibetans, the country would come apart.

"Tibetans were angry at senior government officials and aristocrats," says one Tibetan doctor who had seen corruption firsthand. "There weren't any of them who didn't hold large lands and properties. And the Chinese started paying silver coins to them in this curious way, sending officers with a box on their shoulder to knock on their doors." These public payoffs for cooperation were considered especially brazen.

Inside the palace, time seemed to blur. It was difficult for many officials to grasp what was happening. The Norbulingka hadn't been besieged in this way in living memory. In fact, Tibet had no history of popular movements at all, unless one counted the militias formed only a few years before to fight the Chinese. The country had always been ruled from above, by kings or chieftains or His Holiness. For years, Tibetans had experienced daily humiliations at the hands of the Chinese, starvation, inflation, and religious persecution. They'd absorbed each insult, but now, at the thought of danger to the Dalai Lama, they'd risen up in a kind of unconscious mass spasm. They were presenting the officials with a new proposition: *We are the conscience of Tibet. Are you with us or against us?*

At 10:00 a.m., with the uprising already several hours old, His Holiness was upstairs in his palace with his Lord Chamberlain, who was trying to explain why Tibetans were converging on the Norbulingka. The Dalai Lama had slept badly the night before, uneasy about the visit to the Chinese camp. He'd risen at 5:00 a.m. and gone to his prayer room, where he'd meditated amid the flickering of butter lamps and the smell of saffron water. After that he had taken his daily walk. But then he'd heard shouts and chants from beyond the two walls that separated him from the streets outside. The thick stone ramparts muffled the sounds so that he couldn't make out the words. He hurried back to his palace to find out what was happening. His officials told him that it seemed all of Lhasa was emptying onto the large open space in front of the Norbulingka.  ·

Now the Lord Chamberlain was laying out their possible courses of action. "I remember saying very slowly . . . ," recalled the Dalai Lama, "that this day, March 10, would be a landmark in Tibetan history." His Holiness was more agitated than he'd ever been as ruler of Tibet. One scenario ran through his mind again and again: the crowd turning to attack one of the Chinese military camps, setting off a full-scale PLA attack. "The Lhasan people would be ruthlessly massacred in thousands," he thought. Already, rebels were setting up roadblocks in Lhasa and appearing in Lhasa armed with rifles. "From my window with the help of binoculars I had a clear view of the Potala and the Chakpori [Iron Mountain]," wrote one Chinese observer, Shan Chao. "The sills of innumerable windows of the Potala are usually the favorite playground for doves. Now rifle barrels glint from them." Shan Chao could see Tibetan troops taking up positions on the mountain, which lay between central Lhasa and the Norbulingka three miles away. Others struggled up the slopes carrying the ammunition and supplies needed for a full-scale attack.

His Holiness didn't believe in nonviolence unconditionally. Even in studying accounts of past wars as a young boy in the Potala poring over issues of *Life* magazine, he'd recognized certain exceptions to the rule: self-defense, especially. And he secretly admired the patriots who were at that very moment daring the Chinese to shoot them or building barricades in the street. When he later met with a monk who described how, during the uprising, some Amdo horsemen in a remote corner of eastern Tibet had stormed a PLA camp containing hundreds of troops, resulting in the deaths of "large numbers" of Chinese soldiers, His Holiness didn't flinch. "I was very moved to hear of such bravery," he remembered. The CIA agent Ken Knaus would later tell of the Dalai Lama endorsing the Allied cause in World War II. Bloodshed *could* be justified. But what he felt coming, in premonitions and in the scenes he could see in his mind, could not. That is, wholesale slaughter.

His Holiness listened to the shouting crowd. He'd wanted for so long to talk with his people like an ordinary man. Now he sensed the crowd's "vehement, unequivocal, unanimous" anger pulsating through the walls of the Norbulingka. "I could feel the tension of the people," he said. "I had been born one of them, and I understood what they were feeling." At times in the recent past, he'd shared that rage. But the Dalai Lama felt he couldn't give in to it or Tibet would burn.

He began to pray.


The Chinese had been caught off-guard by the protests. Their two top officials in Lhasa had been called home to Peking just days before, leaving the volatile Tan Guansan in charge. But the Chinese now began to react, and their first instinct was to remove themselves from any possible danger. The PLA's daily patrols vanished from the streets. Barbed wire, some of it electrified, was unrolled along the rooftops of all the Chinese residences and offices. Tibetans reported seeing Chinese technicians perched on top of telegraph poles— either to repair the line or, as the rumor went, to take ranges for PLA artillery gunners. Soldiers could be seen digging infantry trenches on the perimeter of all the military camps that ringed Lhasa. The Chinese had previously built secret tunnels between the office of the commander in chief, the political HQ, and the payroll office, allowing staff to move between their command centers without appearing on Lhasa streets. Now even Chinese civilians carried weapons as they went about their business in town. But the authorities still underestimated the true dimensions of the threat.

The Chinese, most likely, never intended to snatch the Dalai Lama away to Peking or to harm him in any way that spring. Neither would have served their purposes. For one, he was, even for his occasional refusal to obey their commands, an effective conduit for ruling Tibet. He'd signed, however reluctantly, the Seventeen Point Agreement. He hadn't publicly supported the rebels, despite their pleas, though there were suspicions he'd given them private encouragement. He'd even agreed to revoke the citizenship of two of his brothers, Gyalo and Norbu, when they came into disfavor in Peking. The Dalai Lama, like his predecessors, was playing the long game with the occupiers.

It was only in what he considered core matters that the Dalai Lama defied the Chinese. When they demanded that he send the Tibetan army after the rebels, His Holiness refused again and again, each time ratcheting up the anger from Peking. He did send letters to the guerrillas in various parts of the country, asking them to seek a peaceful solution with the Chinese, but he wouldn't send Tibetans to fight Tibetans.

The Chinese diarist Shan Chao toured Lhasa by armored car as both sides prepared for war. He was genuinely perplexed by what he saw: "They are raising such havoc all through the city that it's as if some imperialist invader had entered our land." It was a reminder of how genuine the Chinese belief in their own mission was; they couldn't see the uprising as anything but a bizarre plot against Tibet's future.

At the PLA military headquarters, the minutes ticked by, the tension in the air thickening as morning turned to afternoon. Chinese officers emerged to look toward the Norbulingka and then huddled in nervous groups. Choegyal, the Dalai Lama's younger brother, spotted pro-Chinese monks milling around, guns visible beneath their robes. He could hear the chants of the crowd in the distance, growing louder but still not distinct enough to make out the words. The Chinese officials glared at the Tibetan nobles. "They were getting quite agitated," Choegyal remembers. "And that's when we knew His Holiness wasn't going to come."

The Tibetan guests were anxious to get back to their families, but the Chinese insisted on carrying on with a strained lunch and a shortened version of the performance. In complete silence the locals watched the dancers swoop and pivot while grim-faced PLA soldiers glared at them.

Choegyal watched it all, enthralled and not a bit afraid.

His mother was growing frantic. A squad of twelve PLA soldiers charged into her house, demanding to see her. Making their way toward her private room, the soldiers were on the verge of finding Diki Tsering when her house manager violently pushed them back, claiming that His Holiness's mother was ill. "After a look of hatred," Diki Tsering said, "they left the same way they had come." She took the visit to mean the PLA was looking for hostages close to the Dalai Lama, and her thoughts turned to the missing Choegyal. Again, she felt she could hear him crying for help.

Diki Tsering's son-in-law, the Dalai Lama's chief bodyguard, sent a car for her out of the Norbulingka, but the crowd, seeing the driver's Chinese uniform, rained stones down on the vehicle, nearly killing him. Finally, her son-in-law came himself and was just able to get through the roadblocks set up by Khampa warriors, part of the popular government that had sprung up within a matter of hours. With the help of a permit signed by army officials, he collected Diki Tsering and barely made it back to the Norbulingka.

But now Choegyal wouldn't know where to find her. She sent messengers to the Chinese camp. Hours later, they returned empty-handed, unable to locate her son among the Tibetan aristocrats and PLA soldiers. "We thought," she remembered, "they would take him to China."

At the summer palace, Norbulingka staff and Tibetan government officials met to discuss what was to be done. "Many officials felt that the Dalai Lama was compelled to advise caution because of his religious position (which required him to oppose violence at all times), and because of the fear of the Chinese," wrote the Tibetan historian Tsering Shakya. Others believed that if the Dalai Lama were to support the resistance, the Chinese would flatten the Norbulingka and attack Tibetans at will.

Three senior ministers were hurriedly sent to the military headquarters to explain what had happened. The Chinese officials they met with were initially calm and relaxed. But then the acting head of the Chinese government in Lhasa, Tan Guansan, arrived and quickly became apoplectic. He was later described by the British journalist Noel Barber in deeply unflattering terms: "a pair of stooped shoulders, yellow teeth, extremely thin hands, and a habit of reeking with perfume"—an alcoholic and a rock-ribbed party loyalist whom even the kindly Dalai Lama described as looking "like a peasant," with stained teeth and an army crew cut. Tan slammed his fist onto a wooden table, and his face went beet-red. "Reactionary elements must behave or all will be liquidated!" he yelled. "Up until now, we have been patient, but this time the people have gone too far." The Dalai Lama's absence went beyond a social snub: it was, in the minds of the Chinese, a deliberate act of defiance. The Chinese were convinced that the "imperialist rebels" were being secretly backed by members of the Tibetan government. Tan Guansan and the other officials ranted at the Tibetans for several hours, and by the end they were promising "drastic action" to end the revolt.

In front of the Norbulingka, neighborhood leaders threaded through the crowd, signing up people to guard the summer palace against the PLA. The sixteen-year-old protester Yonten ran up to a man he knew and asked to be put on the list. "You're too young," the man shot back, but the teenager persisted. "I cried and pleaded with him to accept my name by saying that I would be happy to carry a single bullet." As fresh chants rumbled through the crowd, the man looked at him and quickly jotted his name on the paper. Yonten was ecstatic. He was now fully one of the crowd, the movement of his legs locked to its every swivel and rush, his voice hoarse with the day's slogans.

A protester shouted out that the only way the Dalai Lama would leave the Norbulingka was if his vehicle rolled over their bodies. Others roared their approval. Elsewhere in Lhasa, the Tibetan army was actually considering this idea as a tactic. One Tibetan doctor went to morning assembly and received orders that he and his unit of army troops were to line the route from the Norbulingka to the Chinese military camp with their guns unloaded. If they saw His Holiness's car approaching, they were to lie down in the road and stop it.

At 3:00 p.m. the crowd stirred as officials emerged from the Norbulingka. A cabinet member picked up a megaphone. "The main fear of the Tibetan people is that His Holiness will go to the Chinese army base to see their performance," he called, his voice echoing out over the upturned faces under bright sunlight. "But His Holiness is not going to go. You should all go back to your homes." A murmur of satisfaction rippled through the crowd: they'd saved the Precious Jewel, at least for now.

Voices called from the crowd to allow them to see the Dalai Lama. The officials conferred among themselves and agreed. The massed Tibetans, in a scene out of the French Revolution, chose seventeen "people's representatives" to meet with His Holiness and plan for the coming days. To the cheers of the crowd, their leaders were escorted through the gates of the summer palace. Tibet now had a kind of democratic assembly for the first time in a thousand years.

. . .

Around 4:00 p.m., Choegyal was finally released from the Chinese HQ. Eager to find out what had happened back home, he hurried toward his mother's residence. On the way, he passed a pillbox swarming with PLA soldiers carrying black submachine guns. He'd never come across Chinese soldiers so tense before, so clearly ready to shoot.

Soon after, a servant from the Norbulingka found Choegyal and escorted him home. They passed through the gates and into the palace grounds, where his mother was waiting in a small house. Choegyal caught a glimpse of her in a window. Diki Tsering saw him and immediately began clapping. He could hear her voice calling out to him.

"She was very happy to see me," Choegyal said.


As dusk fell, the People's Representatives—along with about seventy members of the Tibetan government itself—convened a meeting inside the grounds of the Norbulingka. They declared Chinese authority in Tibet null and void. The Kusung Regiment, the Dalai Lama's corps of bodyguards, decided they would no longer take orders from the occupiers. Tibetan army troops began to shed their Chinese-issued uniforms and replace them with their traditional khaki.

Perhaps 5,000 protesters remained at the Norbulingka to ensure that the Dalai Lama was not smuggled out to the occupiers. "The officials kept saying that they didn't need more guards, since the army and the Dalai Lama's bodyguards were enough," remembers sixteen-year-old Yonten. But the Tibetans, who a day before would have obeyed the cabinet without hesitation, ignored them. "The choice was in the people's hands."

Yonten wasn't about to go home as evening fell. He felt his section of the crowd move toward the Lhasa road, and he let himself be carried with it, chanting "Tibet Is Free!" along the path open to the plains until the words began echoing off alley walls, and he looked up above the shoulders of his fellow marchers and saw they were in central Lhasa. "The whole city was filled with the sound," he remembered. Soon he found himself standing in front of the Yuthok, the home of the highest-ranking Chinese official in Tibet, an old aristocratic mansion that had been bought by the government but still kept the name of the family that had lived there for generations. Guards quickly pulled the doors shut and soldiers appeared on the rooftop, pointing their rifles down at the swirling masses. Men began pulling open their shirts and asking the Chinese to shoot them in the chest. For ten minutes, they called up to the soldiers before moving off to Barkhor Street, where they "took two turns around" the square and then, as night fell, drifted off to their homes.

Late in the day, the Dalai Lama received a letter from Tan Guansan. "Since you have been put into very great difficulties due to the intrigues and provocations of the reactionaries," he wrote, "it may be advisable that you do not come for the time being." It was clearly an attempt to save face: the decision not to attend the show had been made by the Dalai Lama hours earlier, but with the letter Tan Guansan could claim credit for it.

The Dalai Lama's reply indicates the enormous pressure he was under. He apologized for not attending, saying he was prevented by "reactionary elements." "This has put me to indescribable shame," he wrote. "I am greatly upset and worried and at a loss as to what to do." There was a long tradition of Tibetan leaders writing insincere letters to their Chinese counterparts in order to get their own way; it was seen as a necessary diplomatic device. The Dalai Lama would later dismiss the letter (and two others to follow) as a delaying tactic, but his tone is striking. The protests had clearly caught him off-balance.

Yonten arrived home. His father, whom he deeply loved, was a teacher who ran his own school for the sons of all classes, from farmers to nobles. He was also a longtime Tibetan nationalist who'd fought against the Chinese occupation. He had been chosen as one of the People's Representatives and was at that moment at one of the tumultuous meetings being held at the Norbulingka. Yonten, bursting with the news of what he'd done and said that day, told his sister, the one who'd run out with wet hair that morning, that he'd signed up as part of the volunteer guard for the Norbulingka. He ordered her to pack a bag with barley and flour so he'd have something to eat. His sister just laughed at Yonten; he was an excitable boy who wasn't going anywhere near the summer palace. She told him to wait for their father to get home before he started collecting provisions.

When his father arrived, Yonten begged him for permission to guard the Dalai Lama. His father just smiled. "You're too young," he said. "If war breaks out, what are you going to do?"

Yonten felt that the words he'd chanted all day long—"We shall fight to the last man, even if only women are left to defend the country!"—applied directly to him. He pleaded to be allowed to stand between the PLA and the Dalai Lama.

Finally, moved by his son's persistence or just exhausted, his father relented. He would let the boy come with him to the meetings of the People's Representatives. "At last he understood me," Yonten remembers. "And he said I could follow him. It was Buddha's way."

As night fell, a group of young monks left their vigil outside the Norbulingka and returned to Drepung Monastery. The *choe-ra*, the common area shaded by willows where the lamas would teach the novices, was empty. The entire monastery seemed deserted. Still disturbed by what they had seen in the city, the young monks climbed to the monastery roof and sat there under the moonlight, looking at Lhasa in the distance. As they watched, the sound of a drummer beating a dirge-like rhythm over and over pulsed out from the monastery's Temple of Wrathful Deities. There, in an airless, black-painted room, smelling strongly of rancid butter, with gaping-mouthed demons and monsters painted on the walls, surrounded by costumes made of bones, monks were chanting out prayers for the safety of Tibet. It was a place of horrors designed to protect against horrors, and its drum beat through the night.

None of the young men could sleep.


Over the next few days, the tension rose almost by the hour.

Swarms of women banging pots and kettles and shouting slogans emerged from the narrow alleys of Lhasa and surged toward the Potala Palace. There were young girls, grandmothers, aristocrats, servants, women who found themselves side by side for the first time in their lives. Many of them taunted the Chinese soldiers, newly installed on the rooftops along Barkhor Square, crying, "Go ahead and shoot us!"

Monks at the three great monasteries ringing the city awoke to find their sleepy bastions militarized. Each of the Great Three had a "master of discipline" who meted out punishments for infractions. Now as the monks gathered in the *choe-ra*, these men called out for volunteers to guard the Norbulingka and protect the Dalai Lama. At Sera, three miles north of the Jokhang Temple in central Lhasa, a young monk awoke to the sound of Chinese voices. "The loudspeakers were saying they would kill the three red bugs if we didn't obey them," he recalled. The "three red bugs" was a local colloquialism for the three chief monasteries of Tibet—the Chinese had begun using native slang in their warnings.

The 500 monks at Sera rushed to a meeting, and each house within the monastery was asked to produce 10 volunteers. The young monk stood up. "I was a tough guy," he says. "Only twenty-five years old." He was handed an old British rifle, a World War I relic, serviceable but hardly a match for the Chinese machine guns. The monks were told there was one gun for every two men, and only a hundred bullets for the entire house. At another monastery, Ganden, one of the faithful listened to his abbot speak. "He pleaded with those who were deeply engrossed in their studies not to go, as it was also essential to protect the Dharma." But those who felt their vocation less intensely could abandon their vows. The abbot made it clear that once a monk volunteered for the resistance, the punishment for backing out was death.

Some of the volunteers formally renounced their vows in an odd ceremony, exchanging their maroon-and-gold robes for a gun, or a sword, or just a pledge to protect His Holiness. The monks now entered a kind of spiritual netherworld. Violence against even an insect was forbidden in Tibetan Buddhism; to kill a man was to cast oneself into the realm of demons. "My spiritual comrades and I felt very uncomfortable about choosing the path of violence," remembers one Ganden monk. He was a novice, and he offered back his vows to his mentor, "thinking this would make my sin lesser." But he couldn't deny that he was driven by what Buddhism regarded as repugnant desires. "I was a human being and I felt these negative emotions intensely—I kept thinking about revenging myself over and over again on the Chinese for their brutal killings."

The Lord Chamberlain was leaving nothing to chance. He

issued a command banning the use of electric flashlights, all the rage in Lhasa, which lacked streetlights. The Lord Chamberlain was worried that if His Holiness was forced to escape, a soldier or citizen might flash a torch into the face of a soldier and find it to be the Dalai Lama in disguise. He also sent a messenger galloping to the southeast, to inform Athar and Lhotse—the only connections to the CIA and the Americans—about recent developments and asking them to set off immediately toward Lhasa. "Immediately" in the rugged country of southern Tibet was relative, however—it would take six days for the message to reach the two CIA operatives.

On March 16, Athar was at Lhuntse Dzong, a huge stone fort in the south of Tibet, sixty miles north of the Indian border, that was commanded by the rebels. Having failed to meet with the Dalai Lama, Athar and Lhotse were focused on building up the rebels. On February 22, they'd watched a second load of CIA-bought arms parachuting onto their landing zone, guided by another dung bonfire, and they'd helped hide the munitions in a secret cache for future operations. The pair were in constant contact with the CIA, but they had essentially given up on the Dalai Lama and his government, having had no contact with Lhasa for a year.

Every day, Athar would laboriously encrypt that day's information, using his one-time pad and employing the five digits common to the Chinese commercial telegraph system. At the time designated in his signal book, Athar would then crank up the generator of the RS-1 crystal radio and send the report in Morse code. The transmission would be picked up by the CIA's station at Okinawa, then relayed from station to station all the way to Washington. If it was intercepted, it would appear to be a harmless order for batches of silk or truck parts.

Athar was in far more danger than he realized. A year earlier, just after his first meeting with the Lord Chamberlain, Tan

Guansan had met with the Tibetan cabinet and vented his rage on them. He revealed that the Chinese knew of radio messages being broadcast from a small mountaintop near Lhasa. By decoding the messages—something the CIA didn't believe they were capable of—the Chinese had discovered that the Tibetans had gone to the Americans for help. It was a revelation that played into Peking's deep paranoia about foreign interlopers in Tibet. With this discovery of American aid, Tibet had become far more than a troublesome borderland issue for the Peking leadership. It was now a matter of national security. The PLA had even caught one of the CIA-trained Khampa guerrillas and—it was assumed, though nobody knew for sure—forced him to reveal the details of the entire operation.


Back at the Norbulingka, on March 16 the Dalai Lama again went for a walk as the sun set. He marveled at how normal and serene the Jewel Park was. There were his bodyguards, out of uniform, bent over his flower beds, carefully watering the budding plants from a long-nosed can. His beloved peacocks strutted across the manicured lawns. Brahmini ducks floated on the pond, their kicks under the surface sending a slight ripple across the smooth green-black water.

It was, as Buddha taught him, illusion, all illusion. "I must admit," said the Dalai Lama, "I was very near despair."

## Six

# FOREIGN BROTHERS

houghts of the outside world flitted through the Dalai Lama's mind as the crisis escalated. He understood that Tibet had no reliable friends in the world. He and the cabinet had sought foreign allies as a counterweight to China's massive power, but they'd been bitterly disappointed by the response. His Holiness knew that messages had been sent in secret to Tibetan mutual-aid societies in India and elsewhere, telling them of the uprising and asking them to rally support outside Tibet. And protesters in Lhasa would soon arrive in front of the missions of India and Nepal, the only two in Lhasa, pleading for those nations to back their cause.

Many Tibetans held out hope that America, a beacon of freedom even in this hermit kingdom, would somehow come to their rescue. But the Dalai Lama knew that Washington was thousands of miles away and already fighting its own war in Indochina. Having dealt with a cautious State Department in the past, he didn't believe America would send its sons to die in the Himalayas. But his knowledge of the world was fragmentary at best. "I had an atlas, and I pored over maps of distant countries," he said later, "and wondered what life was like in them, but I did not know anyone who had ever seen them."

As Tibetans dreamt of an improbable victory, the world on March 10 knew nothing of what was happening in Lhasa. Tibet in 1959 was a rumor of a nation, a shadow on the world's collective memory. Off-limits to foreigners for decades, it was the object of a romantic longing that had only intensified during the gray, dreary confrontations of the Cold War. Tibet was removed not only in space, hidden behind the almost inaccessible peaks of the Himalayas, but in time. Prior to the Chinese arrival, there were only three cars in the country, two Austins and a Dodge, all owned by the Dalai Lama (one had been taken apart and carried over the Himalayas on mules before arriving in Lhasa fully assembled). There were no modern hospitals, no railroads, no cinema, no newspapers. After China invaded in 1950, it brought hydroelectric plants, new roads, and a local newspaper that was published every ten days. But the Chinese occupation had also made information on Tibet even harder to come by. Foreign journalists were banned: no footage of the occupation was allowed out, no photos of the uprising spun on the drums of the Associated Press, no radio networks broadcast the latest news to the capitals of the world. The country was practically invisible to all but a handful of *chi-ling*, or foreigners of European descent.

What was known, or imagined about Tibet was alluring. It was "a place of dizzy extremes and excesses," according to the Italian explorer Fosco Maraini. Herodotus had believed monstrous ants burrowed up mounds of gold in its hills, perhaps referring to the Tibetan villagers who collected the earth dug up by the native marmot and extracted gold dust from it. Here mastiffs "as huge as donkeys" could bite off your head in a single gulp, according to Marco Polo, and any Tibetan official who let a foreigner enter was arrested, jailed, tortured, and then tossed into the Tsangpo River. (That last part, in fact, was true.)

The first Western explorer to reach Tibet was probably a Jesuit priest, the Portuguese António de Andrade, who reported on his travels in *The New Discoveries of the Great Cathay or of the Tibetan Kingdom* in 1626. Andrade was convinced Tibet had once been connected to the ancient Christian civilizations, a common belief in Europe at the time. One expert called this the "foreign brother" syndrome, a belief among Tibet-lovers that the nation possessed a culture sympathetic to Europe's own, exiled among brutes and apostates. This distant and mysterious country was believed to retain values and customs cherished by Westerners. A hundred years later, another Jesuit missionary visited Lhasa and found beautiful architecture and an often bizarre justice system. One method of determining whether a suspect was innocent involved "making an iron red hot and commanding him to lick it thrice." If he burned his tongue, the man was guilty; if not, he was set free.

Not all the world thought of Tibet as a sanctuary. Princess Kula of the Himalayan kingdom of Sikkim described a nation consumed by "greed, magic spells, passion, revenge, crimes, love, envy and torture." But the overall tone was one of admiration. The

ESCAPE FROM THE LAND OF SNOWS

massive 1763 *Alphabetum Tibetanum* declared that "according to the theories of many historians, the human race expanded from Tibet and its neighboring lands." There was nothing Tibet was not capable of, including becoming the birthplace of *Homo sapiens*.

At the beginning of the twentieth century, a Tibet craze struck Europe. Sherlock Holmes, after being killed by Professor Moriarty, returned in 1903's "The Adventure of the Empty House" and told Watson he'd escaped to Florence and then Tibet, where he'd wandered through Lhasa and enjoyed "spending some days with the head lama." But the greatest popularizer of Tibet was the English writer James Hilton, whose bestselling 1933 novel *Lost Horizon* tells the story of three Brits and an American who crash-land in the Valley of the Blue Moon, also known as Shangri-La, where the people live long, blissful lives without a hint of cruelty. It was turned into a popular Frank Capra movie in 1937 and became perhaps the most influential vision of Tibet as a haven of peace and sublimity. FDR, who wrote ditties about Tibet and its politics ("I never saw a *Kashag*, I never want to see one . . ."), even named his presidential retreat Shangri-La before it became the more sober "Camp David."

One of the best-known authorities on Tibet in the mid-1950s was T (for "Tuesday") Lobsang Rampa, a Tibetan lama living in London who'd written a book called *The Third Eye*, a memoir of life on the Roof of the World that included descriptions of crystal gazing, mummifications of Lobsang's previous selves, and yetis, or Abominable Snowmen, flying across the Himalayas on the backs of large box kites. The title referred to an operation the lama had had performed to open up the mystical aperture that would allow him to see the "psychical emanations" of people he met. T Lobsang Rampa described the operation:

The instrument penetrated the bone. A very hard, clean sliver of wood had been treated by fire and herbs and was slid down so that it just entered the hole in my head. I felt a stinging, tickling sensation apparently in the bridge of my nose. It subsided and I became aware of subtle scents which I could not identify. Suddenly there was a blinding flash. For a moment the pain was intense. It diminished, died and was replaced by spirals of colour. As the projecting sliver was being bound into place so that it could not move, the Lama Mingyar Dondup turned to me and said: "You are now one of us, Lobsang. For the rest of your life you will see people as they are and not as they pretend to be."

The book became a worldwide bestseller, selling 300,000 copies in its first few years, but Tibetophiles—including the author Heinrich Harrer—smelled a rat. Harrer hired a Liverpool detective to look into the lama's background, and the private eye discovered that T Lobsang was actually Cyril Henry Hoskin, a large-nosed former plumber's assistant from Devonshire who had shaved his head, bought a monk's robe, and changed his name. Hoskin, cornered in Ireland, defiantly said that he'd formerly been a man named Cyril Henry Hoskin but that he'd been possessed by the spirit of Lobsang when he'd fallen down and hit his head while photographing a rare owl in Surrey.

Hoskin was a fraud, but he was a very evocative one. Far from being a gimmick, *The Third Eye* presented a compelling, fully imagined world—the *Times Literary Supplement* said the book "came close to being a work of art"—that captivated readers so consistently that it remained in print and highly popular even after the author was exposed. Unfortunately, this was a fully imagined world, a place that Lobsang/Hoskin and many thousands of others had dreamt into existence out of disgust and boredom with modern life.

In short, the world in 1959 knew almost nothing about Tibet.


Despite the trash about Tibet that was readily accepted in the West, there were a few interested parties, pinpricks of light dappled around the globe who represented a desire to know the country as it truly was. As the Dalai Lama considered leaving Lhasa, these isolated individuals and groups would prove vital.

In Kalimpong, a spy-infested town on the border between India and Tibet, the journalist George Patterson was stirring up a hornet's nest. The lanky Patterson was a Scot by birth, a doctor by training, and an evangelical Christian by the grace of almighty God. The fervently religious expat had been seeking a personal relationship with his Savior for most of his life. "I wanted to be like Moses and Joshua," he said. In 1943, at the age of twenty-three, he'd been reading a book on mountaineering when he heard a voice say, "Go to Tibet." This was the first time his Savior had spoken to him, in a tone so clear it was "like a knock on the door." He'd gone to Tibet, treated the sick, and become a convert to the cause of Tibetan nationalism. "I wanted a cause for which I might die," he wrote. "It was in this cause that I went to Tibet."

Now, in 1959, the pale, rangy ex-missionary was the lead journalistic agitator for the Tibetans. He'd become a stringer for the well-respected British newspaper the *Daily Telegraph,* and he was perfectly placed in Kalimpong to get fresh reports from refugees streaming out of Tibet, whose stories of torture and repression filled his bulletins. The trouble was, very few people in the West believed what he was reporting. The previous year, the London *Times* had run an extensive article by its Nepal-based correspondent saying that the Tibetans *approved* of the Chinese takeover of their country, were profiting under Peking's leadership, and had switched their allegiance from the Dalai Lama to Mao. It was a consistent theme in reports on Tibet. Whenever Patterson published his scathing reports of Chinese abuses and Tibetan resistance, they were called "bazaar rumors."

Many Westerners had taken up the Land of Snows, more as a romantic ideal than anything else. Patterson was different. He was among the first to adopt Tibet as an actual place, to live among the Khampas, to advance their political cause. He'd found Tibetans to be fantastically tough people, excellent horsemen, generous and dangerously playful, men and women possessing a caustic sense of humor. And in the spring of 1959, he spent his days hounding diplomats, heads of state, and editors at the foreign news desks in London to forget about *Lost Horizon* and pay attention to the real Tibet, by which he meant the guerrilla war spreading across the country.

But Patterson's dream had run afoul of one very important person in India: Jawaharlal Nehru. The country's first prime minister had inherited Gandhi's mantle after he'd led India out of the British colonial system, and Nehru was determined to make the country into a new kind of world power, aligned neither with socialist Russian or with the capitalist West. For that, he needed good relations with China—and though he was sympathetic to Tibet's plight, he was determined that it not drag India into conflict with its massive neighbor to the east. The conflict in Tibet, he said, was "a clash of minds rather than a clash of arms."

Nehru and his ministers were incensed by Patterson's often lurid accounts of the Chinese occupation. The journalist was summoned to a government office and threatened with expulsion from India unless he confined himself to "normal and objective" reports.

"George," the British High Commissioner finally broke in, "do you think you know better than Prime Minister Nehru?"

"If what the Prime Minister says is what he knows," Patterson replied, "then I *do* know better than him."

Threats were nothing new to Patterson. In 1951, the Scot realized he was being followed around Kalimpong by two people he assumed were Chinese agents. An Indian security official informed him that the Chinese knew of his activities on behalf of Tibet and offered him a pistol for protection. "I was about to be liquidated," Patterson remembered. He promptly sent back word to the Chinese that "no follower of Karl Marx could intimidate a follower of Jesus Christ" and, relishing the gesture, refused the gun.

In one of Patterson's drawers at his home in the city, there sat a letter from a Khampa leader. Khampa men were being forced to dig their own graves, the letter said, and Tibetan girls were being forced to stab them to death and push them into the earth. "Everywhere there were scenes of slaughter and promiscuous butchery," his correspondent wrote. The man then explained, almost apologetically, that the struggle against the Chinese "was known to be a hopeless fight but we could no longer contain ourselves." The words explained, as well as anything could, the root of Patterson's near-mania for the Khampas.

The Scotsman was a kind of advance indicator of world opinion: the path he was blazing would soon be trampled by thousands of dedicated Westerners.

Tibet had made Patterson a journalist, or a propagandist, depending on whom you asked. And there were other professional journalists spread out around the globe who would soon converge near Kalimpong to get the story the Scot had been pushing, some-times to the point of shrillness, for years. Among them was the greatest tabloid foreign journalist of his time, the *Daily Mail*'s Noel Barber, who in March 1959 was caught in the African hellhole known as Nyasaland as it threatened to explode into a Mau-Mau–style revolt. The hard-traveling Barber, "The Man Who Made Journalism an Adventure," had covered dirty little wars from Algiers to Beirut and had filed bulletins from the wastes of Arabia to the dazzling islands of Oceania. He became the first Englishman to reach the South Pole after Scott, married a Florentine countess, befriended the Duke of Windsor, drank ouzo with Maria Callas on the deck of Aristotle Onassis's yacht, talked women with Clark Gable and the fate of Europe with Churchill. Barber had been stabbed by a Moroccan fanatic in Casablanca, inadvertently eaten human flesh in Singapore, been shot in the head in Budapest, and had a protester die in his arms at the barricades before driving to Vilna to file his story in a bloodied suit, just making his deadline. By 1959 he'd gone beyond Fleet Street legend to become a kind of international symbol of news. "Wherever the action was," wrote the *Times* of London, "so was Barber." The *Daily Mail* ran ads taunting their competition on Fleet Street: *"Where is Noel Barber today?"* This was hell for his rivals. During the Hungarian uprising—a rebellion that would soon draw parallels with the situation in Tibet—a *Daily Express* correspondent received a bluntly worded telegram that read:

BARBER SHOT WHY YOU UNSHOT.

If Barber had one flaw, it was occasionally making things up. "Never check an exciting fact" was one of his maxims, borrowed from one of his boon companions, a foreign affairs editor. It would soon land him in notorious trouble.

As it happened, by 1959 Barber was a charter member of the same tiny brotherhood of Tibetophiles that claimed George Patterson. In 1950, the correspondent had traveled to Tibet overland by way of Nepal to get the truth about the Chinese invasion and had fallen in love with the people. "I'd been there at the beginning," Barber would later write.

If Patterson was the holy fool, Barber was the celebrity. When it came to Tibet, his byline alone would signal that the Dalai Lama and his cause had graduated to the international stage.


That March, in Washington, D.C., a mid-level CIA agent named John Greaney was trying to change the course of Tibetan history without a single journalist knowing he existed. "Publicity," he notes, "was not one of our goals." The amiable Greaney, a native Washingtonian with four children and a pregnant wife, was the deputy chief of an obscure five-man unit called the Tibetan Task Force, known to just a handful of people inside the agency. The men were in their late twenties and thirties and had all served in World War II, and each had come to the CIA mostly out of necessity rather than hard conviction. "In that era, you didn't make plans, Uncle Sam made them for you," Greaney says. "I went to the CIA because I really needed a job." Greaney had started at the agency as a courier at the pay grade of PS3, or $1,700 a year, from which he worked his way up to what he called "the bang and burn side of things."

Around the same time Greaney joined up, Ken Knaus was teaching political science at Stanford when he was called up to do a tour of duty in the suddenly hot Korean theater. The year 1951 was a terrible one for Americans in Korea; on January 4, Seoul was abandoned to the Communists, and the combined Chinese and North Korean forces were blitzing south in terrifying night raids. Desperate to stay stateside, Knaus got to Washington a few days before he had to report for duty and began searching for a job that would keep him out of General Matthew Ridgway's brutal Operation Ripper. "I went over to the State Department," he remembers, "and this very sniffy guy said, '*If* you get back, let us know.'" As a shaken Knaus left the office, the man's secretary caught his eye. "That's the lousiest thing I ever heard," she whispered to him. Then she told him to head over to the CIA. The Cold War was in full swing. Strategists at the Defense Department had even selected a date that the Soviets were expected to invade Western Europe: July 1, 1952. Which meant the agency was hiring. When his interviewer at the CIA learned that Knaus was a former lieutenant in military intelligence and was fluent in Chinese, he murmured, "Oh, *do* come in."

Few on the team came to the agency as a cause. But the man who directed the Tibetan Task Force, Desmond FitzGerald, was cut from a different cloth. "Des was very handsome," said one longtime friend, "with sparkling eyes, color in his cheeks. He could be very smooth, discussing the best restaurants in Paris." FitzGerald came from a privileged background: family wealth, Harvard, a white-shoe law firm after the war. He had impeccable connections throughout the executive and foreign policy community in D.C. He wore safari suits custom-made at Abercrombie & Fitch and sprayed vermouth into his martinis with an atomizer. When it came to the Cold War, FitzGerald imbibed an almost Arthurian sense of honor. His name was apt: his dashing looks and romantic notions—and the hopeless depressions he suffered from—made him seem like a character out of F. Scott Fitzgerald, though some believed he was a dabbler. The CIA agent E. Howard Hunt disparagingly called him "the Instant Enthusiast" for his habit of grasping hold of and then abandoning the latest fads for fighting Communists.

China was a specialty. FitzGerald had fought alongside Chinese troops in World War II and been part of the agency's China Mission in 1954, where he'd seen his clandestine forces chewed up by a far more sophisticated effort directed out of Peking. In 1958 he took on the Far East brief. "Des told me he knew this territory," recalled a colleague, talking about China. "He knew these bastards." In a letter to his daughter, Frances, in 1954, FitzGerald summed up what many felt in watching Communist victories around the globe. It was a kind of creeping spiritual terror:

> I must say that the world is a dark and dangerous place and the dehumanization of man has made terrible progress. I see the worst of it from where I am—nations of blind warrior ants in the making and the world of morality and reason being slowly forced back.

And so Tibet became his cause.

FitzGerald and his counterparts at State didn't believe the Tibetans could eject the PLA from their country. The Chinese advantage in men and matériel was simply too overwhelming. They made this clear to the Khampas: the CIA trainers told the rebel Athar that the aim was to "disrupt Chinese rule," not end it. What they hoped to do was establish a network of guerrilla cells around the country to harass the occupiers.

Late in 1955, President Eisenhower signed a confidential presidential order known as National Security Council Directive 5412/2. It directed the CIA, in part, to:

> Create and exploit troublesome problems for International Communism . . . complicate control within the USSR, Communist China and their satellites . . . discredit the

prestige and ideology of IC . . . and to the extent practicable in areas dominated or threatened by IC, develop underground resistance and facilitate covert and guerrilla operations.

Tibet fell under 5412's rubric. "The Tibetans were people fighting the common enemy," says Knaus. "We ended up falling in love with them."

Knaus and John Greaney and their peers shared with FitzGerald an unalloyed love for their men. "They were the best people in the world," Knaus says of the young Khampas. They were almost oddly perfect guerrillas: adaptable, keenly intelligent, and seemingly impervious to pain. They never snuck out of their barracks at Camp Hale to get drunk in the cowboy bars of nearby Leadville. They didn't complain about long marches in the frigid Colorado air. They were funny and stoic.

The CIA did have to make adjustments. Their trainees had no concept of the twenty-four-hour clock; time in their villages was dictated by the rising and setting of the sun. There wasn't a Tibetan word for "antenna," so Greaney had to improvise a term—"sky-wire" (as planes became "sky-boats"). He was astonished at how quickly the men adapted. And they were as high-spirited as they were tough, constantly playing practical jokes on their trainers. But there was one exception. Around the office and training camp, the CIA men irreverently called His Holiness "the DL." The Khampas never joined in. "They were very reverent toward the Dalai Lama," Knaus recalls. "They would clasp their hands and bow their heads whenever we said the name." Athar, the rebel dropped back into Tibet to contact the resistance, called His Holiness "the heartbeat of every Tibetan."

"Everybody wanted to be on the Task Force," Greaney says,

"and that made all the difference in the world." In talking with frustrated fellow agents working on other operations, such as the one that would become the Bay of Pigs invasion ("the Latinos were not enthused about it"), Greaney was relieved he was working with what he saw as the truehearted Tibetans. The CIA men chanted "Go Go Goloks!" when word came in that the Tibetan Goloks had risen up against the Chinese, and they pushed hard for men and matériel to back them. When the Task Force requested C-130s, the air force's biggest plane at the time, for airdrops into Tibet, they got it. When they needed a training base in the mountains of Colorado, it was built in record time. At times, it seemed as if the notion of Tibet as the lost "foreign brother," the same notion that had obsessed missionaries to the place in the sixteenth century, had taken hold in certain sectors in Washington.

Above all, it was a black-and-white mission in a gray decade. "One of the most romantic programs of covert action undertaken by the Agency" is how one CIA document referred to it.

The Tibetan Task Force sometimes took on an air of unreality. Greaney remembers initial meetings at the Pentagon to obtain hardware for the mission. "When we told the generals we were operating in Tibet, their eyes popped out of their head," he says. "Because they all remembered the movie [*Lost Horizon*]." Allen Dulles, the legendary head of the CIA under Eisenhower, was even less informed about the real Tibet. "We used to call him the Great White Case Officer," says Greaney. Dulles, along with his brother John Foster, head of the State Department, was responsible for everything from deposing Iranian prime minister Mohammed Mossadeq to the mammoth anti-Soviet intelligence work inside the Iron Curtain. When Greaney was called to update him on the Dalai Lama and the resistance, he felt honored. A few minutes into the briefing, however, Dulles interrupted him.

"So where *is* Tibet?" he asked.

Greaney looked at him blankly.

Dulles gestured toward a *National Geographic* map pinned above the office's leather couch. Greaney followed the director over, and together they stepped onto the cushion. The agent then pointed out the relevant territory: the Himalayas, India, China, Tibet. "He joked about it," Greaney remembers. "He wasn't embarrassed that he didn't know where the place was."

For all the passion of those involved, in 1959 in Washington, D.C., the Dalai Lama's plight did not rise to the level of a national priority. "Nobody wanted to go to war over Tibet," acknowledged Frank Halpern, a CIA officer in the Far East division. "It was a flea biting an elephant . . . fun and games." The fight for Tibet was going to be a "pinprick war" in which America's role would be disguised. But the diehards hoped for more. As early as 1947, the American chargé d'affaires in New Delhi wrote that "Tibet may . . . be regarded as a bulwark against the spread of Communism through-out Asia, or at least an island of conservatism in a sea of political turmoil." Others wanted to turn the Dalai Lama from an obscure "god-king" into a global symbol—"the Pope of the Buddhists"— and from there to make him a resistance hero of the Cold War, especially among the hundreds of millions of Buddha's followers in Asia. For that, they needed the Dalai Lama to be free of external controls and accessible to the world and its media. They needed him out of Tibet.

The rebels were occasionally naïve. "They couldn't under-stand how we could limit our commitment to them," Greaney says, "which is something that happens often in intelligence work." One rebel leader, Gompo Tashi, asked for the Americans to send a weapon it was rumored they'd developed: a mirror whose rays would incinerate the Chinese in a burst of fire. The Khampas, who kept a photograph of Eisenhower (signed "To my fellow Tibetan friends"), even believed the U.S. Army might provide them with the atomic bomb.

The Tibetans couldn't grasp their own crushing insignificance on the world stage. Like the citizens of many small nations threatened by huge powers, they believed in the rumors of foreign troops streaming in from the airport, in the single phone call from a European prime minister that would end the crisis in a matter of minutes, in the deus ex machina dressed in the uniform of a strapping American airman.

Even Athar fell victim to it. "We really felt that the gods were with us," he said. "Nobody could beat the Americans." With U.S. support, he and the Khampas believed they would take back Tibet.

# Seven

# ACROSS THE KYICHU

*I*n Lhasa, March 17 dawned clear and warm. Lhasans were used to hearing the bells and the horns that normally rang out from the temples of the Potala just after dawn, calling the monks to prayer. They heard nothing that morning except the chatter of birds. The monks who normally worked the bell ropes were hurrying to the storage rooms of the Potala and other secret places where caches of old British rifles were waiting, or carrying boxes of ammunition to Drepung, Sera, and Ganden monasteries for distribution to the rebels.

As he drove through the streets of Lhasa, the Chinese diarist Shan Chao saw not monks but rebels on Chakpori, the mountain on the edge of Lhasa, building fortifications. "It looks as if there is going to be fighting soon," he wrote. "We cannot sit by and wait." The guerrillas upped the ante, sending a telegram to their compatriots in Kalimpong: "The independent country of Tibet was formed on the first day of the second month of the Tibet calendar [March 10]. Please announce this to all."

With the Chinese withdrawn behind their walls and only emerging in heavily armed patrols, Tibetans were caught up in an almost revolutionary fervor. Posters covered the city's walls, ranging from the nationalistic ("Tibet for the Tibetans") to the warlike ("We Will Wipe Out the Chinese!"). Without any direction from above, locals had formed themselves into proto-military units. Two hundred fifty volunteers from the Do-Sing Chesa (Association of Masons, Carpenters, and Builders) banded together in units of fifty men each, and their wives and sisters were instructed that, if war broke out, they were to take to the roofs of Lhasa and throw rocks and stones at the Chinese battalions. Leatherworkers, painters, and tailors were organized into military squads, with a few guns and a handful of bullets between them. "In our excitement, we had neither doubt nor fear," said the carpenter Landun Gyatso, who signed up for one of the paramilitary squads. "We wanted to be free." Homeowners in Lhasa had covered their roofs with coils of barbed wire and stuffed sandbags and sacks of salt into their windows to stop bullets. Others built makeshift stockades and filled their larders with enough food to last through a siege.

Even as they chanted out independence slogans, the crowds made it clear they had one immediate demand: the safety of the Dalai Lama. Many were beginning to believe he could never be protected in Chinese-occupied Lhasa. "He was in danger," remembers

Narykid, a young Norbulingka official. "If we lost him, we lost everything."

The cabinet had ordered the Lord Chamberlain to make plans for an escape, should one become necessary. His instructions were coded in old Tibetan proverbs: "Snatch the egg," he was ordered, "without frightening the hen."

The Lord Chamberlain had already sent a messenger to Ratuk Ngawang, a Khampa leader in a place called Tsethang, just over one hundred miles southeast of Lhasa. "I received a letter asking for my presence at the Norbulingka," Ngawang recalls, "but heavy fighting was going on and I was needed to lead our forces." The rebels had been battling the PLA near Tsethang, suffering heavy casualties, for nearly a year, and now the letter informed Ngawang that His Holiness would need to flee through the region on his way to safety in the south. The commander sent a messenger saying his men would secure the area of Lhoka, which encompassed Tsethang and some of the oldest cultural sites in Tibet, including Samye, the first Buddhist monastery. "I wasn't worried about the Dalai Lama once he reached Lhoka," Ngawang says, "I was worried what would happen to him on the way. We had reason to fear that His Holiness might be abducted by the Chinese authorities, and we had been worried about that since 1958."

The Lord Chamberlain had summoned his personal tailor and asked the man to make up a Tibetan soldier's uniform to the Dalai Lama's measurements. He'd contacted top Khampa leaders who, on March 15, sent a caravan of horses across the Tsangpo River with what appeared to be sacks of manure on their backs. Inside were supplies for an escape attempt: food, blankets, and other necessities. The Khampas also rounded up the river coracles—basketlike boats that had animals skins lashed over a wood skeleton—so that they would be ready in case the Dalai Lama appeared. They also wanted to prevent the pursuing Chinese battalions from getting their hands on any of the slim craft.

On the morning at March 17, after rising and having his breakfast, the Dalai Lama met with his cabinet. They decided to send Tan Guansan another letter, their third, asking him to be patient. It was another delaying tactic. The guards at the Norbulingka were now forbidding any government official to leave, but a servant was able to convince the soldiers that he was just going to do a bit of shopping in Lhasa. He left, the letter concealed deep in his robes, and made for the Chinese headquarters. Meanwhile, the Dalai Lama and the ministers waited back at the summer palace.

The hours dragged by. At 4:00 p.m. the Dalai Lama stewed, feeling keenly the futility of another letter that would lead only to another delay. He decided to try the Nechung Oracle one last time. With his attendants trailing after him, he walked to the room where the current manifestation of the oracle waited—a young monk named Lobsang Jigme. Like the Dalai Lama himself, the spirit of Dorje Drak-den passed from mortal to mortal in continuous reincarnations, the Buddhist principle of impermanence rendered in the flesh, substance passing into form before departing, endlessly.

The ceremony began as soon as the Dalai Lama seated himself at his throne. Usually, the oracle would perform a sword dance, something the Dalai Lama, who was by nature drawn to flashing displays of military skill, very much enjoyed. But tonight the oracle came directly before him without any preliminaries, his chest heaving, and stood there "like a magnificent, fierce Tibetan warrior chieftain of old."

The Dalai Lama looked into the oracle's mad-looking eyes and asked his only question: Should he stay in Lhasa or attempt an escape?

He didn't know what to expect. Dorje Drak-den might issue

another of his noncommittal answers. But the vacillation that had marked the oracle's behavior for the last week, going back to when the junior official Barshi challenged his useless answers, was now gone. "Go!" the Nechung bellowed. "Go tonight!" He stumbled forward, the mirror on his chest sending glimmers of candlelight into the dark recesses of the room. The oracle grabbed a pen and wrote something out on a paper. When the Dalai Lama leaned over to look, he realized it was precise directions to the Indian border, "down to the last Tibetan town."

As the Nechung collapsed to the floor and His Holiness hurried back to his chambers, two mortar shells exploded inside the palace walls.

The Chinese would always deny firing at the summer palace, with Radio Peking later calling the charge "a blatant, outright fabrication." But many Tibetans heard it, including His Holiness. He realized the shells had struck near the northern gate (according to eyewitnesses, dropping into a tranquil pond and sending sprays of water and mud into the air). And the sound of a mortar shell slamming into water had the effect of sealing the Dalai Lama's fate. "Within the palace, everyone felt the end had come," he said. "I must leave the palace and the city at once."

The bombing of the Norbulingka enraged the Tibetans. The shells only confirmed for them that the Chinese were intent on decapitating the Tibetan state and destroying the Dharma by killing the Dalai Lama. A member of the cabinet had to run to the Norbulingka's front gate and block the guards there from assaulting a PLA position at a nearby transportation hub. Meanwhile, His Holiness performed a last divination. He performed the *Mo* dice ritual and the message was clear: Leave now. He and his ministers made a quick decision. They would escape that night, although "the odds against making a successful break seemed terrifyingly high."

Thirteen-year-old Choegyal had been running wild for days, slipping out of the Norbulingka to sample the mood of the crowd outside. "I roamed all over," he remembers. "I was very naughty." He found the summer palace a study in contrasts. "It was so peaceful inside the walls, but outside there was tremendous commotion." All around him, there was the color and sound of a revolution: the crowd was chanting, waving flags, pleading, eating, marching, drinking, debating. The boy, still dressed in his monk robes, chatted with Khampas, their guns propped against the Norbulingka wall with blue, red, and green tassels stuffed in the barrels to keep out the dust. Choegyal, the reincarnation of a high lama, had inherited a German Luger from his predecessor. "He must have gotten it in Russia," Choegyal says. "He traveled there and to Mongolia." Like his brother growing up in the Potala, the young boy had a fascination with soldiers—"my superheroes," as he called them. Now they were everywhere, perhaps 1,500 regular Tibetan troops and hundreds more Khampas and armed civilians. "The whole scene was astonishing, and I was completely dazed by it," he recalls. "They looked grim, determined, and fantastic, and I felt a shudder of excitement as I watched them."

But on the afternoon of the 17th, Choegyal noticed a change in the already electric air of the summer palace. "Everyone was anxious," he says. "And I kept asking everyone questions, which got on their nerves." Choegyal was the favorite of the family, a kind of exasperating mascot, and he was used to laughter and confidences and a feeling of closeness, his fat uncle grabbing him "and tickling me until I couldn't breathe." Now Tibetans were terrified of what the Chinese might do but also secretly afraid of confiding in their loved ones and friends, in case they turned out to be either gossips or PLA spies. The boy noticed that when he entered a room, his elders would immediately fall silent.

At 6:30 p.m. his mother called him into her room.

"You better go and change into laypeople's clothes," she told him. "We're going to the south."

"To India?" he replied.

"No, to the south. To a nunnery across the river."

Choegyal turned to dash to his room. "But . . .," his mother called.

He turned. She was nervous, her voice trembling.

"You can tell no one."

Choegyal nodded. "I knew we were going to India, even though she wouldn't tell me."

The boy's instincts had outraced the actual plan. The Lord Chamberlain and the Dalai Lama had agreed they would head southward toward a rebel stronghold in the south and try to set up a dissident government there. Despite the mortar shells, they still held out hope for a negotiated settlement. The Dalai Lama had chosen Lhuntse Dzong, the fort where the CIA-trained Athar was stationed at this moment, for their destination. His Holiness wasn't yet ready to light out for India. Leaving Lhasa would make his break with the Chinese occupation clear and unmistakable, but leaving Tibet was another matter. It would be a desperate step, His Holiness felt, one that would leave his subjects without a spiritual leader and give the Chinese carte blanche to unleash the PLA.

Choegyal ran toward his room. He took off the maroon-and-gold monk's robe and put on an old *chuba*, the long Tibetan coat. Underneath, he carefully secured his Luger under a belt. He bounced downstairs and ran to his uncle's room, where he found the fat, good-natured man—one of his favorites in the family—sewing sacks for provisions, "stitching bags like mad." Choegyal was about to ask if India was their true destination when his uncle barked, "Go away! I'm busy!" Eager for gossip, the boy snuck upstairs and found his mother's maid, Acha, looking worried. "Acha, guess what? We're going away to India." She glared at him and snapped, "Keep quiet!"

Choegyal slipped away, hoping to find a soldier to lend him some precious ammunition for the Luger, whose pleasant heft he could feel with every step. He imagined being ambushed by a Chinese patrol on the way south and heroically gunning down a score of PLA soldiers. "I had no doubt in my heart that if we had it out with the Chinese, I would be victorious."

Choegyal climbed the stairs and approached his mother's room. Every lamp was turned on, and the room shone with light. Inside he found a previously unimaginable sight: his mother and his aunt being dressed as ordinary Tibetan soldiers by their man-servants. His mother had on a short fur dress, borrowed from her brother, worn over a shabby pair of men's pants and boots that had mud smeared over the leather to make it look as though the wearer had just come off patrol. "Over my shoulder I slung a little toy rifle, which would have looked ridiculous during the day, but was not noticeable at night," she remembered. The final touch was a commoner's hat borrowed from one of her servants. In the brightly lit space, which looked to Choegyal not like the room he'd left earlier but a theatrical stage on which his mother was being dressed for some kind of farce, the boy began to splutter.

"I just couldn't help it," he protests. "I started to laugh. They got quite mad at me."

Choegyal was soon given a disguise as well. He was handed a wool hat, known as a "monkey cap," that could be lowered over the face. His sister contributed a pink mohair scarf. Someone handed him a bowl for eating on the journey, and a rifle. Choegyal looked at it with rapt admiration before throwing it over his shoulder.

To avoid suspicion, the fugitives would leave in three groups: Choegyal and his family would go first, followed by the Dalai Lama's group, then one composed of tutors and cabinet ministers. A squad of four Tibetan soldiers arrived at Diki Tsering's house around 8:30 p.m. led by a captain in His Holiness's bodyguard. "They said, 'Get ready, we're leaving,'" Choegyal remembers. For the thirteen-year-old boy, the exhilaration building inside him was now tempered by sadness; he felt for the first time not the freedom and excitement of all the upheaval around him but the looming separation from the people pressed against the walls of the rooms, staring at him and the other members of the escape party. "I started saying good-bye to the people who looked after me at the monastery," he says, "a young chap who must have been around fifteen, and an older servant, about twenty-four, who was kind of a butler, who looked after my food. And the older one said to me, 'Don't forget the texts you have memorized so far.' Looking back, those words are kind of moving to me. Why should he care, actually?" The servants were asked if they wished to come along, but they declined. Many had families in Lhasa, while others perhaps thought they would rather take their chances with the Chinese than on a last-minute break to the south. "There was a sadness leaving those people behind," Choegyal adds. "And thinking I would never see them again."

In another part of the Norbulingka, the Dalai Lama was composing a letter to the leaders of the protest movement and to the ministers of his government. Around him, a hundred last-minute tasks were being seen to. His ministers gathered up the Seal of Office and the Seal of the Cabinet that stamped all official orders; whatever food and water was in the Norbulingka kitchen was slipped into the newly sewn bags; and each member of the escape party was hurriedly choosing a minimum of clothing—two full outfits, in the Dalai Lama's case—for the journey.

But everything else would have to be left behind. For the Dalai Lama, the vaults of the Potala were filled with the remnants of his former selves, not only the colossal burial chambers (one of which contained 3,271 kilos of gold and other precious metals) but jewels and gold dust given to him in tribute, the gifts from the Russian czars and English queens, including the ones for his own installation, an intricately worked clock and a brick of solid gold minted by the Calcutta Mint. A thousand years' worth of Tibet's patrimony would be left behind. The Tibetan cabinet had spirited "substantial" amounts of gold and silver out of the treasury during the 1950 invasion, but many millions of dollars' worth of precious objects remained. And the rooms and chapels were filled with irreplaceable manuscripts and Buddhist art that the Dalai Lama could barely begin to think of being handed to Tan Guansan and the Chinese bureaucrats.

The Dalai Lama felt a jolt of sadness but little physical apprehension of the journey ahead—not because it wasn't dangerous but because he'd come to believe so deeply in his own reincarnation. "I have no fear of death," he said. "I was not afraid of being one of the victims of the Chinese attack." But he knew the death of another Dalai Lama would convince the people that "the life of Tibet [had] come to an end." And he feared, intensely, being captured by the Chinese and being forced into the role of a stooge. If they caught him, His Holiness believed, the Chinese would force him to publicly betray everything he cherished.

In his room, His Holiness opened a book of the Buddha's teachings and let the pages fall randomly. His eye dropped to the open page.

"The passages were about temptation and courage," he said. The Dalai Lama closed his eyes and began to think about the words "courage" and "altruism." Then he imagined the escape party winding through the wastes of southern Tibet and someday, in another party with himself leading it, returning to the palace grounds.

As softhearted as he sometimes could be, the Dalai Lama was a decisive man. Once he fixed on a course of action, he rarely regretted it. "No going back," he thought to himself.

As dusk fell, the Dalai Lama walked to the shrine of his personal protector, the six-armed Mahakala, with the five white skulls around his snarling face, each representing a different transformation of evil into good: ignorance into wisdom, jealousy into accomplishment. The heavy wooden door groaned as he pushed it open, and inside he saw "the glow of a dozen votive butter lamps set in rows of golden and silver dishes." He paused before presenting the *kata*, or ceremonial scarf, he held in his hand to the statue of the protector. All of these very ordinary things he was seeing possibly for the last time, and so as his eyes rested on each one in turn, the Dalai Lama tried to stamp them on his memory: the smoke-burnished colors of the religious frescoes on the wall, the chanting monks (most likely aware of him now but, out of reverence, averting their eyes), the small lump of *tsampa* left on the altar as an offering to Mahakala, and a servant scooping out ladles of melted butter into the candleholders. A monk lifted a horn and blew out a "long, mournful note," and raised a pair of golden cymbals and then brought them together. The metallic *passsh* filled the room and then fell away.

His Holiness returned to his rooms to put on his disguise. He took off his monk's robe and, for the first time in many years, put on a pair of trousers and then a long black coat. He was handed a *thangka*—a painted Buddhist banner—of the Palden Lhamo, the same blue-faced protectress who had watched over the divination that had directed him to leave India three years before. He placed it in a traveling container and threw that over his left shoulder. An old rifle went over his right. He took off his distinctive black-rimmed glasses, unfamiliar to those Lhasans who'd managed to get a glimpse of their Precious Protector (wearing glasses in public was thought of as a Western affectation, and the Dalai Lama often avoided it), and slipped them into his pocket, then donned a fur cap and a warm scarf that he could pull up over his mouth. He now looked like a lowly, half-blind Tibetan soldier. The disguise was as much for the crowd of protesters—who were checking the identity of everyone leaving the summer palace—as it was for the Chinese.

The Dalai Lama walked to the ground floor, pausing to pat the head of a dog that, he reflected with some satisfaction, had never been very fond of him and so wouldn't miss him very much. "As I went out, my mind was drained of all emotion," he remembered. Years of meditation had given him the ability to remove himself from the moment. As he walked, he could hear the slap of his feet on the floor and the ticking of a hallway clock, as if he were back in his palace cinema watching one of the films he loved. The partings with the sweepers who had practically raised him since the age of four were more wrenching, though his beloved caretaker, Ponpo, was among the men coming with him. Finally, at the front door to his small palace, he turned and paced down the patio, "pausing on the far side to visualize reaching India safely." As he strode back, he again visualized his eventual return to Tibet. Every high lama in Tibet is believed to be able to see the future "as clearly as you see yourself in a mirror," but the Dalai Lama wasn't so much picturing the future as willing it to happen. Watching the young monk walk back and forth, the gray-haired Lord Chamberlain felt this was "the saddest sight, the most awful moment I have ever known in my life."

Soldiers guided His Holiness in the darkness to the gate in the inner wall, where he was met by his brother-in-law, the chief of his bodyguards. Almost stumbling in the dark, he walked past the tranquil lawns of the Norbulingka, now still and black-green in the darkness, and came to the south gate. Ahead of him he saw the blurred image of one of his bodyguards brandishing a sword, along with a contingent of Tibetan troops. One twenty-nine-year-old Tibetan soldier had been assigned to accompany the Dalai Lama all the way across the Himalayas. When His Holiness walked up, blinking with nearsightedness and dressed as a common soldier, the soldier felt an odd, nameless feeling. Then he became faint. "I felt like blacking out on seeing His Holiness looking like that," he said. "I knew bad times were striking Tibet." As the men waited, he tried to hide his despair, whispering to their friends and checking their gear.

The soldiers opened the creaking wooden doors, and one of them announced in a loud voice that an army squad was going out on a patrol. The protesters guarding the gate turned and looked briefly at the small party before stepping back to let them pass. In the distance, the loudspeakers droned the same message they'd been broadcasting for days: "You are like ants scratching at the elephant's feet. China is as mighty as the sun and wherever there is sun, there the Chinese are also." As he stepped outside, the Dalai Lama felt his fear of capture spike. The thought of being taken, and how awful that would be for Tibet, flashed across his mind. He looked on himself almost coldly, not as Lhamo Thondup, the boy from Amdo, but as Chenrizi, the vessel of the Dharma in Tibet and the world. As he walked over the cobblestones, following the shape of his bodyguard ahead of him, he was anxious about what losing this person, the Dalai Lama, would mean to the people whom he could sense around him, the great mass of protesters whom he could hear and feel more than see. If he was captured, these people whose elbows and flanks pressed against him would simply fall apart.

The party walked out through the ring of protesters—the Dalai Lama sensing the crowd melting away in front of him— and followed in the footsteps of Choegyal's party. The lights of the Chinese camp, just two hundred feet away, were clearly visible, and the Dalai Lama was sure that every stumble on the rock-strewn bank would alert the PLA to their escape. "I needed to be very careful," he said. "We came so near the Chinese that we could hear them. That was dangerous."

A thin moon hung in the black dome of the sky. The wind ruffled up from the direction of the Chinese camp, which the escapees hoped would mask the racket they were making. When they reached the Kyichu River, the Dalai Lama was relieved, and the group quickly began to load into coracles, narrow boats made of yak skins stretched over wooden frames. But the noise of the crossing soon had his nerves peaked again. "I was certain that every splash of oars would draw down machine-gun fire on us," he said.

On the far bank of the river, Choegyal and the first batch of escapees waited anxiously for the arrival of the Dalai Lama's party. After milling around on the dark shore, Choegyal began chatting with the Tibetan guards, but they were too nervous to talk. With the lights of the Chinese camp twinkling in the distance, the boy wandered off a way to relieve himself. He found a place shielded from the view of the others, undid his *chuba*, and looked up. In the distance, he could see the long white line of Drepung Monastery against the bulk of Mount Gephel. As he stood there, Choegyal was filled with a sudden fondness for the place he'd disliked so intensely. He finished up, tied his *chuba*, and walked forward, but he continued to stare at the monastery in the distance. "I don't know what made me do it," he remembers, "but I lay down and prostrated three times to it. And I whispered to myself, 'May I see you again.'"

As he walked back to the riverbank, he heard the splash of oars. The keel of a coracle glided onto the pebbles, and a Khampa grabbed its nose, pulling it in. Another rebel guard watched as the Dalai Lama climbed out. "This was a very emotional moment for us," the guard said. "Here was the living symbol of our nation and our religion having to disguise himself in order to escape the Chinese." Along the route, when the menacing warriors spotted the Dalai Lama, they would immediately fall to the ground and prostrate themselves.

"All of a sudden I heard a lot of people and horses passing in the dark," Choegyal remembers. Then there was the voice of the Lord Chamberlain murmuring, "*Tasbidelek tasbidelek*," a traditional New Year's greeting that means "Good luck." Behind him came His Holiness. The Dalai Lama turned to one of the guards and asked him his name. Startled, the guard gave a hurried reply. "He was young and . . . very different from anyone else," the soldier recalled. "Even when you caught a glimpse of him, there's a special charisma there that you just can't describe."

The third group—with the Dalai Lama's ministers, two cabinet ministers, and the young Norbulingka official Soepa—arrived on the riverbank soon after. By midnight, the fugitives were all together and mounted on horses brought by the Khampas. They set off into the Vale of Lhasa.

There were now more than 700 Khampas gathered to escort the Dalai Lama and his entourage on to the next goal, the Tsangpo, the highest major river in the world. But ahead lay their first geological barrier: the 17,000-foot mountain pass known as the Che-La, which separates the fifteen-mile-long Vale of Lhasa from the Tsangpo Valley, forty miles south of Lhasa. They would ride without stopping.

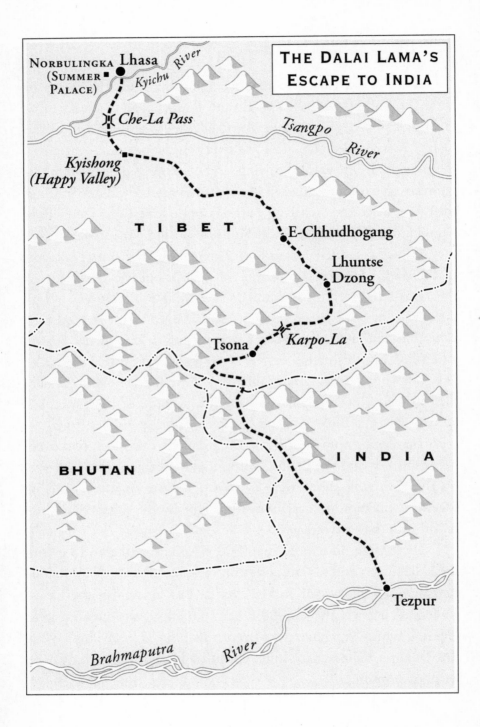

THE DALAI LAMA'S
ESCAPE TO INDIA

NORBULINGKA
(SUMMER
PALACE)

Lhasa

Kyichu River

Che-La Pass

Kyishong
(Happy Valley)

Tsangpo River

TIBET

E-Chhudhogang

Lhuntse
Dzong

Tsona

Karpo-La

BHUTAN

INDIA

Tezpur

Brahmaputra River

*Eight*

# FLIGHT

The fugitives hurried through the night, with the Dalai Lama's group sprinting ahead, putting a full two hours between themselves and the other escapees. They were heading for a place called Kyishong ("Happy Valley"), which lay along a far less-traveled trail than the direct Lhasa-Tsangpo route, in hopes of reducing their chances of stumbling into a PLA squadron. The temperature sank with each passing hour. "My feet grew numb," Choegyal remembers. "And my horse got extremely tired." The Luger was digging into his side, but he refused to remove it from his belt. He'd also acquired a Mauser rifle, presented to him by the men of the Kusung Regiment, and he'd secreted an extra clip of bullets in the folds of his *chuba*. To this collection he'd added an eighteen-inch dagger. "I looked the perfect soldier," he said. "Except I was a bit too short." Later, he was ordered to give up the Mauser, which was replaced—humiliatingly—by the Dalai Lama's umbrella.

His Holiness found that, even on the trail, old habits died hard. As they approached Che-La, he decided to walk for a bit. He slid his right leg over the saddle and dropped to the ground, his soft leather boots kicking up a small cloud of dust as he landed on the dry soil. As he turned to march ahead, he noticed the minister on the horse behind him quickly dismount from his horse and begin walking. Like dominoes, all the tutors and even his family members began to drop off their horses one by one and started trudging forward. One apparently couldn't be seen riding if the Dalai Lama had decreed it was time to walk. "It's OK," the Dalai Lama called back to the other escapees. "Get back on your horses." But, heads bowed, they kept shuffling ahead, old men for the most part who'd been softened by years of court life. Finally, the Dalai Lama gave up and jumped back in the saddle. Slowly, the line of marchers followed suit, and in a few minutes they were all riding again.

The incline of the ground began to rise. The fugitives stopped briefly at a farmhouse, where the peasants had been alerted that His Holiness would be arriving for food (he'd had no dinner) and a short rest. An old man, a former groom to the Thirteenth Dalai Lama, appeared leading a white horse with a white scarf tied around its neck. The man was worried His Holiness's pony wouldn't make it over the high passes ahead. He began to cry as the Dalai Lama accepted the gift. His Holiness comforted the old man and assured him he wasn't going far, all he could think to say on the spur of the moment. The man accompanied them as far as Che-La, which they reached around 8:00 a.m. The sun was high enough in the sky that it lit the plain behind them, but the mountain ahead threw a shadow over the marchers.

They began to climb the sandy incline (Che-La means "Sandy Pass"). As they ascended the slope, the ground shifted under the weight of the animals. For every step forward, the horses would slide back four. Riders began to drop behind the leaders as the horses tired, and the rest found the trail "rough and weary." Choegyal saw his fat uncle ahead nearly topple off his horse. "His saddle was slipping off the horse because he was just too heavy," Choegyal says. "He was yelling and grabbing on to the mane." As the Dalai Lama came to the crest of the pass, an aide sidled over to him and mentioned that this would be his last chance to look on Lhasa. His Holiness dismounted and gazed at the cluster of buildings to the north, tiny in the landscape. From this distance, even the Potala lost its imposing mass. "The ancient city looked serene as ever as it spread out below," he remembered. The Dalai Lama said a prayer and then turned and began running down the sandy slopes, lit by the sun, that led down to the valley of the Tsangpo.

As the sunlight hit their faces and they placed a mountain range between themselves and the PLA headquarters, the mood of the escapees lightened. "I was laughing uncontrollably," admits Choegyal, who couldn't take his eyes off his uncle struggling to stay in his saddle. "But he was such a kind man, he didn't yell at me." Having escaped Lhasa, the uncle began to regain his sense of humor. "Whenever I did something naughty," Choegyal recalls, "he would just shake his head and say, 'Oh my god, he's done it again.' He was a very kind fellow." The escapees dropped off their mounts and began to follow the Dalai Lama, who was running full speed down the side of the mountain. "We were all very happy,"

Choegyal said. "We'd escaped. We were euphoric. Now we could say what was in our hearts."

The Dalai Lama took giant steps down the slope. "The day after I escaped from Lhasa, I felt a tremendous sense of relief. Actually, the danger was still very much alive." But for the first time in years, the constraint he felt in Lhasa was gone. He could curse the Chinese if he felt like it: " 'I have the right to say bad things about them,' I remember thinking. The sense of freedom was very vivid: my strongest reaction following the escape." When he reached the valley on the other side of the mountain, a dust storm kicked up, blinding the fugitives. The Dalai Lama comforted himself with the thought that the dirt would hide them from any PLA troops sent to capture them.

The lead party crossed the Che-La and sped ahead to the Tsangpo River, ten miles away. Rebels were waiting at the banks, with coracles to ferry them across. When they reached the other side, they met a group of villagers who had been told the Dalai Lama was approaching. The sight of Tibetans along the trails was almost always the same: humbly dressed men and women, bowing their heads in prayer, sticks of incense or *katas* in their hands. One villager recalled spreading hay and dung across an expanse of ice that the escape party would be crossing, crying both with joy and with grief at the thought that His Holiness was fleeing to India. Others brought out food and clothing from their meager stocks and offered them to the escapees, "weeping with sorrow at the fate of Tibet." Knowing that this might be the last time they saw the incarnate, they all asked for his blessing. At the sight of the villagers, the escapees' giddiness evaporated.

After twenty straight hours of riding, Choegyal and the second group of fugitives stopped at Rame, one of the earliest Sakyapa monasteries in Tibet, built in the twelfth century. The Dalai Lama's mother was by now the worst off in the party. "I had no scarf or glasses, and since I had on a man's short dress, I froze on the way," she remembered. "I could barely stand, from a mixture of cold, fatigue and cramps in my legs." Her face was covered with a thick layer of dust, and the skin on her face had begun to peel because of the wind and dust storms. Choegyal was cold and tired but over-joyed to see his older brother, who'd arrived hours earlier. He found the Dalai Lama on the second floor of the monastery, dressed in high leather boots and his soldier's uniform. "How are you feeling today?" the Dalai Lama asked. The boy replied that everything had gone well, apart from the sandstorm and their mother's pains.

His Holiness paused for a moment, looking at his younger brother. "Tendzin," he said, "do you realize that we're free now?"

Choegyal nodded.

But the fugitives were still hundreds of miles from safety. The route ahead was treacherous, lined with dangers both natu-ral and man-made. They were leaving the Vale of Lhasa, the heart of Tibetan civilization, and venturing into desolate territory. The Himalayas, still encased in their winter ice, awaited; the passes alone measured 19,000 feet and more and were for part of the year totally impassable. The 500-yard-wide Tsangpo River, cold and fast with the winter snowmelt, would have to be forded. The rebels held the territory ahead, but they were battling with large contingents of PLA forces in places such as Lhoka. Traitors among the Dalai Lama's own people, militants who favored armed rebellion and dis-dained his pledge of nonviolence, could easily be lurking in the vil-lages ahead, or even among his own party, and might deliver him to the Chinese. There were even wolves and leopards native to South Tibet and the *de-mong*, a legendary bear with mustard-colored fur.

There were landslides, deep cold, and rock falls. Travelers on these routes would often find boulders the size of cars blocking routes that had been passable the year before.

The escape parties headed due south through a landscape of flint and sand. "It was all new to me, this land," Choegyal remembers. He had never ventured more than a day's journey from Lhasa, and now he was seeing the ancient seabed that made up the enormous Tibetan plateau. "It reminded me of Palestine, arid and flat."

But the Chinese were the real worry. "We were all thinking they might all of a sudden intercept us," Choegyal says. "That's why we traveled very fast and didn't stop more than was absolutely necessary." One Khampa leader rated the Chinese intelligence network, even in some rural areas, as "excellent." "They knew beforehand what to expect," he said, "and could prepare accordingly."

If the Dalai Lama's party did make it as far as the Indian border, Prime Minister Nehru, who was increasingly anxious about his relationship with the Chinese, might refuse to admit them. The Lord Chamberlain had sent word to Athar and Lhotse, who he knew had radios capable of reaching Washington, but the two guerrillas hadn't yet reached the escape party, and even if they managed to send a request on their CIA-supplied radios, there was no guarantee that Nehru would grant the fugitives asylum. The Lord Chamberlain had tried to notify the Indians before leaving that asylum might be requested, but the message was never received in New Delhi.

To counter any possible PLA attack, the guards on the route went around heavily armed even for Khampas, their *chubas* dripping with swords, jewel-encrusted daggers, pistols, Lee-Enfield rifles, and Buddhist charm boxes that would, they believed, protect them from Chinese bullets. Even the Dalai Lama's cook wore a bazooka over his back and a bandolier of the enormous shells around his chest. At one point, wanting to impress His Holiness with his "magnificent and terrible-looking weapon," he unslung it, loaded a shell into the bazooka, lay down on the ground, and fired at an outcropping. The shell exploded with impressive power, but it had taken fifteen minutes to load the thing. A second demonstration took even longer. "If we're going to use that bazooka during the war," the Dalai Lama commented dryly, "we might want to ask the enemy not to move."

The fugitives rode at a punishing pace, around twenty miles a day at altitudes of 16,000 feet and higher, across rough trails. As they pushed forward, one miscalculation became clear. Some of the horses they'd brought from the Dalai Lama's stables weren't fit for the journey. "We only had 'court' horses, aristocratic animals if you will," said one guard. "All they knew was to eat, drink, and sleep." Even the meager supplies that the guards had loaded on the animals' backs were proving too heavy, and the horses began to collapse on the road. When the fugitives came across a settlement, they asked the villagers for pack animals. "Why do you need them if you can carry the packs yourselves?" the villagers asked—not realizing, apparently, that these were not hardy farmers and nomads but city-bred tutors and old men. Finally, forty peasants, including women, volunteered to take the loads and carry them across the mountains. "I was surprised to see that women were willing to carry such heavy loads," said one fugitive. "They replied that when it came to carrying loads and climbing mountains, the women were stronger than the men."

His Holiness dashed off a quick letter to his sometime rival the Panchen Lama at his base at Tashilhunpo Monastery, informing him that he'd escaped and encouraging the younger incarnate to join him. It had been months since the two had communicated, kept apart not only by centuries-old jealousies but also by the

Panchen Lama's alliance with Peking. But during the winter, the twenty-one-year-old Panchen had sent him a secret note telling the Dalai Lama that the two needed to work together on a single strategy. "This was the first indication he had given of being no longer in the thrall of our Chinese masters," the Dalai Lama said. The Tibetan leader also knew that with him out of the picture, the pressure on the Panchen Lama to bow to Chinese pressure would increase exponentially. Peking would want him to become what the Dalai Lama never had: the Tibetan face of a Chinese occupation.

One of the Dalai Lama's ministers went in search of Tenpa Soepa, an enterprising young Norbulingka official who'd helped arrange the escape. When he found the young man, the minister asked him if he would do His Holiness a service. The Dalai Lama was still carrying the letter he'd written to his ministers back at the Norbulingka—he'd either forgotten to hand it over in the rush to escape or been worried that leaving it would reveal the fugitives' plan. Now someone needed to hand-deliver the letter to the Dalai Lama's personal secretary back in Lhasa. The minister asked Soepa to accept the mission.

Soepa didn't want to leave His Holiness in the wastes of southern Tibet. "A great feeling of sadness and depression came over me," he said. "In my whole life I have never been sadder than at that moment." When the emotion passed, he began to consider what was waiting for him in Lhasa. It was bound to be a dangerous place, especially for someone who'd helped the Dalai Lama flee. "The Chinese are there," he thought to himself, "ready to start the killing. . . . If I go back . . ."

Soepa gathered his things, alerted his servant, and set off for the summer palace.

*Nine*

# THE NORBULINGKA

oepa retraced the escapees' route back north. He arrived back at the Kyichu River, which he'd crossed only hours before. On the riverbank, he found a few poor villagers waiting for a boat to Lhasa, where they would sell some sticks and branches they'd collected for firewood. He advised against it: "I told them that instead of selling their firewood, they were likely to lose their lives." He was melancholy as he stared at the far shore: "I felt that once I crossed the river, I might never make it back again."

Self-preservation told him to stay out of the capital. Soepa considered another way of getting the letter to the Norbulingka—asking his servant to take it. "He could go across and deliver the letter while I waited here," Soepa thought. Unable to decide, he took out the unsealed envelope, slipped the letter out, and began reading. If it was important enough, he would risk his life.

The letter informed the leaders of the escape and appointed two acting prime ministers and a new commander in chief of the army, since the acting one was riding along with the figitives. It instructed the men to negotiate with the Chinese, to avoid violence, and to keep the Dalai Lama updated on all developments. At the bottom was His Holiness's signature.

The letter was obviously crucial. Soepa decided he couldn't just hand it to his servant. "It is my moral duty to go to the Norbulingka and hand this letter over with my own hands," he thought. "Even if I die, then I have to die, but there will be no regrets." He remembered a curious clause that was written into the General Rules and Regulations that all Tibetan civil servants agreed to when they joined up. "For duty and responsibility," it read, "one must jump into hell and leave one's father behind."

Soepa persuaded a soldier guarding the bank to fetch a boat, and thirty minutes later, he was gliding across the river. The coracle touched the sandy bank, and a nervous Soepa headed for the Norbulingka. "The situation seemed delicate and vulnerable," he says. "I felt that the whole place could break into chaos once the Chinese discovered the Dalai Lama had fled." Inside the palace, Soepa knew, only a few people suspected that His Holiness's rooms were empty that morning. The normal chores would be under way. The enormous Tibetan mastiffs inside the palace grounds had to be fed at dawn. The horses in the stable had to be walked, brushed, and combed. The pet monkey had to be given water. Life at the summer palace went on as if it were just another spring day in the Land of Snows.

When Soepa reached the palace, he saw that the crowd around it hadn't changed. The protesters were still clearly unaware that their Precious Protector was gone. Women were cooking *tsampa* over smoky fires, and guards were gossiping or oiling their rifles. As the sun burned off the cold morning mist, men took out homemade kites and ran with their sons, trying to lift the paper craft into the air. At Barkhor Square several miles away, Chinese traders in their stalls blew on their hands as they rearranged their stocks of spicy snacks, loose wool, gorgeous Indian silks, and LPs from the West. The only thing merchants noticed was that the bullets they were hawking at 2 shillings apiece were flying off the shelves.

There was an air of nervous enjoyment, of doing a few last things before the inevitable arrived. "You don't have to ask what's going to happen," wrote the Chinese diarist Shan Chao. "Those who have their eyes and ears open are polishing their rifles and bullets. I have taken out my hand grenades and will put them by the side of my pillow." There were signs in the city that the Chinese leadership suspected that the Dalai Lama had escaped. Chinese officers appeared at the Indian and Nepalese missions and requested permission to search the buildings for His Holiness. Both consuls refused. The Chinese official Tan Guansan later sent a second messenger to the Indian mission, suggesting that the personnel evacuate the building, an ominous sign.

Soepa made his way toward the Norbulingka. He was still sworn to secrecy. Rumors that the Dalai Lama had slipped away from the Norbulingka were rife, he knew, but there were a thousand rumors floating through Lhasa at the time and he tried to treat the questions about His Holiness as just another piece of gossip. When protesters called out and asked what he'd heard, Soepa shrugged. "His Holiness?" he said. "He must still be here. We have all been here together. Where else could he go?"

As Soepa approached the outer wall of the Norbulingka, a gun barked. He paid it no mind. The city was filled with nervous gunmen, and for the past few days "misfirings," as he put it, had been common. But then there was another gunshot, and a bullet buzzed past his ear. He dropped flat to the ground. He had no idea who'd fired the shot. Soepa slowly raised himself up and approached the gate. Just then, a Chinese tank swung into view, rumbling down the road. There was a fixed machine gun on top, and a young PLA gunner pointed the barrel at the protesters. The people around him ducked down, but Soepa reached underneath his *chuba* for his gun. The tank advanced toward the Tibetans for a few seconds more, then swerved away.

Soepa greeted the guards at the gate, and they let him through. He delivered the letter to the Dalai Lama's personal secretary and reported that His Holiness was safe. He had a cup of butter tea, then began the second mission he'd been given by the Dalai Lama's ministers: collect as much ammunition and as many guns as he could and bring them to his house for safekeeping. That night, he had the first decent sleep he'd had since the uprising began.

As the 19th dawned, the streets of Lhasa pulsed to the sounds of another rally. The women's association had planned a huge march, and now thousands of women surged through the narrow streets, shouting anti-PLA slogans, waving prayer banners, and expressing their undying support for the Dalai Lama. It was a matter of honor for many families in Lhasa—from peasants to aristocrats—that at least one member of their clan was there to represent them, the married women in their fine-spun colorful aprons, the single women without. The Chinese soldiers watched from the roofs of the buildings, some snapping pictures of the protesters, others with their rifles pointed down at the march. "I wasn't afraid that the Chinese would fire on us," said one twenty-eight-year-old nun who marched that day. "The situation was very tense, but we couldn't imagine what was to come." The diarist Shan Chao, however, reported something that the Chinese insisted on throughout the protests: that the "spontaneous" marches were actually held at the point of a gun. "The rebels ordered it!" he recalled hearing two Tibetan turncoats shouting as the women marched past. "They said anyone who does not attend the meeting at the Norbulingka will be fined; if he still fails to go, then they will have his head cut off!" The observer even told Shan Chao that Tibetans were being beaten to death for refusing to protest and that "not a single one of the scores of young nuns" staying at the Jokhang Temple had escaped being raped by the bandits.

The reports were almost certainly false. None of the Tibetans who were in Lhasa that day reported being forced into protesting. But the rebels did ask the local merchants and schools to close for the day in solidarity, and many agreed.

Soepa decided to spend the night at the summer palace. At 1:00 a.m., he was asleep in the guard post near the northern gate of the Norbulingka when a huge explosion snapped him awake. Artillery guns opened up in the darkness, accompanied by concussions and the sound of breaking glass. Soepa ran out into the grounds and saw that a shell had hit the Dalai Lama's private residence and left a gaping hole in the roof. He could see chunks of wood and mortar sprayed across the lawn. The Chinese assault on the summer palace had begun.

Soepa grabbed a rifle—a brand-new model that had never been fired—and hurried to the nearest barricade, near the northern wall of the Norbulingka. Already he could hear waves of gunfire hitting a crescendo. He reached the Tibetan position. Machine-gun fire was being directed at the earthen palisade that the rebels had thrown up, and the Tibetans were shooting back with rifles. Soepa unslung his rifle from his shoulder, crouched down, and took aim at the muzzle flashes that were all he could see of the Chinese. But the gun froze up. It still had too much oil and grease from the packing crates. He pulled out his handgun and began shooting. The snap of the pistol was lost in the terrifying drumming of the machine-gun fire blasting at him from across the road, and Soepa thought of a Tibetan saying, "You know who has won and who has lost a battle by the sound of their guns." *It really is true*, he thought.

The thing he'd dreaded when contemplating a return to Lhasa had finally happened. Soepa found himself in the middle of a firefight in which the Tibetans were outnumbered and outgunned. The lights of the Norbulingka had gone out as soon as the PLA barrage started, so he saw only moving figures and shadows around him, lit by muzzle flashes and weak moonlight. But he could see men—Khampas and Tibetan soldiers—fall to the ground when shot and he could hear their rough grunts as they did. Some of them cried out in pain, but there was no medical service, no planning of any kind to help the injured. As he reloaded his pistol, Soepa was terrified he was going to be killed at any moment. But after five minutes, he found his mind clear of any anxiety, almost cold as he continued to shoot at the flashes across the way. "You forget your fear," he said. It helped that he saw more and more Tibetans arrive and pick up the guns of the fallen soldiers and begin firing.

The Norbulingka was the first battleground in the battle for Lhasa, but skirmishes were being fought across the city. The Tibetans largely held the heights. They were dug in on Chakpori, the mountain overlooking Lhasa, and at the Medical College near its summit, with light artillery guns, mortars, and a few ancient cannons that had sat there for decades. Days before, during a protest, sixteen-year-old Lobsang Yonten had witnessed a disturbing spectacle on the mountain. "A thick bunch of prayer flags caught fire, lighting the whole sky," Yonten remembers. "It looked as if the air was engulfed in flames. I was terrified when I caught sight of them." People in the crowd argued whether the burning flags were a good or bad omen, but Yonten felt a churning anxiety in the pit of his stomach.

The rebels also held the Potala and the monasteries that ringed the capital, where hundreds if not thousands of monks had joined the resistance and were now ferrying guns to the rebels or attacking the PLA. The Chinese were at a strategic disadvantage: they held the low ground, always the worst position to begin a battle. But in every other way, they held the upper hand: in manpower, training, equipment, and planning, the PLA outmatched the Tibetans by a degree of magnitude.

The Chinese artillery pounded the Norbulingka grounds. But when the Tibetan rebels at the Norbulingka tried to call the PLA positions in to the mountain gunners, they found that the cables to the army positions at Tez and Chakpori had been cut. The Tibetans had no wireless radios, either, so the only way to communicate with the artillery was to send messengers up the mountain. In the middle of the firefight, a commander arrived from Chakpori in search of fresh ammunition. He told the fighters at the Norbulingka to come with him. "Staying inside the Norbulingka, you have no way to fight back," he told one young government official. "You will just be slaughtered."

Soepa was told the same thing by a rebel: the battle was hopeless and they should abandon the palace and run to higher ground.

"My mouth said, 'Yes, you are right, we should run,'" he remembered. "But in my mind, I really didn't want to flee at that moment. 'His Holiness has sent me back,' I thought." Soepa imagined escaping the battle, fleeing to the south, and there running into the Dalai Lama. "He will ask me, 'What is the situation in Lhasa, at the Norbulingka?' If I had to say, 'Well, they were shooting and when I heard the sound of the guns I ran away,' that would be shameful."

As unprepared as the Chinese were for the uprising, it became clear in the early hours of the battle for Lhasa that they'd at least had a plan for the military endgame. These were supremely disciplined soldiers who'd fought the Nationalists and endured the agonies of the Long March. Many Tibetan fighters recalled that they never saw a single PLA soldier in the hours and days to come, as the troops had dug trenches and constructed barricades that far outstripped the amateurish ramparts that the Tibetans, with little or no military training, threw together.

But the Tibetans were adrenalized with hope. They'd wanted this war ever since the rumor of a threat on His Holiness's life had swept through the market stalls.

Yonten was in a home ten minutes away from the Norbulingka when the bombing began. He fell to the floor. "We lay there as the sky filled with gunfire and bombings," he says. As he pressed his body to the ground, a silver coin fell out of his pocket and slowly rolled away. He watched it swivel and turn on the stone floor. "Being a boy, I was more worried about my silver coin than anything else."

He soon turned from protester to gunrunner. Now that open battle had broken out, he and his father hurried to the Tibetan army headquarters to retrieve guns and ammunition for the fighters. They managed to load eleven heavy English rifles and 1,200 bullets into their arms. Returning to the city center, Yonten was running along the cobblestoned streets when a huge artillery gun opened up nearby. The pressure wave knocked him to the ground. His companions picked him up, and they went searching through the alleys and barricades for the fighters who were expecting the guns. But the streets were locked in cross fires between gunners and had become impossible to navigate without getting shot. The air above the city turned "dark and horrible," with acrid smoke from fires lit by shells. "The situation was so chaotic and frightening as the battle was erupting all around us," remembered Yonten. "The people of Lhasa were frantic, saying, 'The war has started.'"

Finally, Yonten and his father made it to the Shöl, the small village below the Potala, and began handing over the rifles, with the din and concussion of the bombing all around and the loud prayers of old women gathered with the soldiers. Loudspeakers around them sounded the Chinese line: "Unless the Tibetans surrender and give up their arms, the Chinese will fire with more powerful weapons and raze the Potala to dust." The announcement alternated with the voice of Ngabö, an adviser to the Dalai Lama who was fast becoming an arch-traitor in the minds of the rebels. The voice told them to lay down their guns. If they didn't, he said, Lhasa would be blown to bits.

In the chaos, Yonten's beloved father calmly handed out the rifles and asked each fighter to sign a receipt for every bullet.

It was soon clear that the Chinese guns were indeed aimed at the Potala above them, the symbol of the Tibetan state. Yonten looked up the hill at the palace as it disappeared behind a cloud of dust thrown up by the shells. "I was extremely worried," he remembered, more concerned for the moment about the palace than about the men around him. Onlookers running from the city would see the smoke and tell the Dalai Lama days later that the Potala had been destroyed, causing him deep distress. But when the smoke cleared after a barrage of ten shells, Yonten could see the Potala's distinctive white buildings standing nearly undamaged.

It was a rare victory for the Tibetans.

After a few hours of exchanging gunfire with the Chinese at the transport station, Soepa realized the PLA was winning. "Their bullets were finding their mark and many were killed on our side." As morning approached and the first rays of the sun lightened the sky, Soepa looked around and counted ten corpses nearby, "blood oozing from everywhere," with many more injured, crying out for water or moaning as they lost consciousness. He ran back into the interior of the Norbulingka, ravenously hungry now, and found a spot behind the office of the Tibetan cabinet that seemed sheltered from the shells falling across the gardens and government buildings. Another fighter sat and ate with him, but minutes later, a mortar shell dropped a few feet away, sending shrapnel and a huge cloud of dust over the crouching figures. Soepa shook the dust off as his companion staggered off, cup still in hand, then collapsed and died.

The sculptured grounds of the summer palace became a killing zone ruled by randomness. No one was in charge. No Tibetan commander had a battle plan or really an objective other than holding the Chinese off. There was no chain of command to consult. No one, it seemed, had any sense of tactical street warfare or an idea of the PLA's vulnerabilities. The enemy was not even visible, only his victims. The Tibetans, wholly unprepared for war, were slowly being blown up by the Chinese artillery and picked off by its sharpshooters. Yet few ran away. The rebels felt they had to stay to defend the palace and His Holiness, who many believed was still hidden on the grounds. Soepa and hundreds of other brave and utterly confused men ran back and forth from the gates to the buildings in the interior, as the smoke drifted from the Chinese artillery batteries and fires broke out in the palaces and chapels. Soepa remembered conversation after conversation with people who emerged out of the darkness and the billowing dust, each reciting his own fragment of the war situation, only to disappear again on an errand or to be scattered by a shell dropping from the sky.

The dead were now "everywhere":

There was one man who had his backside ripped off, and he was breathing, I could see blood spewing out. He called me and asked me to shoot him, but I couldn't bring myself to do it. Shells blew human bodies into pieces. Legs, hands and broken pieces rained down with the dust.

Another fighter told Soepa they were leaving and he should come with them. As Soepa stood on the Norbulingka lawn asking himself what he should do, a shell exploded yards away and a young Norbulingka servant standing next to him collapsed to the ground, killed by shrapnel. "I thought, 'All right, if they kill me, that's it. There is nothing I can do.'" The group of fighters left without him, and many would follow the Dalai Lama across the Himalayas to India. But Soepa, nagged by a sense of duty to His Holiness, stayed on.

He headed back toward the north gate. As Soepa approached it, a Tibetan militiaman emerged from the smoke and stuck his rifle muzzle into Soepa's chest. "I am going to shoot you!" he cried. "You people in the government—we have been pleading for guns, but until now you wouldn't give us anything." The man blamed Tibet's fall on bureaucrats like Soepa. Now he'd make Soepa pay the price.

Soepa quickly reached for his gun. As his hand closed on the butt of his pistol, another shell landed nearby and kicked up a cloud of dust. Bodies toppled left and right. The militiaman who'd been about to kill him was nowhere to be seen. Half-deafened, Soepa ran. When he'd recovered from the concussive power of the shell, he found he'd suffered only one wound: shrapnel had cut into his left shoulder, sending a steady stream of blood down his arm and causing it to throb painfully. Still, he was alive. His "weapons protector," the amulet he wore around his neck, with a holy image and a few bits of the remains of a high lama, had saved his life. He said a silent prayer of thanks.

The Chinese were fighting and dying, too. A ferocious battle was under way on Chakpori, located between central Lhasa and the Norbulingka. A PLA company was advancing on dug-in Tibetan rebels above them. As the Chinese forces sent flares up to illuminate the predawn sky, Fu Lo-min, a squad leader with the first PLA platoon up the mountain, charged toward a machine-gun nest that had been installed in a flat-roofed home. "The hill was very steep but in eight minutes we got on the roof," he remembered. "I was hit in the leg by a bullet but continued to give command till other units stormed up and covered our advance." The rebels fled.

Even the eyewitness accounts from PLA soldiers were glazed over with the Chinese insistence that the Tibetans were united *against* the guerrillas. Behind Fu Lo-min's platoon, a soldier named Chang was sweeping the hill with machine-gun fire to cover the platoon's advance. "We wiped out strong rebel points," he said, adding, "the local Tibetan people encouraged us and helped carry our equipment to wipe out the bandits."

Certainly, there were Lhasans who were furious at the rebels for their uprising. Tibetans were never a monolith, and there were pro-Chinese sprinkled throughout the population, low and high.

There were undoubtedly people who believed the Chinese had brought prosperity and even freedom from the elites and the bureaucrats. But the claim that the rebels made up a tiny minority of the population and were the plotters of an unpopular coup d'état is simply not credible. The photos of the massive protest crowds alone disprove it. No Tibetans in Lhasa for the battle remember any of their neighbors helping the PLA. To do so would have been unimaginable.

The Jokhang Temple, near Barkhor Square, its roof guarded by hideous statues of bird-men with infant heads and vulture wings and ringing wind chimes under their chins, had become a combination rebel headquarters and refugee station. About 200 Tibetan army troops and 100 Tibetan police had taken refuge in the enormous, white-walled temple, with its golden roofs and Buddhist sculptures covered in gold leaf, along with hundreds of women and children fleeing from the fighting. The two-story walls of the holy place concealed large courtyards, where smoke rose from open fires and Lhasans waited nervously for news of what was happening outside.

A tall, thin monk flitted through the courtyards as the sounds of battle echoed outside. He was Narkyid, twenty-eight years old, an official who served on the Council of Lhasa along with three elderly monks and a quartet of lay officials. The quick-minded Narkyid had become the key figure on the council, the man whom the elders turned to when something needed to get done. He even spoke some Mandarin, which made his dealings with the Chinese that much easier.

Days before, members of the Dalai Lama's cabinet had approached Narkyid and said, "You must stay in the Jokhang and take responsibility for it," he remembers. "They said, 'This is one of our most important places.'" It was an understatement: the Jokhang was the Tibetan St. Peter's. In the days after March 10, Narkyid had shuttled between the Norbulingka and the temple, organizing defenses and getting the latest palace scuttlebutt. When he'd visited the summer palace on the 18th, though, he'd immediately noticed a difference. "I felt something missing," he says. "There was no energy in the palace. Truly, it was gone." The officials kept up a regular schedule of meetings and appointments, but "we knew, we knew" that the Dalai Lama had fled. That morning, Narkyid had been relieved to feel the curious spiritual emptiness of the place. And now that His Holiness was gone, the Jokhang was the spiritual locus of Tibet.

The flagstones in the courtyards were lifted up and wells drilled down to the water table. Hundreds of women flocked through the wooden doors and lit campfires, brewing tea and roasting *tsampa*. Narkyid ordered enormous balls of thick Nepalese wool to be brought in and soaked with water, which made them even denser; when they were saturated, the balls were stuffed into the slits that pocked the Jokhang's walls, to protect against bullets penetrating into the interior. Supplies were brought in: enormous quantities of barley, butter, and meat—carcasses cured in the mountain air—were stacked along the inner walls. Narkyid saw to the building of two barricades. Soldiers filled sandbags and stacked them across the rear gate, adding wooden beams and packing the holes with mud and clay, while a second barricade went up at another entrance, this one thrown together out of heavy flagstones, furniture, and junk scoured from the Jokhang and nearby homes. The troops set up a machine gun in the center of the rampart and distributed a dozen Lewis guns—light machine guns first used in World War I—and small mortars around the temple grounds.

There was no way to tell from which direction the Chinese would come, and the light arsenal was all the hundreds of Tibetans packed into the chapels and open squares of the sprawling temple complex had to resist them.

When the PLA's guns opened up in the early hours of March 20, Narkyid was in the Jokhang. He knew the sound was the opening barrage on the Norbulingka and the rebel positions. The Jokhang, for the time being, was left unscathed. At dawn, when the guns died off for the moment, he climbed to a roofed walkway of the temple. From there he could see Lhasa laid out at his feet, smoke rising from fires and the smoldering summer palace in the distance. But it still held an unearthly beauty, framed against the low mountains, everything vivid even at a distance. "It gave you the impression you were looking at a picture."

Now, with the battle still raging miles away at the summer palace, Narkyid sent soldiers to cut the telegraph and electrical wires leading to the Chinese loudspeakers that ringed the Barkhor, just steps from the Jokhang's front gate. "Every time they climbed the pole and cut a wire, they would hang there and yell, 'Ah, we've done it.'" But the Tibetans could never seem to silence every speaker, and the Mandarin-inflected voice kept up its mantra: "Surrender now." In other ways, the Jokhang had returned to the days before the occupation. The electricity that the Chinese bureaucrats had brought was off now; as dusk fell, the temple was lit by cooking fires and torches, the shadows licking across the rough stone walls. The Chinese, installed at the cinema across the street from the temple, exchanged barrages of machine-gun fire with the rebels manning the temple barricades. But the PLA's bullets sent tiny jets of sand up from the bags or sank without a sound into the water-drenched balls of wool.

Late that night, Soepa acquired a machine gun, and as he was hurrying toward a rebel position to begin using it, the Dalai Lama's
secretary ran up to him and said that Chakpori, the main Tibetan
artillery position, had been taken by the Chinese. The rebels must
assemble some fighters and retake it, the secretary told him. Soepa
agreed, changed into fresh clothes, and went to collect ammunition
for the coming fight. "I waited with a thousand rounds of ammunition, but he didn't show," the secretary remembers. Another man
grabbed Soepa and said, for the fifth or sixth time in twenty-four
hours, that the fighters must escape the Norbulingka. Finally convinced that the rebels' position was hopeless, Soepa ran to get horses
for the journey. Arriving at the stables, he saw all the stalls were
empty. "What happened to all the horses?" he shouted at the stable
master. "Others took them," the man answered. "They were threat-
ening to kill me if I didn't give them the mounts." Soepa pulled out
his pistol and pointed it at a man leading a horse away. "He gave
the horse to me at once," he said.

More rebels came running to the stables and told Soepa
that the Chinese had taken over the only rebel-held positions that
might offer them refuge and were at that moment advancing on
the walls of the Norbulingka. Again, Soepa's plans reversed in a
moment. He and the other fighters decided to fight until dusk, and
then escape via Ramagang, a crossing on the Kyichu River close to
Lhasa.

A shell slammed into the stables. Soepa was thrown to the
ground and knocked unconscious, the machine gun crashing down
on his back as he fell. A young Tibetan aristocrat was standing yards
away. Shrapnel ripped open the aristocrat's right thigh and cut a
vein in his face. Blood gushed out and covered his clothes; after a
while, he could feel blood squishing inside his shoes as he tried to
force his way out of the shattered building. "Many people inside

the stables, as well as horses and mules, were killed or injured," he said. "Those still alive shouted for others to help pull them out of the wreckage." As the bombardment, which always seemed to come in waves, dropped away again, the aristocrat emerged into a charred, burning landscape. Buildings were on fire, and gray smoke was drifting through the poplar trees. But what caught his eye was a monkey, one that had for years been a centerpiece of the Dalai Lama's private zoo. The animal was tied to a post in the stable courtyard, "scampering up and down in terror." When there was an explosion, the monkey would hide its head in a cotton awning. "It stared around wide-eyed at the dead and wounded people and horses and became more terrified still." The young man tried in vain to free the monkey, but the animal was too frightened to let him approach. Finally, he left it where it was and staggered away.

The "Tibet Military Committee of the People's Liberation Army" issued an offer to the rebels: "No account will be taken of the past misdeeds of those who desert the rebellion bandits and return to us; those who make contributions will be rewarded; all those captured will be well treated, they are not to be killed, insulted, beaten, or searched and deprived of their personal effects." Men approached the monasteries surrounding Lhasa and told the monks to come out—later, the monks would realize that the men were traitors working for the PLA and trying to lure the Tibetans out so they could be arrested.

As night fell, Soepa found himself trapped in the wrecked stable, unable to get up. There were dead and dying all around. Taking the machine gun slung across his back, he used it as a walking stick and made his way to the room next door, where survivors were trying to recover their wits. Then another round hit. "The roof came down on top of me," he remembered. "I was pinned down and it was only with great effort that I dug myself out." His left leg was mangled by the falling timbers, and he couldn't stand on it. Suddenly thirsty, Soepa began to crawl, looking for water.

There was none to be found. Gasping and bleeding, he lay on the floor of the shattered building and considered his predicament. "I can no longer fight," he thought, "and now I have no chance to escape. If I am captured they will surely torture me." He concluded that it was best to die, and so he stopped trying to find shelter from the bullets that came winging in from the Chinese positions and the procession of mortar and artillery shells. But after an hour, he'd been hit by nothing larger than pieces of mud. "Finally, I decided that a Chinese bullet was not going to kill me, so I took out my pistol and decided to shoot myself in the head." But he changed his mind. In Buddhism, the ideal way of death is in water, which ensures that in one's next incarnation, one will be granted a "clear and lucid mind." The Buddhist suicide must consider his next stage in life, and the Norbulingka's lake, where the Dalai Lama had nearly drowned twice in his life, offered the most advantageous method. Soepa holstered his pistol and began to crawl toward the water. The peaceful gardens of the summer palace were now a torn-up abattoir of dying animals and men, but the pond was still as it always was, its surface calm and coolly inviting. Soepa crawled to the edge and toppled in. He felt himself drift down until his boot touched the silt of the muddy bottom. The young official tried to stay there, suspended in the murky green water, his eyes open, but he felt himself rising up. Breaking the surface, Soepa took a breath and dove back down to the silt that sucked at the soles of his boots, but natural buoyancy kept popping him back to the surface.

His amulets were *too* powerful. "I just wouldn't die," he realized. Finally, Soepa let out a breath, took a large gulp of water, and sank back down. He felt the bottom underneath his feet and grabbed the silt with his hands. But there were no plants to hold him. He began to ascend.

Thirty minutes later, he gave up and decided to live.


Some Tibetans took advantage of the chaos enveloping Lhasa to settle old scores. One of them was Ugyen, a young man in his mid-twenties, a member of the lowest class in Tibetan society, the *Ragyabas*, men and women who were doomed to perform duties left to outcasts: cleaning sewers, begging at weddings, and butchering dead bodies that were then fed to vultures at ceremonial sites. They were ruled by a hereditary lord, the Dhaye, who collected their earnings and had them lashed mercilessly with a split-end bamboo cane. "I really can't begin to count the number of times I was beaten," Ugyen told the writer Patrick French. "You would usually be bleeding . . . and sometimes bits of flesh would come off on the bamboo." Unable to escape their fate, the unclean *Ragyabas* weren't considered fully human by other Lhasans much the way the Dalit class of India were considered untouchable. If there was one group of people who embodied the Communists' charges against Tibetan society—that it was oppressive and feudal—it was Ugyen's people.

When the bombing began, Ugyen watched the puffs of dust erupting from the walls of the Potala and decided this was his chance. "I thought, this is it, Lhasa is in revolt, and I am going to take my revenge on the Dhaye," he said. Ugyen grabbed a knife and under the cover of night snuck to the lord's home, where he planned to kill his master. But when he got to the address, Ugyen found the man had fled with his family. Many aristocrats knew that if the Chinese took over complete control of Tibet, they would be the first targets of the PLA. Later Ugyen heard that the Dhaye was killed by a Chinese bomb as he made his way toward the Kyichu River. "I was very happy when I heard that news," Ugyen remembered.

The young *Ragyaba* was left at loose ends. The very model of an oppressed proletariat, he should have been cheering the sound of explosions from the seat of Tibetan power, the Potala. But instead he did something the Chinese, had they even been aware of him, wouldn't have understood: he joined the resistance. Ugyen was loyal to the Dalai Lama and convinced in his heart that the atheist Chinese would destroy the Dharma. And he was willing to lay down his life to prevent it happening. "The Communists wanted to take away our monasteries and temples," he said. "They wanted to destroy our gods." It was a sentiment that thousands of Tibetans identified with. What the Chinese failed to understand was that this was an uprising of Buddhists even more than it was one of Tibetans.

The war did change one fact of Ugyen's existence. When he escaped Lhasa and joined up with the guerrillas in Nagchu, northern Tibet, he found that his status as a *Ragyaba* made no difference. "Nobody cared," he remembered. The battle had erased, if only temporarily, the hereditary bonds of his family. He fought as a free citizen. More important to him, he fought as a man of faith.

## Ten

# OPIM

As the Tibetan rebels fought and died, the Dalai Lama's party was following the old trader's routes south. They were now in some of the most desolate country on earth and saw few people as their horses and ponies clipped along the rock-strewn paths for hour after hour. The route would enable them, if they were intercepted, to veer toward the border of Bhutan. "If worse came to the worst, we would always have a line of retreat behind us," the Dalai Lama said. Now that they had put a fair bit of distance between themselves and the PLA camps in Lhasa, their most acute fear was of getting caught between Chinese squadrons moving up from their camps at Gyantse and Kongpo.

On March 20, the fugitives arrived in Drachima, where they found waiting a dozen mounted rebels led by the tall, imposing Khampa leader Ratuk Ngawang. His Holiness, "young and energetic" in Ngawang's words, immediately struck up a conversation. "He told me there was no need to feel upset by the various statements issued against our resistance fighters," says Ngawang. "He told me that what we were doing was necessary and our hard work would not go as a waste." The Khampa leader nodded, moved by this assurance. The Dalai Lama was finally revealing his true sentiments about the rebellion.

"Have you heard any news of Shudup Rimpoche?" the Dalai Lama asked, inquiring after a guru from Lithang Monastery, Ngawang's "native place." The Khampa, a man who'd killed scores of PLA soldiers and watched his own men die, attempted to speak but was overcome with emotion. "My eyes swelled with tears." Shudup Rimpoche was his "root lama," a figure close to his heart, and Ngawang knew he was trapped at Lithang.

"It was wrong of me to ask," His Holiness said, gently. "I'm sorry." He looked down at the rebel leader's sword.

"How many Chinese have died from this dagger?" His Holiness asked.

"Two severely wounded Chinese had to be killed with it, Your Holiness. Purely out of mercy, to put them out of their pain."

The Dalai Lama nodded. His eyes moved to the Khampa's rifle. Seeing how intent he was on the gun, Ngawang unslung it and offered it to His Holiness.

The toy weapons and the soldiers the Dalai Lama had played with as a child were now suddenly quite real. His Holiness reached for the rifle.

"Don't play with your weapons so close to His Holiness!" the Lord Chamberlain shouted. "There might be an accident."

"Don't worry," the Dalai Lama said calmly. "These men know how to handle them."

At that moment, Athar and Lhotse were riding north to link up with the fugitives. They reached the Dalai Lama's party on March 21 at Chongye Riwo Dechen, about a third of the way from Lhasa to the Indian border, carrying the RS-1 set, rifles, and another gift from the CIA—a small movie camera, which they would later use to shoot footage of the escape. They found the fugitives at a small monastery. Athar immediately requested an audience with His Holiness, but the Lord Chamberlain replied that the Dalai Lama needed to rest first. The guerrillas could see him the next morning. Now that the Dalai Lama's break with the Chinese occupiers was out in the open, the tables had turned: it was the Lord Chamberlain who was eager to talk to the rebels and hear the CIA's plans for Tibet. Athar told him about the rebels' strengths and recounted some of their recent exploits. He also revealed for the first time that the Americans were air-dropping planeloads of weapons into Tibet and were training guerrillas at Camp Hale for reinsertion into the country. The Lord Chamberlain was delighted. The Tibetan government would need every ally it could find simply to have a chance at surviving. After the meeting, Athar dug out his CIA codebooks and began composing an urgent message to go out over the RS-1 radio.

In Washington, D.C., the members of the Tibetan Task Force were unaware that the Tibetans were in the midst of rising up. They had bits of information that suggested resentment against China was growing even in Lhasa, but no way of knowing that a rebellion had exploded and that His Holiness was on the run. The agents' days were spent in bureacratic routines: planning drops, requesting airplanes from the CIA, drawing up budgets—"like running an import/export firm," says John Greaney. The deputy head had been tasked with the rather dull duty of translating Athar's incoming messages in the early days of March: reports on PLA infrastructure, rebel morale, and troop numbers. It was vital, in its own way, but it had little of the "bang and burn" quotient that Greaney relished.

Every day, Greaney would trudge down to the agency's postwar headquarters, a rat-infested set of temporary buildings by the lovely and placid Reflecting Pool, between the Washington Monument and the Lincoln Memorial. Even though they were located at the heart of the city, the CIA huts were ugly, shoddily built, and manned with sleepy guards desperate to escape the boredom of their assignments. With Tibet thirteen hours ahead of Eastern Standard Time, the messages from Athar invariably came in the middle of the night, which required Greaney—on the rare occasion an urgent bulletin arrived—to leave his young wife in bed in their Chevy Chase home, jump in his Ford station wagon, and travel through the deserted streets of Washington to the Sig (Signal) Center.

To translate Athar's incoming messages—the cryptonym on the bulletins was "ST Budwood"—and send the agency's own instructions, the CIA had a Mongolian monk, Geshe Wangye, stashed at a safe house not too far from the Reflecting Pool. The monk was dedicated to the mission but too recognizable for the agency's liking. "Geshe would walk down the street in these saffron robes and an overcoat and a fedora," Greaney says. "We tried to keep him off the streets as much as possible." And the work was often tedious, translating messages loaded with lines such as "35 cases of guns and 2 of recoilless rifles and explosives." With the monk the only Tibetan speaker in the room, it was also a bit unnerving. "I remember one time Des FitzGerald says to me, 'How do I know what he's putting into those messages?'" Greaney remembers. "'He could be telling them to kill each other for all we know.'" Greaney had nodded. The same thought had occurred to him. But over time, he'd come to trust the patient Geshe, who was deeply grateful for a chance to live in the United States and wouldn't, Greaney felt, double-cross the men who were now trying to help his people.

Ever since Athar's abortive attempt to reach the Dalai Lama and get his approval for the rebellion, the CIA, however, had been less than enamored of His Holiness. He "was such a pacifist," in Greaney's view, "that he refused to endorse the freedom fighters, making the CIA's efforts on their behalf almost moot. There was some feeling among the Task Force members that the Dalai Lama took nonviolence too seriously for his people's good. They longed for a man of action—or at least someone who appreciated their efforts. "This was the hard thing for us to understand," Greaney admits. "Here we are trying to help the guy resist the Chinese, *and he doesn't like it at all.*"

Still, there was no question in Washington that the young monk was the linchpin to the resistance. The goal of the Tibetan Task Force's mission at that point was simple and Greaney knew it: "to protect the Dalai Lama and get him out."

But Athar's messages in the middle of March had been as dull as dishwater. Tibet was seemingly asleep.

Until the night of March 21. Some 7,600 miles away from Lhasa, in Chevy Chase, Maryland, Greaney was deep in dreams when his phone rang. It was the CIA Sig Center. "They had an OpIm from Tibet," he says. An "OpIm," or "Operation Immediate," was the agency's second-most-urgent classification for incoming messages. Only "Flash" was higher. "And in all my years at the CIA," Greaney added, "I never once saw a 'Flash.'" The agent jumped into his Ford station wagon, backed it out of his driveway, and headed into the sleeping city, the radio tuned to his favorite country and western station, which was playing Red Foley's hit "Chattanoogie Shoe Shine Boy." Twenty minutes later he arrived at the Sig Center, flashed his ID at a half-asleep guard, and grabbed a sheet filled with clusters of five numbers in purple-colored ink. Glancing at it, he hopped in his car and sped through the deserted streets to Wisconsin Avenue, where Geshe Wangye, the Mongolian monk and translator, was waiting.

Wangye began to transpose the numbers into Tibetan and then from Tibetan into English. "He would sit there and scratch his head and say, 'I think the boys were saying this, but they might have meant that.'" Greaney sat with him at the kitchen table, puzzling out the words as they appeared through the fog of coded language. He was nervous. This bulletin would be conveyed to the president of the United States in a few hours' time and could conceivably hold the fate of the Dalai Lama and Tibet itself in its net of seemingly random numbers. "There was no verbatim to what they said," Greaney acknowledges. "It was 'What are they trying to say?' It was by guess and by God that we got those messages done."

Athar's message included details of the rebellion in Lhasa. The CIA was elated. The fact that the Dalai Lama had escaped the control of the Chinese would be an enormous boon to their efforts to delegitimize the Chinese occupation. Having the Dalai Lama in the south of the country gave their backing of the Tibetan resistance instant credibility. How the Dalai Lama went, so went Tibet.

On March 22, Athar and Lhotse were ushered into the Dalai Lama's presence. His Holiness inspected the men who had been to America, looking at each piece of equipment and weapon they carried. "He particularly wanted to see the radio equipment," Athar recalled, "but we said it was hidden in the mountains." In fact, the set was nearby, but the CIA had told Athar not to show the RS-1 to anybody. The CIA operative then asked the Tibetan leader what his plans were for the immediate future, and His Holiness told him that he would lead the escape party to the stronghold of Lhuntse Dzong, renounce the Seventeen Point Agreement, and set up a provisional Tibetan government. "There . . . I should stay," the Dalai Lama said, "and try to open peaceful negotiations with the Chinese." It was obvious to Athar that His Holiness wanted to remain in Tibet and didn't foresee crossing the border to India, a step that would perhaps lead to his permanent exile. When the Dalai Lama asked about the rebels and the CIA, Athar told him about Camp Hale and about the weapons that the agency had sent into Tibet on parachutes, and described the RS-1 radio that gave the rebels a direct link to Washington and the waiting ears of President Eisenhower. "You could see that he was very excited about this," Athar remembered.

Athar dashed off a message to the Tibetan Task Force, and the CIA quickly responded, saying they planned more airdrops for the Tibetan rebels in the near future, including one involving two planeloads of munitions with enough firepower to supply 2,000 soldiers. The planes were waiting at an airstrip in East Pakistan, and Athar radioed back that the arms should be dropped at Tsethang, close to the rebels' headquarters. But the base would soon be over-run by Chinese battalions, forcing the drop to be canceled. The escape had reenergized the PLA onslaught against the guerrillas. The gloves had now come off in the battle for Tibet.

His Holiness and his party left the Khampa leader Ratuk Ngawang and his rebels at Chongye Riwo Dechen. The men had safely guided them through their area of operations and were turn-ing back to fight the PLA. His Holiness pulled the rangy leader aside and told him he and his men could accompany them south if they wanted to.

"I told His Holiness that it was my duty to go back and lead the Tibetan fighters," Ngawang explained. "I also said I had no regrets if I died fighting."

The Dalai Lama nodded. "But there's no reason to sacrifice your life simply out of bravery," he replied. "We will need men like you. Stay alive if it is at all possible."

His Holiness knew that Ngawang and his men would most likely die if they returned to fight the better-armed PLA, especially while the Chinese ramped up their efforts as news of his escape spread. He sadly gave Ngawang his blessing and the men bowed, then whipped their horses' heads around and clattered down the trail heading north.

As he watched them go, it was as if the legends and tales that His Holiness had studied as a child on the walls of the Potala were now happening in front of him, to men whom he'd touched and spoken with. He'd stepped out of a fable into the middle of a red-blooded war.

The Dalai Lama's escape had raised the temperature on the question of Tibet—for the Americans, who saw the Dalai Lama coming into their fold; for Peking, which saw foreign intrigues behind every move His Holiness was making; and for the Tibetans themselves, who had finally found a semblance of unity along the trail to India.

For now it was a journey conducted in secret. That was about to change.

*Eleven*

# "GODLESS REDS VS. A LIVING GOD"

As the Dalai Lama made his way south, the Scottish reporter George Patterson sat in Kalimpong, India, awaiting his forthcoming expulsion from the country for his "misleading reports of the situation in Tibet." But events were moving too fast for the Indians to make good on their threat. Nehru had previously denied to the Indian Parliament that there was "any large-scale violence" happening in Tibet, but it was clear that Lhasa was now in open warfare. Patterson was allowed to stay—perhaps because

163

Nehru was embarrassed by opposition politicians demanding to know why he'd been "misleading the House" on the whole situation in Tibet—and he went right back to stirring things up, filing pieces about the revolt for the *Daily Telegraph*. Soon Patterson's sources were telling him that Lhasa was in flames and that the whereabouts of the Dalai Lama were unknown. And, for once, Patterson wasn't alone in reporting the spreading revolt. Reports of massive violence coming out of Tibet were seeping into the world's major newspapers.

The news of the Lhasa uprising broke in the West on March 21, as Athar linked up with the Dalai Lama a third of the way to India. The story hit the headlines of the English and American dailies and soon led the hourly radio bulletins and TV nightly news around the world (although the Soviet media declined to cover the story). The first take on the story in the West was a variation on the David and Goliath theme: "sword-swinging priests" were battling "Chinese soldiers with machine guns," according to one newspaper. The Dalai Lama was portrayed as a "gentle mystic," a bespectacled monk who loved to laugh, and who was now being forced to flee for his life across the wastes of southern Tibet.

Reporters struggled to come to grips with Tibet as a real place and often failed. In the New York *Daily News*, under a headline that screamed "Godless Reds vs. A Living God in Tibet," the first report opened:

> In the windswept highlands of Tibet—the Shangri-La of book and screen—the Marxist bosses of Communist China are fighting a force never envisaged in Marx's rulebook—the fanatic soldier-priests of a smiling, 23-year-old living god. He wears spectacles, tells jokes and loves to take motion

pictures and run them on his own projector. At the same time, he is a Buddhist scholar who debated a learned abbot on equal terms at the age of 14.

But the outline of the longer struggle was also being drawn. "According to knowledgeable Tibetan sources," London's *Daily Telegraph* reported, "he is no religious exile fleeing to some safe retreat . . . but a God-king of a proud, angry and courageous people coming to demand moral recognition and help in the name of religion from those who profess to believe in it against the forces of materialism."

In the kitchen of his small apartment in New York City, where he'd come to push for American assistance to his homeland, the Dalai Lama's oldest brother, Norbu, was stirring soup on the stove. He was half-listening to a news program on the wireless when the announcer reported that fighting had broken out in Lhasa. "I forgot my soup now and listened eagerly," remembered Norbu. "I stood there with my mind in a whirl. What I had most feared for many years had come about at last."

The broadcast brought back memories of his first encounter with the Chinese, when Communist cadres had spent seven months living, eating, and talking with Norbu, who was then an abbot at a monastery. The cadres had been assigned to convert him to Mao's philosophy. He'd found them to be curious, oddly persistent people. "They kept talking, kept asking questions," he remembered. "They kept saying Communists are good, Stalin is good, British and Americans no good." His Chinese handlers asked him bizarre questions—how many pieces of underwear he owned, for example—and dug for the names of his friends and contacts, trying to suss out a picture of the monastic elite and how it functioned. But mostly they'd extolled the virtues of communism.

Having escaped to America, Norbu now called up Tibetan friends in the city—in a city of obscure immigrants, Tibetans were among the rarest—and then at midnight rushed down to the street when he heard the newsboys calling out a special edition with the news of the escape on the front page. He bought every one he could find. "What was going to happen now?" he wondered, thinking particularly of his brother. Norbu felt he had, by virtue of those seven months of close contact, a special insight into the Chinese capacity for relentlessness that his gentle brother didn't share. And he knew how much Peking wanted His Holiness. "The Chinese would clearly move heaven and earth to prevent his escape," he thought to himself. He didn't sleep the entire night.

When the news of the Dalai Lama's escape got out, a horde of twenty of the world's top foreign correspondents gathered in Kalimpong and Darjeeling, the point of what was going to become a very large and unwieldly spear. For journalists, the escape was becoming one of the "stories of the century," a career-altering happening much like the race for the South Pole and the conquest of Everest, in which getting the scoop became as much of a quest as Hillary's climb. For foreign editors around the world, the story seemingly had everything: an exotic locale, a hazily understood potentate who was both "god" and "king" (at least to Western eyes), a villainous oppressor, a cliff-hanger ending still to be decided. The murky issue of Tibet now had a clear and compelling narrative and an immensely appealing character to humanize the cause.

The escape of the Dalai Lama made Tibet a major international news story. Without him, the fighting there would have been relegated to the back pages and taken its place alongside Burma and Mongolia as another obscure Far Eastern controversy.

But larger, darker anxieties also fed the appetite for news on His Holiness. Westerners saw in the Dalai Lama's fate a mirror of their own possible futures. What was happening in Tibet had already happened in places such as Budapest and East Berlin, and there was a very real worry that it would happen in London and Paris and New York. The week the escape hit the headlines, stories ran in American newspapers with titles such as "An Inspiring Message from the Mayor of West Berlin: Never Let the Russians Think You're Weak!" The Dalai Lama was, as odd as it sounds, a kind of doppelgänger for the West, a man culled from the pack who was on the run from the vicious and godless Communists. The old concept of the "foreign brother," the Tibetan who shares the West's values, was resurrected once again, in an atmosphere of paranoia about the West's very survival.

On March 22, a *New York Times* editorial blasted Peking: "This is a complete indictment of the Chinese Communist on the charge of genocide. . . . Complete absorption and extinction of the Tibetan race is being undertaken." Protests erupted in Asian cities such as Bombay and even reached to New York, where Buddhists who considered His Holiness their leader took to the streets. Guards at the Bhutan border reported "panic-stricken Tibetans" almost unable to speak appearing at their border posts. Expats in India were told to sell all their belongings and to head to Delhi to fight for the Dalai Lama. In Bombay, demonstrators cried out for the world to resist China and pelted a portrait of Mao with eggs and tomatoes.

Outside the United Nations, one of the more remarkable demonstrations took place when a group of Kalmuks, descendants of Genghis Khan, appeared on First Avenue, led by six lamas in "flowing purple, pink and yellow robes." They carried signs reading "Protect the Dalai Lama from Red Terror" and patiently explained to reporters they were the remnants of a group of Mongolians brought out of World War II displacement camps after their tiny republic had been liquidated by Stalin. Deeply familiar with the methods of state terror, they feared for His Holiness's life. Meanwhile, the Dalai Lama's older brother Gyalo announced in the *Times of India* that the escape of the Dalai Lama was the prelude to genocide. "We are going to be wiped out by the Chinese," he said. Henry Cabot Lodge, the chief U.S. delegate to the United Nations, spoke of "unspeakable brutalizing" and presented Tibet as a warning to the rest of the continent: "Tibet is proof to the people of Asia that there is imperialism in Peking which seeks to enslave other Asian peoples and does not hesitate to use war and treachery in the process."

The Chinese, stung by what they felt were misleading stories, quickly hit back. "These rebels represent imperialism and the most reactionary big serf owners," the New China News Agency reported. "Their rebellion was organized by the imperialists, the Chiang Kai-shek bandits and foreign reactionaries. Many of their arms were brought in from abroad." They accused the Tibetan rebels of a long list of atrocities: "plunder, rape, arson and murder," to which the American journalist Anna Louise Strong added the crime of "gouging out eyes." The line out of China was that the PLA had patiently and humanely put down a coup d'état of Tibetan sellouts who had attacked their own people for not joining their coup. Peking spit poison: "The spirit of these reactionaries soared to the clouds and they were ready to take over the whole universe. . . . The reactionary forces of Tibet finally chose the road to their own extinction."

The Chinese understood what the Tibetans had not yet grasped: The fight for Tibet was reaching its climax in Lhasa. The battle for how Tibet was *perceived* was just beginning.

The story was made for star reporters such as Noel Barber. But the outbreak caught the *Daily Mail* correspondent in Nyasaland, the British protectorate soon to be known as Malawi, which was being rocked by nationalist violence. When he checked in with his London editors and heard the news from Tibet, he flashed back to his 1950 Tibet expedition. "I was whisked back in time to the exciting days when I climbed across the Himalayas," he recalled, "to try and find something of the truth about the hidden war in Tibet. . . . Now it was as though I had returned to see the last episode in a terrible and true story." And, he could have added, to shape it—for the Tibet story was being transformed daily, from a war narrative in an obscure part of the world into the search for the man whose fate would soon come to represent the tragedy of Tibet itself.

Barber raced to the scene. He flew to Salisbury in Southern Rhodesia to catch a flight to Nairobi. The plane was delayed for two hours, which would cause the reporter to miss his Nairobi-Bombay flight. That, for a man of Barber's stature, was unacceptable, so he called some well-connected friends in London and asked them to request Air India to delay the plane until he could make it, which they promptly did. ("Very considerate of them," Barber said.) The journalist slept all night on the plane, landed in Bombay, showered, and jumped on a twin-engined Dakota to Nagpur and from there to Calcutta at 6:00 a.m. He then flew to Bagdogra, hopped on a bus occupied by chickens and Indian peasants, drove ten miles to Siliguri, and finally jumped in a taxi for the ride to Kalimpong before hiring a single-engine plane for the last leg of the trek. "It was one of the most wretched journeys I have ever made," Barber sighed. It was also a trip that dozens of journalists were making from points all over the globe as the story exploded in the world media.

Meanwhile, George Patterson had become a marked man in Kalimpong. Because he was seen as the reporter with the best local sources, some of the freshly arrived Western journalists hired locals to spy on the Scotsman, standing outside his house in the boiling heat and watching his every arrival, then trailing him through the city when he went to meet with his sources. Desperate to know what had become of the Dalai Lama, Patterson gambled that His Holiness would follow the route his older brother, the tough-as-steel Gyalo, had taken when he fled to India in 1952. Patterson himself staked out the brother's house, and when Gyalo slipped out of his house and made his way to the airport in Siliguri, the Scottish journalist decided that India was indeed the destination of His Holiness. He calculated that the escapees would "come out" around Tsona Dzong on the Indian-Tibetan border, which would place them in the North East Frontier Agency, a huge borderland between China and India that was off-limits to everyone except the Indian military. And that is exactly where Patterson decided he would go.

The next night, Patterson awoke in the early hours, packed his things, checked the darkened street for the "watchers" hired by his competition, then slipped out into the streets of Kalimpong. He made his way to Darjeeling, where he chartered the private plane of a friend, a plantation owner, taking off from a landing strip in the middle of an enormous tea garden and flying to Tezpur, a sleepy city on the Brahmaputra River in Upper Assam in the northeast of India. Patterson not only wanted to get the story first and to make his name, he also wanted to reach the escape party before Nehru's bureaucrats grabbed the fugitives and "shut out and shut up the Dalai Lama from making his country's predicament known while he was on Indian soil." Patterson knew all too well how ferociously the Indians guarded their relationship with Peking. The Scot wanted the Dalai Lama to express what he'd been hearing for years from the rebels and give the reports of atrocities legitimacy in the eyes of the world. Nehru would, Patterson knew, do everything he could to prevent that happening.

Tibet was going through a remarkable transformation. It was becoming famous just as it ceased to exist. As the PLA asserted control, Tibet was slowly becoming not a physical place with set borders and lakes and mountains but a cause, a place of the mind. And this was due mostly to the figure of the Dalai Lama, to the romance and tragedy that surrounded the story of a young ruler driven from his throne by the hated Communists. It was people like Noel Barber—who with his celebrity, his manic thirst for adventure, and his cutthroat competitiveness in some ways epitomized a certain idea of the West—who were doing the introductions. What he and his ilk wrote, how they presented the Dalai Lama, would have remarkable staying power.

The fugitives were now seven hundred miles from their target, the rebel fort known as Lhuntse Dzong, which lay over some of the toughest terrain they would face. They knew almost nothing about what had happened in the capital; Radio Lhasa was still off the air, and although their radio had briefly been able to tune in the Voice of America, it spoke only of "unrest in the city," which could refer to the protests in front of the Norbulingka. But as they set out for the stronghold, with Athar now sending their location to Washington daily, the Dalai Lama received the first of three severe shocks.

Navigating one of the stony trails that led south, the Dalai Lama saw that the escapees were being pursued by a group of horsemen. It was led by a Tibetan official who months earlier had been sent to the rebel leaders to ask them to give up their armed resistance. Instead, the official had joined the rebels. Now he appeared out of the bleak landscape to tell the Dalai Lama that the Chinese had attacked the Norbulingka, Lhasa had been the scene of terrible fighting, and hundreds if not thousands were dead. His early reports were a mix of wild gossip (including the false assertion that the Potala and the Norbulingka had both been completely destroyed) and accurate secondhand reports of a major battle.

"My worst fears had come true," the Dalai Lama said despondently. The news ended any hopes that he could reach an understanding with the Chinese. The bond with Mao that he'd formed during those remarkable days in Peking had been irretrievably broken: "I realized that it would be impossible to negotiate with people who behaved in this cruel and criminal fashion." The Dalai Lama listened to the gruesome reports and realized that if he'd stayed at the summer palace, he would not have survived. "The Chinese would have considered me expendable. But even if they kept me alive, Tibet would have been finished."

The Dalai Lama's belief in compassion wasn't formed on the trails to India, but it met its most severe test there. Even the Chinese invasion hadn't shaken him like the news from Lhasa did, because he'd grown to believe it was a necessary evil for modernizing his country—the occupation, he'd told himself, would lead to progress in the end. For his entire life, the Dalai Lama had been raised in a bell jar. He'd had only the briefest glimpses into people's real lives, their sufferings, the injustices they faced. Apart from the loneliness he'd felt as a child, he'd known pain only secondhand. Even the realities of something as enormous as World War II he'd had to work out through bad translations of second-rate reference books. He had no personal experience of hatred and ambition. Evil to him was a figure in a book, or a prisoner in the lens of his telescope at the Potala. The whip hanging on his tutor's wall, never to be used, was an apt image for his early life.

Now His Holiness found it difficult at first to comprehend what he was hearing. "Why did the Chinese do it?" the Dalai Lama asked himself again and again. He could come up with only one answer, and it lay in the Chinese desire for power over his subjects. "Our people—not especially our rich or ruling classes but our ordinary people—had finally, eight years after the invasion began, convinced the Chinese that they would never willingly accept their alien rule. So the Chinese were trying now to terrify them, by merciless slaughter, into accepting this rule against their will."

The first instinct of his boyhood, the violent sympathy for the weak, returned to him, and the Dalai Lama became enraged. Now it was Tibet itself that was being victimized, torn up, bloodied. The old adversary, the wild temper he'd worked so hard to tame, returned to him as he sat in the cold and damp along the trail and contemplated the murder of men and women who had fought to protect him.

He closed his eyes and recited to himself Buddha's teaching: "One's enemy can be one's greatest teacher." It was horribly difficult. The anger rose like bile in his throat. The savagery of his young self wished to be released.

The bitterness of the moment, indeed the entire trip, was accentuated by the history of the places he and his fellow fugitives were trudging through on their exhausted ponies. In escaping toward India, the Dalai Lama was in a way reversing the history of Buddhism in Tibet, hurrying down the trail on which the faith had entered the country centuries ago. His Holiness was the culmination of the lama-obsessed state, and now he was retreating to the place the religion had begun, but as a refugee, a man without a country. Each step he took along the route, leaving Lhasa in the hands of a power that was vehement in its denial of religion, was an erasure. The Dharma in Tibet had been shattered. The Dalai Lama had been carried to Lhasa on a golden palanquin, but he had left it as a fugitive.

This wasn't the first time Tibetan Buddhism had come under

siege. In the middle of the ninth century, forty years after the death of the great Buddhist king Trisong Detsen, a clique of believers in the old religion of Bön struck at the throne and installed their favorite, Lang Darma. Followers of Buddhism were persecuted, killed, forced into hiding, or exiled, just as the Dalai Lama was being exiled by a rival ideology. Monasteries were burned and the Bön pantheon of devils and gods reappeared from one end of Tibet to the other. Lang Darma became the dark eminence of the nation's history, always described as having horns and a black tongue. (The ancient Tibetan custom of sticking one's tongue out as a greeting was meant to show that it lacked Lang Darma's nefarious color.) It wasn't until a monk named Paljor Dorje was told in a vision to kill Lang Darma so that the faith might survive that Buddhism's fortunes changed. The monk dressed in a special robe, black on the outside and white on the inside, covered his horse in charcoal dust, and then rode to the palace, where he entranced the enemy king with a whirling dance. As he spun, the monk pulled out a bow and arrow and shot Lang Darma through the heart, then escaped by reversing his cape and riding his horse through a river, washing off the black dust. It was no small irony that Buddhism, the faith of pacifism, survived in Tibet through an act of regicide.

But a mythical solution wasn't available to the Dalai Lama. His people had believed in fables for too long. As had he.

*Twelve*

# THE JOKHANG

As the Dalai Lama struggled to come to terms with the deaths of his subjects, the battle for Lhasa was reaching a crescendo. Narkyid, the twenty-eight-year-old monk who'd inherited responsibility for the Jokhang Temple and the hundreds of Tibetans inside, was so close to the enemy he could almost listen to them talking. The PLA soldiers were fortified behind sandbags at the corner of Shagyari Street, and Narkyid could see individual soldiers sleeping on the roof, while others broke down a machine gun and cleaned and oiled it. The calmness, the bored expression of the soldiers, the rote chores they were doing, all contrasted with the utterly chaotic and haphazard defense the Tibetans had managed to patch together. Like so many Tibetans, Narkyid had never considered the Chinese brutal until the uprising began. Now he realized how naïve he'd been. "The Chinese were always ready to kill us," Narkyid realized. "They were *prepared*."

Suddenly, a machine gun opened up in the street beneath him. Narkyid ran down from the temple roof to one of the main courtyards and saw soldiers and civilians running pell-mell for the main gates. "The Chinese were coming," he says. "That is what we believed." But when the Tibetans peeked between the slits in the barricades, they saw only the sandbags and the flash of a machine gun. The disciplined PLA soldiers were remaining behind their fortifications, attempting to lure the rebels out into the open.

More gunfire erupted from the nearby streets. The Chinese emplacement visible in the gaps in the barricade was coming under sustained fire. But from where? None of his men was shooting off rounds. Narkyid soon learned that, overnight, Tibetan rebels had managed to sneak into one of the nearby homes and set up a mortar and machine-gun nest on the roof. He ran back up to the roof of the Jokhang to watch the battle unfold. Fully exposed to the PLA guns, the rebels began firing at the Shagyari Street outpost, putting round after round into the gap above the sandbags. One rebel dropped a mortar round into the tube and ducked. The *whooomp* of the shell exiting the tube was followed seconds later by an explosion inside the PLA position. A huge cloud of dust billowed out, and Narkyid knew that the men he'd been looking at minutes before were now dead. He and the others waiting with him understood that the rebels on the rooftop were doomed, that the PLA would soon spot them and hunt them down. And, he was convinced, they would soon finish with the Norbulingka and turn their attention to the Jokhang.

"We never slept," he says. "There was always danger."

At the summer palace, the Norbulingka official, Soepa, was still alive on the afternoon of the 21st. He pulled himself to the base of a set of stone steps that led up from the lake. He felt spent by the effort to kill himself. The water had soaked through his clothes, and, loaded down with grenades and bandoliers of bullets, he couldn't manage to pull himself up the steps. He threw off his *chuba* and as much of the hardware on him as he could. Finally, the young Tibetan was able to drag himself out of the lake.

But he still expected to die, and it occurred to him that the throne of the Audience Hall where the Dalai Lama sat to meet his most important guests would be an auspicious place to do it. He dragged himself along, "leaving a trail of blood and water streaming behind me."

Bullets were still ricocheting off the trees and buildings around him. In a display of raw courage, the rebels were still forcing back every PLA attempt to enter the summer palace. The diarist Shan Chao, watching the waves of soldiers being beaten back, offered perhaps the only note of admiration in the Chinese accounts of the uprising: "When the rebel bandits in the Norbulingka were cornered, they put up a desperate fight, knocked out corners of houses, broke down walls, dug holes and put their rifles through." But they could do nothing against the mortars and artillery shells that continued to loft over the walls into their midst.

Soepa made it to the Audience Hall and crawled toward the throne, then laid his head briefly on the seat. Finally, he lay down and went to sleep. He slept until the next morning. At sunrise, he awoke to voices. They were coming from outside the Norbulingka's outer wall. "The Chinese are at the gates! They are going to occupy the Norbulingka! We should fire the place!" And then, "Let's burn it down!"

He made his way outside, toward one of the palace gates. Suddenly a spent bullet glanced off his forehead and dropped inside his shirt, burning the skin on his chest. He searched frantically for the cartridge until it dropped on the ground. It seemed his amulet was preventing the death he now wished for, as if the spirits were mocking him with near misses.

He found his brother-in-law striding through the palace grounds. Seeing his awful condition, the man took off his *chupa* and wrapped it around Soepa's shoulders.

"You can't stay here like this," his brother-in-law shouted above the gunfire. "Get across the river. If you can't, you will just get killed."

But Soepa felt so close to death that he ignored the advice. He didn't think he could make it to the Kyichu, let alone across. If he was going to die, he wanted it to be in the Norbulingka, the home of His Holiness, the whole reason he'd come back to Lhasa.

"I can't go," Soepa said. "Please shoot me."

But his brother-in-law refused. He walked away, and Soepa turned and staggered back into the Audience Hall. He cadged a cigarette from a teenager, who told him all the ways out of the Norbulingka were being blocked by the PLA. Soepa took a few puffs, then passed out.

At Drepung Monastery, the monks listened to the battle unfold five miles away. "At dawn you could smell gunpowder in the breeze," remembered one. "The noise of gunfire and mortar shells went on relentlessly." Overnight, squadrons of PLA soldiers had appeared at the foot of the mountain below Drepung. And as the fighting raged, a Tibetan man appeared walking up the path to the monastery gate. The messenger told them that the rebels had overwhelmed a Chinese military camp and that the monks should stay where they were for the time being. That told them that the Tibetans were winning the battle for Lhasa, and the monks brightened at the news. But when other reports of the taking of Chakpori and the deaths of hundreds of Tibetan fighters trickled in, the monks soon realized that the messenger had been a turncoat sent by the Chinese to keep them in their quarters and out of the battle.

The young men of the monasteries threw themselves into the rebellion. One group of Sera monks braved the gunfire to retrieve guns for the battle. Dressed in their maroon-and-gold robes, they picked their way over the mountain paths they always used to visit the Potala Palace on special days. Once they reached the gates, they took out hand mirrors and signaled their fellow monks that they had made it, using a prearranged code. Then the volunteers quickly made their way to the storeroom where they knew rifles were cached. "While we were removing the guns from the storeroom, the Chinese were bombing the Norbulingka below and Iron Hill, on the other side of the mountain from where we were," one of them said. As the monks made their way to a storeroom on the top floor of the palace, where there was a supply of bullets waiting, the Chinese gunners turned their sights on the Potala. And it was clear from their aim that as the rumors had suggested, the PLA had sighted the palace many days before, because the shells immediately began hitting their target, sending up plumes of chalky smoke.

Emerging into one of the palace courtyards, gasping for breath, one of the Sera volunteers saw bodies splayed on the cobblestones.

"There were dozens of people dead, and others groaning in pain, covered with blood," he says. "I thought to myself, 'Oh, so I am going to die too.'"

The PLA now turned its attention to the holdouts at the Jokhang Temple. Machine-gun fire rose in pitch until it was a high whining roar. Narkyid, the monk official in charge, and the others with him decided it was time to leave the Jokhang. If they stayed, it would only encourage the PLA to bomb the temple as it had the Potala and the Norbulingka. Lhasa had fallen, the Dalai Lama was gone, and prison or death was all they could expect if captured. He and a group of Tibetan soldiers searched for a way out. They found a small gate unknown to the PLA in one of the Jokhang's walls. They gathered themselves, the soldiers clutching their rifles, then opened the gate and emerged out into the street.

As the group hugged the temple wall and turned the first corner, they came under fire. Unarmed, Narkyid began to run. Even as he moved forward, the young monk was fatalistic. "Once three or four bullets went by, I didn't worry anymore," he says. But he did feel oddly worried about the men shooting at him, a Buddhist impulse too deeply ingrained to surrender so quickly. "Those soldiers were so young," he remembers. "I shouted in Chinese, 'Please don't come forward, because we don't want to kill you! You are so young. Please don't shoot!'" The PLA soldiers came on, and the Tibetan soldiers with Narkyid opened up with their Lewis guns and the soldiers twisted and fell. "They didn't have a choice," Narkyid realized, "because behind them were others who would have killed them if they didn't move forward."

The randomness of the battle struck Narkyid as he searched for a way out of the city. He would turn a corner and find the cobblestoned street ahead littered with corpses and freshly wounded civilians, but a couple of blocks away his party would run into a group of women calmly proceeding on their daily errands, or a family sitting down to a meal of *tsampa* and tea, boys running up after having collected spent shells and showing them to their bored fathers, everyone completely oblivious to the mayhem two streets away. Near the Jokhang, shells and bullets were cutting through the air, and each corner brought a new tableau. Chinese tanks spurting fire. Four men lying, legless, in a spreading pool of blood. "One shell had cut off their legs," says Narkyid. "I went to hold the hand of two of them, but I couldn't do anything for them."

Another young monk didn't make it beyond the Jokhang's walls. As he fled, a squad of PLA soldiers caught and arrested him. He shuffled ahead with the Chinese soldiers behind him, seeing "the marks of bullets and shell explosions everywhere, and countless bodies." One corpse stood out. It was a beggar who'd been caught by a bullet as he tried to run from the fighting and was now lying facedown on the cobblestones. He'd been carrying blankets on his back, perhaps to sleep out in the cold nights. But what caught the monk's eye was a dog that the beggar had been pulling along. It too had been shot, in the back— the monk could see the wound— and was lying next to its master, still attached to the leash.

At the same time, Narkyid was making his way around the eastern wall of the Jokhang, angling toward the Kyichu River. He watched as several women ran up to a Chinese tank, Molotov cocktails in hand, and threw them at the turret. Others poured kerosene in front of the houses and shops where the Chinese were hiding and lit it on fire, only to see the sandbags snuff out the flames. They were cut down by Chinese gunners behind the barricades, some of the women, he swears, with babies in their arms. "We lost so many," he says. "The women were so brave!"

As Narkyid ran through Barkhor Square and toward the river, wounded Tibetans on the cobblestones called out to him: " 'Please kill me,' they were saying. But we couldn't stop or we wouldn't have made it." Navigating the streets, Narkyid imagined that the scenes he encountered weren't real, that they were bits of a movie he'd seen long ago.

The escapees crossed the link road in the northeastern corner of Lhasa and ran toward the mountains. They made their way across a barren field, moving one at a time to avoid detection by the PLA. A Chinese spotter must have caught the group in his binoculars, because a shell suddenly landed ahead of Narkyid. "I only heard the sound and I saw the image of my protector in the Potala and I saw her altar and I said, 'Deity, protect me' and I immediately lost consciousness." When Narkyid woke up after about an hour, he began running again.

There were no soldiers around, no more shells dropping from the PLA batteries. The Chinese had apparently forgotten about his group, one of hundreds of escape parties that made their way to the mountains or across the Kyichu that night. The survivors hugged themselves, brushed off the dirt clinging to their clothes, and began walking. The days ahead would be a nightmare. "We lost so many on the road," remembers Narkyid. The monk found himself part of the exodus following their protector to India.

As Tibetans streamed toward the Kyichu, the river's banks became a killing ground, the survivors caught in enfilading fire from the new PLA outposts at the summer palace and their stronghold halfway between the Potala Palace and Chakpori. The Kyichu was engorged with spring runoff, and the Tibetans linked arms as they began pushing their way into the currents. Many were ripped away and dragged downstream. Others arrived on the far side, half-naked and shivering from the cold.

. . .

Soepa awoke, lying on the floor inside the summer palace. A furious barrage had roused him. In the darkness, he could see figures of PLA soldiers, their crouching bodies silhouetted against the whitewashed wall, now gray in the night. The wooden gate had been shattered and was hanging crookedly on its hinges. The Chinese had finally breached the Norbulingka gates.

A machine gun opened up with a terrifying burst of noise. Soepa peeked out the door and saw that the shots were coming from a large storage room used to keep firewood. It was a Tibetan gunner aiming at the PLA soldiers flooding the palace grounds. The gunner sprayed the garden with bullets, the muzzle of his gun flashing orange. The PLA soldiers seemed to disappear, either dropping to the ground dead or running away. It was the first time Soepa had seen the Chinese soldiers die in numbers, and he felt happy about it.

The Chinese soldiers regrouped and advanced on the gunner, firing as they went. Soon the position went silent, and the PLA troops fanned out over the grounds. Between bursts of gunfire, Soepa heard Chinese voices and Tibetan voices, interpreters surely, calling for the men inside the Norbulingka buildings to give up. The PLA soldiers were afraid to storm the structures and preferred to strafe the windows with bullets and then call for surrender.

Soepa took out his amulet box. He opened it and took out the small precious substance, the *byin rten*, and placed it in his mouth, swallowing it. He then reached around in the darkness, searching for a gun. He thought he would kill one or two soldiers and then be killed himself. But there was nothing there, just the cool stone of the floor, polished by the rags tied to monks' feet.

He crawled outside. Two Chinese soldiers standing near the

door called out and came over with a flashlight and inspected him. Soepa was covered with blood. They pointed at the main gate, now open, and barked at him to walk toward it. Instead, he waited for them to turn their attention elsewhere, then made his way slowly toward a guardhouse. He found five Tibetans lying inside, and he called to them, "Please give me some water." But the men didn't stir. He looked at the figures on the floor more closely and realized they were all dead. A shattered Bren machine gun lay next to one of the bodies, and hundreds of empty bullet shells were scattered across the floor. These men had obviously fought.

Soepa lay down with the dead. A PLA squad came in, flashlights in one hand and rifles in the other. They began kicking the bodies, then bent over to look at the faces, shining their lights and looking for flickering eyelids. They kicked each corpse, but none moved. When they came to Soepa, playing dead, a soldier booted him hard in the hip, but he didn't even breathe out. He was safe for the moment.

Another trio of soldiers entered the building, and the inspection of the dead started again. This time Soepa was kicked in the stomach so hard that he almost screamed. But the men soon left. He crawled onto a mattress set on a makeshift platform of bricks and, exhausted and thirsty, fell asleep.

Hours later, he was captured by PLA soldiers and imprisoned in the summer palace.

Across Lhasa, it was clear the battle was being lost. "In order to encourage the people, the rumor was spread that the American Air Force would be coming on the next day to help us," remembers the sixteen-year-old protester Lobsang Yonten. "Till then we needed to stand steady and defend ourselves." But early on the 22nd, three days into the fighting, Tibetans began to hold up white pieces of cloth and prayer scarves tied to sticks. The shelling and the gunfire slackened and finally stopped. The shocking loss of the capital was softened by news that the Dalai Lama had successfully escaped the ruined Norbulingka. "I felt a huge relief," Yonten says, "as if I'd been set free from an enormous burden."

By the end of the day, the rebellion was over. The voice of the Chinese official Tan Guansan came across the loudspeakers and echoed off the cobblestones and the stone walls of the city. He told the last of the rebels that if they surrendered, they would not be punished. There were pistol shots across the city and hooting as some of the Tibetan fighters sent a mocking response to the Chinese demand. The general's voice was followed by that of Ngabö, the Tibetan minister by now widely considered a notorious traitor. "My name is Ngabö, and you know I am a member of the cabinet." The beautifully modulated aristocratic voice announced that the Dalai Lama was alive, kidnapped by counterrevolutionaries. Ngabö urged the rebels to surrender, by order not of General Tan but of the Tibetan government itself. "Lay down your arms and you will be free," he told listeners all over the city, who struggled to believe that one of their own could really be saying these things.

More and more white scarves appeared, waved on the ends of sticks or rifles. To these were added Chinese flags, hoisted by Tibetans surrendering at last. The sight was a bitter one for many fighters: "We felt let down by this unexpected submission," remembers one.

All over Lhasa, the rumors of the Dalai Lama's escape were finally confirmed by Norbulingka officials and rebel leaders. There was, just as with the news of his imminent kidnapping, a strangely uniform response to the news. "I was hit by two extreme emotions," said one Tibetan doctor, "extreme joy that His Holiness escaped safely and the extreme sorrow that he had to leave his own land." A Sera monk, injured in the battle, felt his sacrifice had gained meaning. "I felt fulfilled," he explains. "We had lost our land but not our king." Others remember saying that they could die happily now, as death no longer mattered. Those who had fought at the Norbulingka and on Chakpori realized that they'd given the Dalai Lama cover to make good his escape, as well as pinning down forces in Lhasa that might have been used to pursue him.

On the afternoon of the 23rd, the PLA raised the flag of the People's Republic of China over the Potala Palace. The authorities announced that the new colors, "symbols of light and happiness," would usher in a rebirth for the capital.

For Yonten, there was no time to mourn his fallen city. His father, a longtime nationalist who'd thrown himself behind the rebellion, met with the commander in chief of the Tibetan army, and together they decided to make their escape along with Yonten and three other men. The teenager and his father went home to say their good-byes and to collect *tsampa*, butter, tea, two bayonets, rifles, and a first-aid box. Yonten's younger sister, just seven, begged to go with them, but they didn't feel it would be safe. "We had to leave her in tears," Yonten remembers. But when they arrived at the rendezvous, they found that the commander in chief had already fled without telling them. There was an air in Lhasa of every man for himself.

As they slipped through the city with their three companions, the father and son could hear the loudspeakers, now broadcasting the same message over and over: "All Tibetans should surrender and hand over their weapons. Anyone found with arms will be charged as a criminal." By the eastern side of the Potala, they were spotted by the PLA, and gunfire immediately erupted, the tracers arcing out at them from the Chinese outpost. "We stood still and did not move a step," Yonten recalls. His father prayed loudly.

The gunfire stopped, and PLA soldiers emerged to arrest the group, taking their names and ranks in the Tibetan government. The Chinese troops led them back to the Norbulingka, and there the captured men joined a long line of prisoners who were throwing their rifles onto a huge stack of rebel arms near a government building. The prisoners were lined up in rows and told to face forward. A jeep crawled by, and a Chinese officer pointed at each man, naming him: "This is Muja, this is Tsarond, this is Sumdho. . . ." Finally, the men were marched toward the city center in two files, passing piles of dead: horses, monks, rebels. The bloodshed was not quite over. "As we passed by the Ramoche shrine," Yonten remembers, "we saw monks from the Tantric College being executed."

A group of Tibetan women began shouting angrily. As Yonten got closer, he realized they were not yelling at the guards but at the rebels, furious at them for starting the uprising and enticing the Chinese to bomb their city. "Some cruel Tibetan women made fun and spit at us," he says. "They shouted, 'You deserve to be arrested for defying the Communist Party.'" The prisoners were led to an open field, and the army cordoned off the temporary holding camp. Yonten and a family friend immediately began gathering the dry grass and making a makeshift bed for his father. But when the older man arrived, he ignored the grass and chanted a prayer, then started to remove the turquoise-flecked earrings that he always wore. Yonten watched him, knowing what this meant.

"I have decided to sacrifice my life," his father finally told Yonten, handing him the earrings. "If you are freed, return home and tell our family not to worry about me."

Yonten began to cry, holding the earrings in his open palm.

"You should live in harmony," his father continued. "Do not change your faith. Be steadfast in your stand." Overcome with grief, Yonten could only nod while tears streamed down his face.

They slept in the frigid night air and woke with dew on their clothes. They were given food, and Yonten watched as a high Tibetan official ate *tsampa* held in his scarf, which was shocking to him, as it was such a common thing for an aristocrat to be doing. "This will be the end of our civilization," the teenager thought. Then the Chinese ordered the men to take off their hats. They were looking for the traditional haircut, the *pachok*, worn by all government officials. Two men were ordered to stand up and step out of the crowd. His father was the second.

Yonten jumped up and grabbed his father, holding him around the waist. "Please take me too," he cried to the Chinese officer who was advancing on them. His father turned and pushed his son away. "Do you want to die?" he cried. Yonten refused to let him go. The Chinese officer asked Yonten who he was, and he explained that he was the man's son. "Our condition is the same," he said, nearly sobbing. "We share a common fate. Please take me with my father." The officer came up and began to pull his father away. Other prisoners called to him, "Dear boy, why are you going? Stay with us."

Yonten's hands were finally pulled away from his father's clothes, and the prisoner was marched off. Yonten felt a premonition: he was looking at his father for the last time. Oblivious to the voices, which were calling for him to sit and have some tea, he stood and watched as his father was brought to a jeep, the door was opened, and his father was put in, looking straight ahead.

The defeat of the rebels shattered some Tibetans' belief in the powers of the Dalai Lama. His Holiness was, after all, supposed to be a superior being with miraculous powers. He and his protectors, it was said, could dispatch demons and ghosts, to say nothing of mere humans. How, then, had the Chinese beaten their protector and forced him to flee like a peasant? Some Lhasans took down their portraits of His Holiness and replaced them with images of Mao, who became a deity in certain Lhasa homes. "I remember some of my neighbors . . . wondering if the Dalai Lama was really the kind of powerful monk they had come to believe in," said one Tibetan who fled to India, "or was he really just a myth?" But the events of March only strengthened the belief of other followers. Many felt that, even if the Dalai Lama had not by some divine act defeated the PLA and freed Tibet from occupation, his escape proved that he was capable of wondrous things. "He performed a miracle when he fled without letting the Chinese know," asserts one monk. "It was impossible for him to leave the Norbulingka any other way."

Tibetans often comprehend the events of life in a multilayered way. Mahayana Buddhism posits that there is "ordinary perception" (*thun mong pai snang ba*) and "extraordinary perception" (*thun mong ma yin*), which reveals hidden truths about even the most mundane occurrences. The Dalai Lama's escape, to some believers, was an occurrence that needed to be contemplated with *thun mong ma yin*. They believed, as one monk-artist later said, that the journey across the Himalayas was "part of a larger divine plan" that had not yet unfolded in its entirety, only the first act of a story with many acts. In this interpretation, the occupation and the PLA's trampling of the rebels could be seen not as a defeat of Chenrizi but as a test of Tibetans' ability to overcome their attachment to transitory things, a blow that would force them to fully embrace supreme detachment from the material world. Or it could be a way to spread Buddhism all over the world, as the Tibetan exodus sent lamas to every corner of the globe.

For many Tibetans, the defeat was simply the beginning of a time when their lives would be, as one survivor put it, "broken beyond repair."

# Thirteen

# LHUNTSE DZONG

s the Dalai Lama and his compatriots hurried toward Lhuntse Dzong, the trail got more difficult. The fugitives were forced to cross a Himalayan pass every day, the lower ones covered in thick mud from the melting snows and the higher ones frozen in ice and snow. They were riding for ten or more hours a day, and they grew more and more exhausted as they traveled mile after mile across the wind-whipped plains. One stop they made, a village called E-Chhudhogang, was the subject of a Tibetan saying:

"It is better to be born an animal in a place where there is grass and water than to be born in E-Chhudhogang." At Sabo-La, they struggled up the pass and found the temperature dropping as they climbed. The soft life of the Norbulingka hadn't prepared the tutors and the ministers for such a rugged trek. "I began to be deeply worried about some of my companions," the Dalai Lama remembered.

The escapees reached the rebel stronghold on March 27, ten days into the escape. There they rested their horses, weakened from the constant riding and the scarcity of food along the way. They bunked down for the night, with the Dalai Lama and his ministers eager to announce the formation of their temporary government headquarters.

The next day, the Dalai Lama bent down to hear a faint broadcast on a battery-powered transistor radio the fugitives had brought with them. There he received the second shock of the escape. Before he could announce his rejection of the Seventeen Point Agreement, Peking nullified it. His Holiness listened as the faint voice of the Chinese premier, Zhou Enlai, announced that the uprising had "torn up" the agreement and that the Tibetan cabinet and all local government institutions had been dissolved, effective immediately. The Panchen Lama would now serve as chairman of the committee that nominally ruled the country. (The Dalai Lama's letter to the young Panchen Lama, asking him to join up with his rival in exile, had never reached him.) Ngabö, the seductively brilliant aristocrat who'd gone over to the Chinese side, was named vice-chairman. For the second time in his life, the Dalai Lama learned of Tibet's fate over the radio.

Tibet had ceased to exist.

Zhou Enlai then read out eighteen names of the key conspirators who'd kidnapped the Dalai Lama, including the Lord Chamberlain, the Khampa leaders, and the cabinet ministers who'd accompanied His Holiness on the escape. As the Tibetans bent down to hear the last of the message, the Chinese premier announced their punishment if they were caught by the PLA: life imprisonment, or death.

The newly elevated Panchen Lama sent a cable to Mao on March 29. It was, by any measure, a shameful message:

> The crimes of the upper-strata reactionary clique show that they are traitors to the motherland, enemies of the Tibetan people and the dregs of the Tibetan nationality. . . . I shall spare no earnest effort to . . . smash all the shameless traitorous intrigues carried out by the upper-strata reactionary clique in Tibet with the support of the imperialists and the Chiang Kai-shek clique. Long live the great motherland! Long live the Chinese Communist Party! Long live Chairman Mao Zedung, the great leader of all nationalities of our country!

Ngabö spoke next, completing his betrayal of Tibet with an even more galling message. "We have deep affection for the People's Liberation Army and oppose the imperialists and traitors," he said. "The rebellion has not led to a split of the motherland. On the contrary, it has promoted the national unity of the country, thus bringing limitless light and happiness to the broad masses of the Tibetan people."

Even as the Dalai Lama digested the news, he received another blow. With Athar on the trail with the Dalai Lama, the CIA had begun searching for any evidence that the Chinese were pursuing the escape party. And they soon found it. "Through various intercepts, the CIA learned that Mao had put out alerts to 'nail' the Dalai Lama," said Roger McCarthy, head of the Tibetan Task

Force during the escape. The reports coming in to the Task Force indicated that the PLA was sending troops and planes after the Tibetans, and that Chinese troops were now gathering north of Bhutan, almost directly to the east of Lhuntse Dzong, and would soon start marching to cut off the Dalai Lama before he could reach India. "It wouldn't have taken many bombs to wipe them out," says CIA officer John Greaney. "The way the Chinese were operating at that point, I don't believe the Dalai Lama would have survived, because the Chinese did not want him in the outside world as a symbol."

The rebels vowed to hold off any Chinese advance. When word came that His Holiness was fleeing toward India, a guerrilla leader told a group of Tibetan fighters that they had to form a rear guard: "We were told that we had to block mountain passes and bridges, and that we should fight as much as possible," remembers one rebel. But the lightly armed guerrillas found themselves matched against PLA troops with mortars and air support, planes that unloaded "bombs and big bullets." In one lethal encounter in which the rebels, armed only with swords, fought against PLA infantrymen with rifles and machine guns, the Tibetan ranks were decimated. The remainder of the unit turned and fled toward the Indian border.

The Chinese announcement and the news of PLA advances toward Lhuntse Dzong meant that lingering at the rebel fort was no longer an option. The Dalai Lama would have to make for the Indian border, just sixty miles away, immediately. Time was now the enemy. The bulletins from Athar shortened considerably: the rebel could now only dash off the Dalai Lama's current position in latitude and longitude, hand-crank the radio, insert the correct crystal for that day, and send the message off. Back in Washington, John Greaney would drive down to the Sig Center and receive the numbers, which he transposed onto a map of Tibet. He would then rush the new location to the Office of Current Intelligence, where in the early dawn hours the staff were preparing the president's daily brief. Every day Eisenhower could track how many miles the Dalai Lama had made and survey the territory ahead, which he could see was difficult, with passes up to 19,000 feet. The escape had put Tibet at the head of President Eisenhower's Current Intelligence Bulletin. "Eisenhower was delighted, sticking pins in his map," says the CIA's Ken Knaus. CIA director Allen Dulles met with the president and gave him a message: "We have every reason to hope that the Dalai Lama will get out of Tibet soon." But he almost spoke too soon.

Early in the morning on the 28th, Athar was asleep inside the fortress at Lhuntse Dzong when he felt someone shaking him roughly by the shoulder. He opened his eyes: it was the Lord Chamberlain. The official hurriedly explained to him that reports had come in that the PLA was marching toward the area in numbers that would overwhelm the Khampa guards. They needed to leave for India, but they still didn't have permission to cross the border. Without that offer of asylum from Nehru, any advancing Chinese troops could pin down the fugitives at the Indian border and kill or capture the Dalai Lama and his family. The Lord Chamberlain asked Athar to radio the Americans and ask them to request asylum from India.

Athar immediately brought out the RS-1, checked the codebook, installed the correct crystal, and began typing out his message.

In Washington, it was six o'clock Saturday evening. John Greaney was at home in Chevy Chase, Maryland, preparing to go out with his wife and three other couples for a rare night of socializing, when the phone rang. It was the CIA Sig Center. A message had come in from Athar. Luckily, the restaurant Greaney was going to that night, the Silver Fox, was near the CIA's headquarters. Greaney and his wife drove into Washington, and the deputy chief picked up the coded message on the way to dinner, briefly scanning the contents as he left the CIA hut. He immediately knew something major had happened; instead of the single line with time, date, longitude and latitude, the sheet was filled with set after set of five numbers each, a torrent of coded prose compared with what he usually received. Greaney got back in his Ford station wagon and drove with his wife to the safe house where the Mongolian monk, Geshe Wangye, was waiting. Greaney left the purple-inked sheet for him to translate, then took his pregnant wife, impatient by this time, to meet their friends for cocktails and light gossip.

All through dinner, Greaney wondered what message Athar had sent. None of the other men at the table was a CIA operative, let alone a member of the Tibetan Task Force, so he couldn't talk shop with them. When the check arrived, he told the couples he had to meet a friend and dashed off to the safe house. "So I got there," Greaney says, "and there's this message that the Dalai Lama requests us to ask for asylum in India." Greaney was taken aback. He knew the history well: the last time the Dalai Lama had been in India, Nehru had resisted offering asylum. Something drastic must have changed for the escape party to be tapping out this request from the rebel fortress.

By now it was the early hours of Sunday morning. An asylum request from the Dalai Lama would, under normal circumstances, have required approval from the State Department. There the issue would be debated for hours, if not days or weeks. "State could have been the biggest hangup," Greaney says. "There was no way we were going to get approval that night." The agent called his boss, Roger McCarthy, who told him to wake up Des FitzGerald, the debonair head of the East Asia Task Force. Reached on the phone,

FitzGerald didn't hesitate. "Do it," he instructed. He was telling Greaney to bypass State altogether and send the request directly to New Delhi. Greaney went back to the monk, and they began composing a message, sitting in the safe house's dining room on the CIA's rented furniture. Within an hour, they had the request prepared; and Greaney rushed back to the Sig Center, handed off the sheet with the coded language on it, and went home to his wife in Chevy Chase. When he walked through the door in the early hours of the morning, he found some of his dinner companions sipping cocktails in his living room. "I swear, today they'd think I was either a terrorist or a drug dealer," he says. But, deep into their glasses of Cutty Sark, the other couples barely batted an eye.

At four in the morning, the phone rang again. A message had been received back from New Delhi. "Somehow, in a matter of hours, they'd managed to reach Nehru," Greaney remembers. "And he said, with these conditions, I'll grant asylum. He even told the escape party where to enter India, through the North East Frontier." Greaney and FitzGerald and the other Tibet hands at first had trouble believing the response. "I didn't think Nehru wanted him there," he explains. "We were shocked."

With the sun rising, Greaney again jumped in his Ford and made the trek to Wisconsin Avenue, where he and the monk bent over the kitchen table cobbling together one last message. At nine in the morning, he rushed back to the Sig Center, nodded at the sleepy guard, and handed over the code to be sent to Athar: The corridor to India is open. Proceed to the North East Frontier Agency.

Greaney walked down the steps of the Sig Center, got into his car, his suit rumpled and his mind groggy, and went home, half-asleep, marveling at the vagaries of history. The fact that the request for asylum had arrived on a weekend had allowed the CIA to get it to Delhi and approved in record time.

"If it hadn't been a Saturday night," Greaney says, "the Dalai Lama might still be in Tibet."

The escapees, now 350 strong, were ill-prepared for the trek to India. They had no money, first of all. They hadn't been able to take any cash from the Potala funds, and they had no access to the monies sent ahead to India after the Chinese invasion. "We were paupers," remembers Choegyal, the Dalai Lama's younger brother. "We had nothing except the clothes on our bodies." All the fabulously rich Dalai Lama had to his name was a donkey, an extra set of clothes, and a few sackloads of Tibetan paper dollars, which would be almost worthless in India. Fortunately, the famous extravagance of the American intelligence system reached all the way to the trails of southern Tibet. In a message from John Greaney, Athar was instructed to give His Holiness's party 200,000 rupees from the stocks of Indian currency the CIA had air-dropped into Tibet. The Dalai Lama would make his way to India on American cash.

The event that the Dalai Lama had so looked forward to—the formation of an independent Tibetan government—now seemed anticlimactic. But it needed to be done; the Dalai Lama wanted to enter India as the head of a sovereign authority and not as a refugee. In front of 1,000 monks, soldiers, villagers, and ministers, His Holiness inaugurated the new government, which now had no country to administer. Then he quickly set off for India.

The journey was increasingly miserable, and it had begun to take its toll on the Dalai Lama. Incessant riding had given the fugitives saddle sores, and there was so little shelter in the arid country that they had to sleep in cowsheds or tiny peasant huts. The feeling of being pursued was fraying their nerves. The Khampas reported that the PLA had crossed the Tsangpo in numbers and that another contingent of troops was moving from the south to cut off the escape party.

There was another obstacle, or rather two. A pair of the highest passes on the route awaited them, both towering above 18,000 feet and cloaked in winter ice. Largo-La came first, and as the fugitives labored to the top of the pass, a snowstorm swept down on them. Choegyal struggled to climb the icy slope. The party's eyebrows and mustaches froze and caked with ice; their hands and feet went numb with the first signs of frostbite. To keep warm, the escapees had to dismount from their ponies and push forward on foot, boots coming out of the fresh snow with a sucking sound, then plunging back into the swirling powder. If they'd stayed mounted on their horses, they would have frozen in their saddles. On the other side of Largo-La, they stopped for a quick meal of bread, hot water, and condensed milk to get their blood flowing again.

As they pushed ahead, the weather began to deteriorate further. "We had difficulties," His Holiness said. "High mountains . . . breathing difficulties. There was too much cold. Our hands and feet became frozen." As the trail dipped and rose thousands of feet in altitude, blizzards alternated with sandstorms, heavy rain, and then dazzling sunlight. Avalanches pushed snowdrifts into their path. "Horses were unable to walk on the snow and even for humans it was difficult," remembered one soldier. Tibetans have a phrase for heavy snowfall—"the sky is broken." As they got closer and closer to India, the heavens seemed permanently cracked.

The next day, March 29, they faced Karpo-La, the last summit standing between them and India. As they climbed the slope, the sky darkened and snow and howling winds battered the escapees. Finally, the storm passed and the sun emerged from behind the clouds, nearly blinding them with its rays bouncing off the crystal white snow. Some of the party tied rags around their eyes to block the intense sunlight, while others used braids of their hair. They stopped on the slope to have their lunch when suddenly a dust storm came twisting through their little camp, blinding them again.

And then the plane appeared.

Like a mythical beast, everyone remembered it differently. Some remember a "biplane, flying low over the long line of the struggling caravan." The military-obsessed Choegyal thought it was a Douglas DC-4 model, the Skymaster, which had become famous for its part in the Berlin airlift. Others thought it was a Chinese military plane. "If it was Chinese, as it probably was," the Dalai Lama said, "there was a good chance that they now knew where we were." But all agreed the unmarked plane appeared out of nowhere, droning down from a blue sky to sweep over the escape party. "We didn't know whether it was Chinese or from another country," Choegyal recounted. "But it flew directly overhead and couldn't have failed to see us, hundreds of men and horses on the pure white snow."

Guards began to panic, jumping off their horses and struggling to get the machine guns off their backs. Suddenly, the Dalai Lama's voice floated across the slope.

"Be quiet," he called. "Don't move."

The fugitives stopped and waited, their breath visible in the frigid air. The Dalai Lama ordered the men to take off the red saddle blankets, which would be an easy mark for any gunners on the plane. In the confusion, his almost preternatural calm had eased the tension. It was a small moment, but the young monk was now ordering Khampa warriors around like he'd been born to it.

The plane was an ominous sign to the fugitives. "We thought it was over," Choegyal concedes. Certain they had been spotted, the escape party broke up into smaller groups that would give at least some of the Tibetans a chance to make it to India. His Holiness took the plane's appearance as a sign that no part of Tibet was safe for him. "Any misgivings I had about going into exile vanished with this realization," he remembered. "India was our only hope."

When they made camp, the fugitives took out their wireless radio and tried to pick up any news about Lhasa. Often they could only get Radio Peking. "The ancient city of Lhasa," the official news agency reported, "is bustling with life again":

> As Tibetan peasants drive their donkeys loaded with fuels and cereals into the city, students with satchels hanging from their shoulders walk to school, the postman on a bicycle begins distributing the day's newspapers, and gradually more and more vehicles of all descriptions come on the streets. In the center of the city, the shops which had to close in the rebellion stand open, their shelves once more stocked with merchandise. The reek of leather curing comes from the tannery and the din of metal sounds from the coppersmiths and silversmiths.

The reality for those who'd stayed behind in Tibet was, however, far different.

## Fourteen

# IN TIBETAN PRISONS

One pregnant Tibetan remembers the worst moment of the rebellion came in a simple gesture. She was being pulled away to prison by PLA troops when her mother came running out of their house to beg the soldiers not to take her daughter away. Her mother, a high-born aristocrat, prostrated herself at the feet of the peasant Chinese boys in their pea-green uniforms. The soldiers turned and left. "I was so ashamed that things had come to this, that my mother was bowing to the invader of our country," she says. "But she did it so that we might be safe."

Tibet was being remade by the Dalai Lama's escape. The Chinese began arresting Tibetans en masse. Lhasa became a city of women, as the only men on the streets were PLA soldiers and Chinese civilians. "We used to get so scared when we heard any sounds of men's footsteps," explains the pregnant woman, "as most of the Tibetan men were being kept in custody at the Norbulingka, and barely a few were left in Lhasa." An aristocrat whose husband was one of the government officials in the pay of the Chinese occupiers, she was later arrested despite her mother's pleas and tossed into a shelter, crowded in with the peasants and the poor. There she sat on the filthy floor thinking about her maid, whom she'd sent to the first protests and who was now imprisoned—for obeying her mistress's order. "I felt so guilty and uncomfortable about it," she admits. "Later I met her in exile; I welcomed her at home and showed her my respect and asked for her forgiveness."

A Tibetan nun describes the conditions at one Lhasa prison in those first days: "We were kept in a small cell with many people, and later on they brought more and more people so that there was barely any room for standing. They started interrogating each one of us one by one. . . . According to how you answered, you received a sentence. I was totally petrified and could not feel much either physically or spiritually. I was without sensation." The nun received five years for helping the rebels.

Others escaped before they could be arrested. One escapee who fled Lhasa remembered feeling as if he were stepping on dried peas as he hurried away, as there were so many empty rifle cartridges littering the streets. In one Tibetan army division, the original force of 500 men had been reduced to only 37, with most of the missing now dead. The Chinese were piling corpses in front of the Norbulingka and in other places where the Tibetans had put up the fiercest resistance. At a place called Tsuklak-khang, an army doctor saw the bodies of women and children lying among the rebels: "The whole city was smoking from burning houses and it stank, especially at the Norbulingka side where the Chinese burned the piled corpses of humans and animals." PLA officers were going from prisoner to prisoner, questioning them on the whereabouts of the Dalai Lama. "They had no idea where he was."

The Sera monks who'd ferried guns from the Potala were caught and arrested. Some were wounded in the battle. "When the bullet hit me, I felt satisfied and had no regrets about dying," one remembers. "It wasn't for myself I was wounded but for the cause of the nation." He was brought back to Sera Monastery, which was now a temporary prison for "counterrevolutionary" monks. "I was held in a dark room," he says. "The Chinese authorities would come every day and ask me to confess to what I did. They said if I confessed, they would let me go." The normally placid monk argued fiercely with them. "I told them that I didn't have anything to confess as we Tibetans didn't come to their land, instead you Chinese had invaded ours." The Chinese interrogators shot back that Tibet was part of China. "I responded that if it was so, then where were they when the English invaded?"

The interrogators had no answer for that.

The fall of the Norbulingka made two things clear to Tibetans: the Dalai Lama was fleeing the country and the Chinese would now exert complete control over their lives. In the next few days and weeks, 80,000 refugees flowed south to India or Bhutan in the wake of His Holiness. Almost every family in Tibet had a member leave for the border or knew someone who made the trip. Others stayed where they were, burning incense and placing lamps with fresh butter in front of their Buddhist shrines, and praying for the Precious Protector, the Dalai Lama, to survive.

Some who lived close to the border made it to exile in a day or two of nothing more than vigorous hiking by moonlight (many of the escapees traveled by night to avoid Chinese patrols). Others suffered horribly—one escapee recalls his wife giving birth prematurely on the road. The baby died of exposure and hunger on the route to Bhutan. Few had prepared for leaving Tibet, setting off without adequate supplies of *tsampa* or clothing. And in regions where there were no telegraphs or telephones, they made their decisions in complete ignorance about what had really happened in Lhasa. Rumors abounded. After airplanes flew over one escape party, the next morning its members were told that the aircraft were the first sign of an American invasion. "There is no need to escape to India," a young man told them. "American troops have come to take back our country.'" The people were overjoyed.

One refugee who followed the Dalai Lama's exact route to the south remembered that the PLA was everywhere. "The Chinese were pursuing us," he says, shooting at them from planes and dropping bombs on their party. Their food was rapidly running out, and the paths were so clogged and steep that they had to abandon their horses, whose bodies lined the route. "We had to walk over them," he says. "There was no time for compassion."

In the stony village of Kongpo Tham-nyen in the rebellious province of Kham, Cho Lhamo marked her life into two sections: before the Chinese and after. Before, she'd been the beautiful daughter of a local farmer and *genpo*, or Khampa leader. She played mah-jongg, wrestled with her brothers and sisters, circled the local temple hand in hand with other children, and rode a horse like a true Khampa child. "I would catch hold of a horse with a rope and ride it without a saddle," she remembered. "I rode into the woods clinging on to the mane of the horse with my head bent against it." She'd been to Lhasa once, in 1956, where as a fifteen-year-old she had gazed upon the young Dalai Lama. "I looked up and thought he was so fair and rosy," she said. "I thought he was really God."

When the Dalai Lama fled for India, Cho Lhamo's family—fearing they would be targeted as prosperous Tibetans—hurried to join him. They walked during the night and hid during daylight, always heading south, meeting hundreds and then thousands of other refugees in the mountain passes. Finally, her father, without telling her or her mother and siblings, dropped behind to join a group of fighters. When Cho Lhamo and her mother found out, they hid in a cave, waiting for her father to rejoin them. Two days later, his dog wandered into the mouth of the cave. "The dog would never leave your father's side," her mother told her. "He has been killed by the Chinese." But they couldn't leave their patriarch behind without knowing for sure. Holding a long knife in her pocket, Cho Lhamo, her mother, and her brothers and sisters walked north until they came across the site of a recent battle, finding empty bullet casings and ground that had recently been disturbed. They also found her father's protective amulet, its contents spilled out in the dirt.

The Chinese caught them on the mountainside. A squad of soldiers advanced on Cho Lhamo and shouted, "Kill! Kill! Kill!" But the family members were arrested instead, their hands bound. Interrogators asked them, "Did you listen to the reactionaries and decide to go?" Cho Lhamo responded, yes, nudging her mother to keep quiet in case she gave a different answer. Instead of making it to India, she and her siblings were forced to march along the escape route back home. On the ground they saw bundles of clothes and food tossed away by Tibetans trying to lighten their load. "The region was entirely deserted," she remembered. The Chinese kept questioning them, "Will you escape again? Will you think differently?" Cho Lhamo told them, "We will never flee again."

It seemed like half of Tibet had left for India, and Cho Lhamo was left to see the aftermath. In her home village, the fugitives' possessions had been given away, their sheep and cattle stolen. And there she learned the fate of her father, who had indeed been killed defending their escape party. "I wept and wept and wept, so that I almost died," she says.

In southern Tibet, a man named Norbu Dhondup was fleeing with his two wives. A simple nomad, thirty years old, he was leaving a land that had become bitter to him. His father, a wealthy landowner, had been subjected to a series of *thamzins*, or reeducation sessions, after the Chinese charged him with supporting the rebels. In fact, when the rebels had ridden into their village and asked for "guns if we had guns, swords if we had swords, horses if we had horses," his father had refused. But the rebels had taken them anyway.

The villagers turned on his family. Norbu's father had lent them grain and money when times were hard, but now they took advantage of the Chinese invasion to erase their accounts. Poor peasants even walked into his father's home and looted it. Sold out by his neighbors, the elderly man was arrested by the Chinese along with five or six other prominent men (including a monk) on charges of helping the rebels. Norbu's father was marched to the public square and made to kneel. The Chinese then pulled his father off the ground by his hair and made him bow to the entire village, gathered in a circle around him. The crowd shouted that Norbu's father had given the horses and guns to the guerrillas.

When prompted by the Chinese guards, they came up close to the elderly man, looked him in the face, and then spit in his mouth. The PLA even demanded Norbu *thamzin* his own father. "It was so bad," he says. "I said I would not do it."

His father received a sentence of twenty years in prison. The elderly man was taken to a small room in Upper Khamba and left there until he could be transported to the prison. Alone, unable to bear the shame, he drew out a long knife he'd hidden in his *chuba*. With it he sliced off his testicles.

"I couldn't think," Norbu remembers. "I felt terribly depressed." The poor villagers came and took the rest of his possessions, his food and silver cups, even stealing his *chubas*. They stopped to complain to Norbu that the coats were made of inferior wool. Norbu began to hate his fellow Tibetans.

He watched them walk away from his house, numbed by the image of his father alone with a knife. "Something had happened to me," he says. He didn't regret losing the furs and the *chubas*. He didn't seem to have any feelings left at all. But he did have an urge to leave Tibet. One thought dominated his mind: "I thought it would be enough if I could see His Holiness the Dalai Lama even once." He started off for nearby Bhutan with his two wives, whom he'd never really been happy with. But they were all he had left.

As Lhasa fell, Soepa, the official who'd returned to the Norbulingka out of a nagging sense of duty, was a prisoner of the PLA. He lay in a huge prayer hall called the Offering Temple, which had been made into a makeshift hospital, or at least a storehouse for the injured and dying: "The floor was a puddle of blood, and the room was filled with stench and groaning." Freezing now, dressed only in his pants and a thin shirt, Soepa shivered as night came on. As the temperature dropped, he noticed lightly wounded Tibetans watching the critical patients, waiting for the moment of death so they could pull the clothes off the fresh corpse. Lying next to Soepa was an old man, a Khampa with white hair, badly wounded in the fight. He was breathing heavily, struggling for air. The desire for life had returned to Soepa, and when the man's breath got shallower and shallower and it appeared he was near death, Soepa did a shameful thing: he pulled off the heavy cloak the man was wearing. He was about to wrap it around himself when he noticed it was drenched in blood. He put it on anyway.

The next afternoon, Chinese military doctors arrived. The bone in Soepa's injured leg was shattered, and he was loaded onto a jeep for the ride to a hospital. The road was filled with ruts and bumps, and Soepa writhed in pain as the jeep smashed its way along. When he got to the hospital, he was left on the floor of a bare room (there was no bed). An armed PLA soldier was stationed at his door. Soepa lay there all night in a thin white hospital dress, covered by a blanket. The cement wall was pockmarked with bullet holes from rounds that had come in through the windows during the uprising. The next morning, a Chinese doctor came in to treat his leg, which he did while jabbing his finger at the bullet holes and telling Soepa that the Han had come to Tibet to help the natives and this is what they'd gotten in return. The doctor was so rough that during the examination, he reached down and pulled a piece of flesh from the wound and held it in his fingers. Soepa instantly passed out.

*Fifteen*

# THE LAST BORDER

While Tibet was being turned upside down, the Dalai Lama raced toward the Indian border, certain he would encounter a Chinese patrol at every turn in the path. As the fugitives got closer to the dividing line, they began to descend from the Tibetan highlands to the tropical landscapes of northeast India. The air turned from bitingly cold to almost sultry. It started to rain on the exhausted travelers, which at first was a relief but soon bred colds and illness in the escapees. On the 30th, they reached the village of Mangmang, a tiny outpost that represented the last

Tibetan settlement before India. It was a place that seemed firmly ensconced in the thirteenth century. "There were very few houses available," remembers Choegyal. "Those that we did find all had stables underneath and the living quarters above, with wood planks for floors. It was how people in Europe lived centuries before, and they were filled with bad odors."

The Dalai Lama was forced to sleep in a tent. Rain lashed the tarpaulin. As with so many of the thousands of Tibetans who were flowing in a huge exodus behind him, the warm air seemed to attack his constitution. The next morning, he awoke feverish and weak. "My stomach's not well," he told his younger brother, then lay back down, unable to travel. On the cusp of freedom, His Holiness had caught dysentery. "I watched him grow sicker and sicker," Choegyal recalls. Dysentery is usually caused by a *Shigella* bacillus or an amoeba, *Entamoeba histolytica*, which most often enters the body through polluted water or rotten food. The illness is a familiar one in Tibet, and often fatal: it is the leading cause of infant mortality in the nation's rural villages and hamlets. Traveling through some of the most isolated and poorest parts of his country, the Dalai Lama had caught one of his people's biggest killers. And there was no medicine to treat him.

His Holiness lay in a high fever all that day, thirteen days into his escape. His handlers moved him to a nearby house, where he tossed and turned before finally falling asleep. It would have been ideal to keep His Holiness resting and drinking fluids, the only treatment his ministers could offer him, but soon word arrived that the Chinese were approaching the nearby town of Tsona, to the rear of the escape party. The next morning, the Dalai Lama was taken from his bed and put on a black *dzo*, a hybrid of a yak and a male cow. He leaned forward in the saddle, "in a daze of sickness and weariness and unhappiness deeper than I can express."

As they approached India, he began to say good-bye to the Khampas who had guarded him on his escape, many of whom were now turning back to fight the Chinese. Tears stung his eyes as he blessed the men. "That was a powerful moment for me in my life," His Holiness said, "as I watched those Khampa horsemen who had saved me and were the patriots of my country." He pulled the reins on the *dzo* and began trudging toward the border, knowing he would never see the Khampas again. "I turned my back to Tibet and looked toward India. I looked around me and I didn't have a friend in the world."

Without his protectors, the Dalai Lama was left with some elderly ministers and tutors, his family, and a skeleton crew of guards. He was dressed in clothes that stank from the journey, and he was sick with a poor man's disease. The young incarnate had truly been stripped bare.

The trails dropped down toward India, crossing into forests lined with burbling streams. The escapees began to relax. Whatever it did, the PLA wouldn't cross the Indian border. And the weather was languorous compared with what they'd faced. "We didn't have to pull on the reins, just lean back in the saddle," remembers Choegyal. "Some of our guys, they got so relaxed, they fell asleep and fell off the horse."

As he traveled the last few miles in Tibet, the Dalai Lama, sick and depressed, listened to a small battery-operated radio. He heard a report on All-India Radio that he'd fallen from his horse and been seriously injured. It was the latest rumor that had emanated out of the press corps. The *Times* of London had led with the story on the morning of March 30: "The 24-year-old Dalai Lama has been seriously injured while making a fantastic day-and-night trek to safety across the perilous mountain passes of Tibet," read the front-page story filed by a Kalimpong correspondent. "He slipped while making a detour on a lonely 19,000-ft.-high footpath at dusk." The story went on to report that His Holiness had suffered "multiple fractures" and was being carried on a "makeshift stretcher or hidden in mountain caves by five members of his Cabinet escaping with him." The Dalai Lama smiled.

His Holiness knew he had to compose himself for his emergence into the world. He had to arrive at a way of expressing who he was and what his philosophy was toward the Chinese. He'd left Lhasa still believing that cooperation with Peking was possible, that their humanity, which he'd been so relieved to discover on that first meeting with the Chinese general, overrode all other considerations. But he'd left that naïveté on the trail. The Chinese had attacked and killed thousands of his countrymen. The events of the past two weeks had forced him to confront evil in the world, really for the first time.

Watching him, the thirteen-year-old Choegyal understood that his brother was facing a life he knew nothing about. "It was a reality check for him," his brother acknowledges. "Before, no matter how practical he wanted to be, the atmosphere he grew up in as the Dalai Lama was not in any way realistic. Now he had a taste of real life." Narkyid, the Norbulingka official, concurs. "He got experience of how things are. He thought people are so good, but what they are saying and what they are doing are not the same thing. Now he saw the truth." The Dalai Lama knew that the uprising and escape had washed away any lingering fantasies of his boyhood. "You discover a cynical brutality, the crushing use of force, your own weakness." With his ministers scattered, his palace occupied, his place in the world gone, the struts of his former life were knocked away.

At around 4:00 p.m. on the last day of March, the Dalai Lama and his party emerged into a small clearing where a group of six Indian guards—Gurkhas in pebbled leather boots and jungle hats—waited at attention, silent against the guttural monkey calls and the singing of birds that emerged from the jungle behind them. As the Dalai Lama came up to them on the awkward *dzo*, the Gurkhas presented arms crisply and their commander advanced toward His Holiness, a *kata* in his hands. The Dalai Lama climbed down, took the scarf with a small bow of his head, then began to walk, followed by his ministers. He was in India now.

The Dalai Lama was unaware that thousands of Tibetans were now following in his tracks and that he would soon head a large exile community inside India. But he did know that the court of Lhasa had in effect disintegrated, that a way of life was gone, perhaps forever. And he didn't mourn all of it. He'd been happy in India before, during a 1956 visit to pay tribute to Gandhi, and he knew that the stifling and often vicious politics of Tibet, the rituals that had kept him from expressing himself as a simple and compassionate monk, could now be remade. As painful as the fall of Lhasa was, it had sprung him from the gilded cage of the Potala.

"His Holiness was very happy to be free," says Choegyal. "Now he could really say what was in his heart."

The escape had been a kind of dream fulfillment for Choegyal. He'd played soldier, he'd mixed with the Khampas as a kind of mascot, if not an equal. But as they passed by trails lined with Tibetan peasants standing and weeping, he couldn't ignore the tragic aspect of what was happening. "The villagers were welcoming, but there was so much sadness in their faces." And the images of those he'd left behind in the Norbulingka had stayed with him and were paired with the stories of the violent deaths so many of the palace's defenders had met. The escape had been the great event of his boyhood. But it had, in some ways, brought that boyhood to an end.

"It forced me to grow up," he reflects. "I think those two weeks had given me a crash course in life." He'd lived out an adventure, but he was now rootless and unprotected by the layers of staff and minders who had watched over him from birth. In later years, he would mark a change in his character to those days on the trail. "The whole experience had a very transformative effect on me—it made me decisive, practical," he explains. "And it taught me that anything can happen. The mind becomes more pliant, more flexible." From being a pampered brother to His Holiness, he was now a penniless refugee. He took the warm clothes that he'd brought with him from Tibet and sold them, earning 15 silver coins. But instead of going out and spending the money on toys or ammunition for his Luger as he would have done just a few weeks earlier, he bought food. "I can still remember what I got: cream crackers, butter, and jam," he says. "They were delicious."

The race for the story of the escape, and to explain who the Dalai Lama was, only ratcheted up once word got out that His Holiness had crossed the border. His Holiness was safely in India, but he was still in the remote North East Frontier Agency, a huge border area that was off-limits to foreigners, especially journalists.

George Patterson was the first to reach Tezpur, forty miles south of the frontier region. The village lies on the Brahmaputra River, usually somnolent under the heat of northern India and bordered by dangerous, leech-filled swamps. It was prime tea-growing territory and had been invaded by a species unknown to the rich landscape for thousands of years: sunburned, portly British plantation owners, who congregated in the Station Club, drank Boodles British Gin, played billiards, and gossiped about the next hunt for Bengal tigers. As Patterson made preparations to go north, further infuriating the Indian government, three other journalists arrived, including the legendary Noel Barber. Patterson was deeply annoyed. The chances of one or two men making their way through the "forbidden zone" of the military-only region were slim. With five (counting Patterson's loyal servant), they were next to none. But Patterson and the others felt they had to try. Their foreign desks were baying for news of the Dalai Lama, and for Patterson and Barber, at least, there was a personal stake in getting the story of His Holiness out.

At nine o'clock in the evening, the journalists hopped in a car and headed out to meet some Indian guides who would spirit them through the North East Frontier Agency. The rendezvous spot was wild. "On the way the headlights of the car picked out the gleaming eyes and form of a tiger," Patterson remembered, "disappearing into the jungle beside the road." When they reached the meeting place, the guides learned the foreigners wanted to make the journey unarmed. The Indian men protested loudly. There were not only tigers in the jungles ahead, there were herds of wild elephants and leopards, not to mention the border guards, the Assam Rifles, who "would shoot at sight anything or anyone moving at night." The arrival of the Dalai Lama had deep political ramifications for India, and anyone hiking through the outlawed zone would be considered a spy or a terrorist. Patterson and the others bid up the price to an astronomical 10 English pounds a head. Finally, the locals went off into the jungle to debate the matter. After a few minutes, the journalists realized the men had taken off, leaving them stranded.

Disheartened, the reporters made their way back to Tezpur, which had become, according to the *New Yorker*, "briefly, the news capital of the world." By mid-April, there were 200 journalists and photographers gathered there, and people from San Francisco to Marseilles were waking up to their daily newspaper to find bulletins about Tibet on the front pages. The small outpost was becoming a rat's nest of the world's most highly paid newsmen. "Famous correspondents were sleeping on couches, billiard tables and wherever they could put up," Patterson said. The newspaper war had begun in earnest: Deep-pocketed hacks had hired out Tezpur's only two (barely working) taxis, for the exorbitant price of 50 rupees per day plus gas money, in part to have them on hand and in part to keep them away from their competitors. One desperate journalist "priced an elephant" as a possible substitute. The tea planters were offered outrageous sums to rent out their private planes, which they happily did. Nothing happened in Tezpur, ever, so to be ground zero in the story of the moment brought with it a gust of British life that the locals would never forget.

In fact, in the absence of real news coming out of Tibet, the coverage of the escape became near-deranged. One correspondent reported 100,000 dead in the Lhasa uprising, more people than the city held. Another wrote that the Dalai Lama's psychic powers had caused him to fully insure the Norbulingka palace, and that as soon as His Holiness arrived in exile, he'd be handed a check for a cool one million dollars. The Dalai Lama was reported to be documenting his flight on a solid-gold Leica. Noel Barber contributed a story about an imaginary group of rebels who had acted as decoys, allowing His Holiness to escape: "Almost to a man . . . ," he reported, "the suicide squad were wiped out in a terrific battle astride the 15,000-foot Himalaya pass." What the *Times of India* called the "maddest competition in journalistic history" caused foreign editors to ring up their correspondents four or five times a day, demanding fresh copy. "Fiction is what they want," one journalist said. "Pure fiction. Well, by God, fiction is what they're going to get."

Barber outdid them all. While waiting in Calcutta, he'd arranged to charter a plane to fly over southern Tibet and get the world-exclusive picture of the Dalai Lama's escape party. Remarkably, before he'd even gotten to Tezpur, the star correspondent had actually *filed a story* saying that he'd spotted His Holiness on the snow glaciers of the Himalayas—misidentifying the monk's robes as yellow, not maroon—and written a wildly colorful description of his daring feat of airborne journalism. On the way to the tea plantation, Barber tormented the other journalists with his world scoop. "He gloated over the fact that there was nothing they could do about it now," Patterson remembered. Now all Barber had to do was jump on a plane, find the escapees, and actually report the story he'd already written and filed.

But when Barber arrived in Tezpur, he was horrified to learn that the North East Frontier Agency was so secret and sensitive in the eyes of the Indian government that planes were not even allowed to fly over it. Anyone caught doing so faced five years in an Indian jail. None of the local pilots would take the job, even for a small fortune, and it was too late to cable the *Daily Mail* to tell them to kill the story. When the story ran, Barber faced prison for something he hadn't actually done. The world's most famous foreign correspondent had risked his career to get one of the greatest stories of the midcentury. And it would prove his undoing as a newspaperman.

The coverage of His Holiness's escape became one of the legendary journalistic farces of the twentieth century. The press abandoned any semblance of truthfulness in its race for the scoop. But even as they drank themselves silly at Tezpur's Paradise Hotel and made up scandalous fictions as they ran down to the telegraph office, Barber and his mates did a few things that proved important. They sketched out the idea that Tibet was being overwhelmed by a power it couldn't hope to defeat. And they made it clear that this tragedy was happening to people very much like the men and women reading about it. The melodramatic way the journalists wrote about the uprising and the escape, as inaccurate as it was, had the virtue of humanizing a people the world barely knew existed.

Tibet was no longer another world. It was like a lot of other places in 1959. Barber and his ilk brought it close.

The avalanche of press also indelibly stamped Tibet on the world's consciousness, even as "Tibet" became—to borrow a term with a later vintage—almost virtual, a movement instead of a nation. The plight of the Tibetans caused a wave of sympathy around the world. The liberal Supreme Court justice William O. Douglas and the right-wing journalist Lowell Thomas formed the American Emergency Committee for Tibetan Refugees (which some alleged was funded by the CIA, though no definitive proof ever emerged), and contributions poured in. Within a few years, twelve agencies—with home bases ranging from Liechtenstein to Australia—were assisting the Tibetan exiles. The Dalai Lama would appear in 1959 before the United Nations, which insisted that China respect Tibetans' demands for self-determination, the first time a world body had ever put its weight behind the tiny nation. Norbu, the Dalai Lama's brother who'd heard about the escape on the radio in his tiny New York apartment, saw the effects of all the attention. "It's funny," he said, "but before this thing nobody knew what a Tibetan was, or even what one looked like. They think the Tibetans are like the Chinese, but with a third eye." The Dalai Lama's face would soon appear on the cover of *Life* and *Time* (under the headline "The Escape That Rocked the Reds"), and his story was retold in hundreds of magazines and newspapers. The press, though it made up half the details of the journey across the Himalayas, had in a matter of a few weeks fused the story of Tibet and the image of the young man in the maroon robe.

Noel Barber later paid dearly for his fictionalized account of the Dalai Lama's escape, which ran under the headline "Noel Barber

Moves Up to the 'End of the Line' as Dalai Lama Prepares for Next Lap to Freedom." Soon after it ran, he left the *Daily Mail*—there were rumors that it was because of the fake story—and turned to writing books. The dashing foreign correspondent had vanished from the front pages. "I don't think he ever covered another major story," one veteran journalist recalled. In his own way, Barber too was stripped of his position and all its glory.

But Tibet remained with Barber, as it did with so many who brushed up against the place. Even as he was spinning out exotic yarns, he turned out two books on the escape and its aftermath, *The Flight of the Dalai Lama* (1960) and *From the Land of Lost Content* (1969). The accounts were filled with barbs against the evils of communism, which was the lens through which most of the world saw the Dalai Lama's escape. Barber wrote about China:

> One day it will, like other empires, crumble; and meanwhile Lhasa, the distant city unlike any other in the world, still stands, despite the Chinese who strut its streets, a symbol (for those who do not forget) of defiance by the puny against the mighty, of the unquenchable spirit of men who, however far away from us, are now welded by a common bond with their brothers in Budapest and in Prague.
>
> For they also asked only for freedom.

The Gurkha guards escorted His Holiness and the other refugees through the Indian jungle to Bomdila, a town a week's march away. There he received a telegram from Nehru that assured him "the people of India, who hold you in great veneration, will no doubt accord their traditional respect to your personage." His Holiness spent ten days in Bomdila, recovering from the last traces of his dysentery, and then was driven to a road camp called Foothills. His next stop would be Tezpur, where the world's press awaited him.

As the Dalai Lama journeyed into the interior of India, thousands of Buddhists lined his route, crying *"Dalai Lama Ki Jai! Dalai Lama Zinda-bad!"* ("Hail to the Dalai Lama! Long live the Dalai Lama!"). At Tezpur, the by-now world-famous Sherpa named Tenzing Norgay, who six years earlier along with Edmund Hillary had been one of the first two climbers to summit Everest, stood waiting to greet His Holiness. He'd carefully avoided crossing into the special VIP section that held diplomats and luminaries and stood behind a wooden barricade, among the common people holding white scarves and praying. Norgay had come down from Darjeeling to greet the Dalai Lama because "I was so worried about him."

On April 18, the Dalai Lama emerged into the glare of the world press. As His Holiness appeared, monks blew conch shells and struck a note on brass gongs, the sound vibrating in the air as the young Dalai Lama, his face drawn but smiling broadly, walked ahead. Attendants held an enormous yellow, red, and white umbrella over his head, and six Brahmin priests chanted Sanskrit hymns. He looked "sick and fatigued," according to the *Times of India's* correspondent. "He seemed very high strung," observed Robert Thurman, an American Buddhist scholar, who met the Dalai Lama months later, "and did not radiate the sort of calm and massive presence that he is today, but he was very alert and aware of you."

Two sealed letters from President Eisenhower were handed to him, congratulating him on his escape and pledging assistance. The next day, Eisenhower received a memo from Allen Dulles at the CIA. For Dulles, the escape proved not only that the Dalai Lama's people wanted to fight but that "the Tibetans, particularly the Khampas, Goloks and other tribes of East Tibet, are a fierce, brave

and warlike people. Battle in defense of their religion and the Dalai
Lama is looked upon as a means of achieving merit toward the next
reincarnation." With the Dalai Lama safely in India, Dulles told
the president, a new insurgency could be planned.

But His Holiness was not yet truly free. The irony of his exile
was that Nehru was no more eager to have the Dalai Lama speaking
out than Mao was. The Indians built a fourteen-foot barbed-wire
fence around his bungalow in an Indian town called Mussoorie and
kept all journalists and visitors away. His first public statement was
actually written by bureaucrats in New Delhi.

As the Dalai Lama arrived at his final stop, an intriguing new theory of his escape was broadcast in London. "It is far more likely
the Chinese allowed him to slip through," stated the left-wing *New
Statesman* magazine, "believing a reluctant Dalai Lama in their
hands would be more trouble than a Dalai Lama in exile, whom
they could make responsible for any troubles they have in Tibet."
The idea that the Chinese had wanted the Dalai Lama out of Lhasa
was also circulating among Asian capitals and embassies in the
weeks after the escape. The Chinese would later endorse the idea.
From the state archives, a telegram emerged in which Mao ordered
his bureaucrats in Lhasa to allow the Dalai Lama to escape, since
his death would "inflame world opinion," especially in Buddhist
Asia and in India.

The theory made sense, on one level. Exiling the Dalai Lama
would demoralize the Tibetan people and rob the resistance of its
greatest rallying point. The clique around the young Panchen Lama
seemed ready to become willing puppets of Peking and to back a
far tougher line toward the rebels than the Dalai Lama had. And
there was a record of dissatisfaction with His Holiness among the

Chinese leadership. In 1956, when the Dalai Lama was in India and deciding whether to return to Lhasa, Mao told an audience, "You can't have a husband and wife [relationship] simply by tying two people together. If a person no longer likes your place and wants to run away, let him go. . . . I will not be sad if we lose Dalai." He reiterated the thought later, telling a member of Provincial and Municipal Party Secretaries that "even if the DL doesn't return, China will not sink into the sea." Later, the Chinese leader Jiang Zemin even claimed that the PLA had had the Dalai Lama surrounded on a hill outside Lhasa but had let him go.

But the theory that the Chinese let the Dalai Lama leave Tibet doesn't align with their behavior either before or after the escape. Mao and his lieutenants had been intent on co-opting, not eliminating, His Holiness. The minister of China's United Front Work Department said in 1950 that "winning over the Dalai will be our greatest victory." And during the Dalai Lama's sojourn in India in 1956–57, Chinese premier Zhou Enlai had charmed and threatened the young Tibetan leader into returning to his palace in Lhasa. The objective of the Chinese diplomatic approach during that crucial time was to get the Dalai Lama back to Tibet. And if the Tibetan leader's death would inflame world opinion, as Mao suggested in his telegram, what would his exile and his ability to speak freely about the abuses inside Tibet do? The Chinese leader was a phenomenally gifted propagandist, and surely he knew how much damage His Holiness could do—and, as it turned out, did—once he was in India.

Other sources contradict the telegram. After the escape, Mao met with Soviet leader Nikita Khrushchev, and the subject of the Dalai Lama came up repeatedly. The discussion was brutally frank. Khrushchev called the Dalai Lama "a bourgeois figure" but then blasted Mao for letting him escape. "The events in Tibet are your fault," he told the Chinese leader. "You ruled in Tibet, you should have had your intelligence [agencies] there and you should have known about the plans and intentions of the Dalai Lama." Mao shot back that Nehru was also blaming him for the incident and that "our mistake was not disarming the Dalai Lama right away." (Presumably, he's conflating the Tibetan leader with the Tibetan resistance.) Khrushchev was having none of it:

> As to the escape of the Dalai Lama from Tibet, if we had been in your place, we would not have let him escape. It would be better if he was in a coffin. And now he is in India, and perhaps will go to the USA. Is this to the advantage of the socialist countries?

"This is impossible," Mao fired back. "We could not arrest him then. We could not bar him from leaving, since the border is very extended, and he could cross it at any point." Later on, the Chinese leader nastily accused Khrushchev of being a hypocrite, as the USSR's bitterest enemies had escaped its borders. "I cannot understand what constitutes our mistake?" he said. "Kerensky [referring to Alexander Kerensky, a Russian politician who'd eluded capture by the Bolsheviks and ended up in Paris] and Trotsky also escaped from you." The Trotsky affair had been a black mark on early Soviet history. Khrushchev conceded the point.

The sense of what Mao was saying is clear: the Chinese did not want the Dalai Lama to escape, but the logistics of keeping him in Lhasa were daunting and his eventual escape took them by surprise. The best evidence tells us there was not a Chinese plot to get him to India.

*Sixteen*

# MEETING A POET

The escape left trails of turbulence in its wake. The Chinese followed the Dalai Lama toward the border, pushing south into territory formerly held by the rebels and overwhelming the small bands of resistance fighters there. Many Khampa warriors crossed the border, handed their weapons to the Indian officials, and went to live in the tents provided to the exiles. When their leader, Gompo Tashi, crossed over on April 28, the broad-based rebellion was over. All that was left were small rebel forces in Kham and in southern Tibet who now relied on hit-and-run tactics to harass the Chinese.

George Patterson looked on the destruction of the Khampa rebellion with despair. He couldn't forget Tibet. On June 20, two months after the escape, he finally met with the man whom God had, in a way, led him to. "I have heard many things concerning *Khamba Gyau* [the Bearded Khampa]," His Holiness told him, "and of the great help you have been to Tibet. But even more than in the past you must help us now, in whatever way you can."

But after the heady days of March 1959, Patterson felt that the issue of Tibet, which had blazed forth during the Dalai Lama's escape, had disappeared from the world's consciousness. He grew depressed. "I had lived for years with a daily expectation that an unknown but divinely prepared set of circumstances was waiting for me, out of which I would learn something new about God," he wrote. He had also expected to help save Tibet. Neither had transpired. In his disappointment, Patterson fixed on a new, radical plan—to slip back into the Chinese-held territories and film an actual Khampa attack on PLA troops, and then broadcast it to the world. He wanted to prove that the Khampas, given the right support, could challenge PLA control of Tibet and that "they were a far worthier ally for the West than either Korea or Vietnam," the latter of which by the early 1960s was sucking in American troops and matériel at an alarming rate.

In May 1964, Patterson and his documentary team took seventeen days to reach the remote Mustang region in neighboring Nepal, where a group of guerrillas based their raids into Tibet. The CIA, which was supporting the Mustang guerrillas with food and weapons, heard about his mission and sent orders that the documentary team be stopped at all costs. Patterson was back in a familiar role: annoying a great power. The last thing the CIA wanted was advertisements about its covert aid to a mortal Chinese enemy. But

Patterson, as usual, outwitted the authorities. Hiking to altitudes of 20,000 feet, he and his team arrived on a mountain slope as the Khampas prepared to attack a convoy of four PLA trucks on the valley road below. When the rebels opened up, Patterson filmed the deadly encounter—in which all the PLA soldiers were killed and a Khampa seriously wounded—and then dashed for the Nepalese border, plunging "suicidally down that vertical moving mountainside in a long, sliding, striding dash for the narrow valley beneath." He and his crew smuggled the sixty cans of film out through the 20,000-foot Khojang Pass, back into Nepal. There they walked into a firestorm: the king of Nepal sacked several cabinet members when he heard about the mission, the CIA cut off funding to the Tibetan guerrillas (a ban that lasted six months), and Patterson was placed under house arrest while authorities scrambled to find— and presumably burn—the film he'd brought back from Tibet. But he'd been expecting that, and the film was smuggled out successfully. The thirty-minute *Raid into Tibet* debuted two years later, "caused a sensation on British television," and was syndicated to forty countries.

Patterson had failed to save Tibet. But he'd transformed the role of the Tibetophile, that collection of melancholy dilettantes and serious ethnographers who'd looked to the Land of Snows for another vision of life. He'd helped create the idea of the Tibet activist, the men and women in San Francisco or London who today devote their lives to actual Tibetans, instead of lamas on carpets.

Back in Washington, the Tibetan Task Force celebrated the escape. "We were overjoyed in our little unit," says John Greaney.

The reaction from the State Department, as expected, was less positive—the Task Force members got the distinct impression that the diplomats there would have preferred the status quo. But for the CIA, it was, as Ken Knaus called it, "a great coup." "If you had to plan an operation to go into Tibet and rescue him," John Greaney clarifies, "that would have been an extremely difficult thing. It would have entailed an invasion of Chinese sovereignty."

After the escape, the Task Force turned its attention to the remaining bands of Mustang guerrillas. But the resistance faced horrible problems—the difficulty of dropping enough food to supply the men was so great that some of the Mustang force had to boil their own shoes and eat the soft leather. And the bands of guerrillas inside the country often brought their families along on the campaigns, making them more vulnerable and far less mobile. When Richard Nixon began planning his diplomatic breakthrough with China, the message from the White House to the CIA was clear: end the Tibetan aid. The Americans knew—either because Mao told them or they could read tea leaves—that a rapprochement could never occur when the U.S. government was supporting the rebels. By 1971, the CIA had cut its lifeline to the guerrillas.

They did so honorably. They alotted 10,000 rupees for every one of the 1,500 fighters left in the Mustang region, to rehabilitate the rebels, buy them land, and open businesses in India. But the Khampas were devastated by the pullout. "They were incredibly disappointed in the whole outcome of things," says Knaus. "And understandably so. I'm sure there were those who had great expectations of us and our power."

One of those left distraught by the endgame in Tibet, and the efforts at dialogue by His Holiness, was Athar, the CIA-trained guerrilla who'd done so much to help him escape. Living in an Indian refugee camp near the end of his life, he was "cantankerous," angry at how things had turned out. "Peace, peace, what is this talk of peace?" he wanted to know. "Are the Chinese peaceful? I want to kill them." The guerrillas had expected to return to Tibet in triumph. When the Mustang rebels finally laid down their arms for good in 1974, several fighters committed suicide rather than give up their weapons.


Back in Lhasa, one Sera monk who'd joined the rebels was sentenced to ten years in prison, the "earth hell," as he calls it, for what he did during the uprising. Like so many of the survivors, he is not sorry for having taken up arms against the Chinese. "I have no regret regarding what I did," he says, pausing to add, "though I mounted up more demerits in my karmic account. The Chinese came to Tibet to capture our land and destroy the Dharma."

Palden Gyatso, a monk from Drepung who was arrested and spent thirty-three years in Chinese prisons and labor camps, would go on to write perhaps the most affecting memoir of the Chinese occupation. He would become, in a way, the Solzhenitsyn of Tibet. He wrote at the end of his memoir, *Fire Under the Snow*:

> Oppressors will always deny they are oppressors. All I can do is bear witness and set down what I saw and heard and what the strange journey of my life has been. Suffering is written now in the valleys and mountains of Tibet. Every village and monastery in the Land of Snows has its own stories of the cruelty inflicted on our people. And that suffering will go on until the day Tibet is free.

Yonten, the sixteen-year-old protester who had wanted to follow in his father's footsteps, was taken to the Ngachen labor camp.

His first day there, a Chinese official gave a speech, in which he called the Tibetans "barbaric cannibals" and "exploiters of the common people." Around Yonten were the men and women who'd played such a large part in the uprising: monks, lamas, the women who'd marched through Lhasa, daring the PLA to shoot them. The faces of the people that he'd remembered from that morning of March 10 when the uprising began, vivid with daring, now looked shell-shocked. The prisoners spent their days carrying rocks, drilling, and setting TNT charges as they helped build a dam as part of a huge hydroelectric project. When the sounds of explosions died off, the voices from the loudspeakers strategically placed around the camp could be heard talking about the motherland and sacrifice.

"I suffered a lot of pain, torture and was so terrified," he remembers. Prisoners were forced to compete against one another to see who could do the most work. Rockslides buried several Tibetan workers under tons of stone, and falling boulders came tumbling down the slopes into the work parties. Many prisoners were lost in a twilight of depression. "On the way to the toilet, we saw each other's pale faces and limbs and wondered whether there was any drop of blood left in our body," Yonten said. The Tibetans suffered the same fate as dissidents sent away during the Cultural Revolution: beatings, starvation, "reeducation sessions," torture (including being hung by their hair), forced confessions.

Four years into his sentence, Yonten learned that his father had died years earlier in a hard labor camp at Kansu, in China. "Many prisoners died from extreme hardship and starvation," he was told by a cook who'd been at Kansu. "Your father was among the first group of prisoners to die." Soon after, he was told that his older sister had also perished in another far-flung prison.

After his capture, Soepa, the Norbulingka official who'd

returned to deliver the Dalai Lama's letter, lay in a hospital, his damaged leg slowly growing infected. He began to dream of a returning army of Khampas and monks and Tibetan soldiers swinging into view through his window, back to smash the PLA and free the prisoners. "I mused that, for the moment, we had lost," he said. "But since the rest of our forces were on the other side of the river, I hoped they would be supported by international assistance, including India, and come back." Sometimes he would lift his head and look out his window, which faced the Kyichu River, to see if he could spot the troops arriving en masse. His neck began to cramp from his constant vigil. He wasn't the only one waiting for a miraculous return. In southern Tibet, a young Tibetan recalls the effect that a plane passing over his village during this period would have on the local people. "We used to bow down at once," the young man wrote, "and pray that it was His Holiness returning to us."

The Chinese began to interrogate Soepa. He recognized one of them. Soepa had regarded him as a rare Chinese friend, but now he realized the man had probably been a spy, assigned to report on his activities for the last five years.

Soepa told his interrogators that he hadn't done anything during the rebellion. He claimed to be a low-level servant in the Norbulingka, "in charge of the tea," and that he'd stayed at the summer palace only because he'd been unable to escape before the shooting began. The questioners asked about His Holiness's escape, but Soepa said he knew nothing at all about the matter. "If you don't cooperate," his interrogators threatened, "it will be easy to finish you off with a single shot." One of the officials unholstered his pistol and laid it on the table.

Soepa looked at the gun. He'd lost his fear of death inside the

Norbulingka, when it had eluded him despite a dogged pursuit. He left the gun where it was.

"You can kill me if you want to," he told them, "but I have nothing to say."

Soepa was taken to the Jiuquan labor camp. He soon saw a number of his fellow fighters begin to disintegrate under the harsh conditions—forced labor, constant interrogations, and *thamzins* in which prisoners were goaded into beating their fellow convicts. After one grueling session, Soepa found the Dalai Lama's personal physician on the veranda of the prison. He'd been thrashed so badly that he was unable to remove his bloody shirt, which was now rubbing against his open wounds and causing him fresh pain. Soepa tried to help him, but the man's torso had swollen so much from the beating that it was impossible. Finally, the younger man simply tore off the shirt. He could now see the doctor's back, "blue, black and reddish-brown from beating . . . it looked as if it would burst there and then."

Food was often scarce or inedible in the camps and prisons. Of the 76 men transported to Jiuquan with Soepa, only 22 lived. "All but one of the others, 53 men, died of starvation," he says. A military doctor captured by the Chinese remembers that he and the other Tibetan prisoners would scavenge for dried human excrement to eat, hoping a few nutrients remained. "We ate little balls of excrement as if we were eating those little pastry balls we make for the New Year," he says. "We chose Chinese shit rather than Tibetan shit because the Chinese were fed better!"

Prisoners began to break down, including one former cabinet minister who'd secretly asked Soepa if he thought escape was possible. When Soepa replied that the Chinese had at least three layers of security around the prison, the minister looked despondent—he'd been hoping to make it as far as the Kyichu River, where he could drown himself and begin an auspicious reincarnation. The man later cut himself in the head with a broken bottle and was led away by guards, screaming, "The Communist Party is lying!"

Soepa was sent from Lhasa to a Chinese prison. The day of his departure he remembered as the worst in his life. His family, hearing of his transfer, came to see him off. The Chinese warned the prisoners against saying anything remotely controversial to the visitors, so Soepa barely spoke to his loved ones. His mother "could not utter a single word and cried, holding my hand tightly in hers." The next morning, the prisoners were loaded into a line of idling Japanese-made trucks, painted oddly bright colors against the dun-colored winter hills. Thirty men and two guards went into each vehicle. "We were allowed neither to talk nor to look about," Soepa remembered. "As we left, my mind turned completely blank."

At the prison they were taken to, Soepa met a famous Tibetan intellectual, who told him that imprisonment had caused a change in the thinking among many rebels. They were now "openly accepting their roles in the uprising with the hopes of being pardoned." It was an alluring thought. Soepa gave in, telling the interrogators about his efforts in the battle for the Norbulingka, but withholding any information on his role in the escape. About that, he feigned complete ignorance. The Chinese questioner blew up at him, his face scarlet with anger, but Soepa insisted he didn't know a single detail. His allegiance to the Dalai Lama remained, stronger even than his sense of self-preservation.

The confession did no good. Soepa was transferred to a tougher prison, Chiu-chon, "a deserted and forlorn place with no other human habitations nearby." Here he mixed with hard-core Chinese criminals, pimps, thieves, and murderers serving life sentences and was forbidden to talk to his fellow Tibetans. A high-ranking PLA officer, marked by a harelip, would make sudden inspections carrying a thin metal wire. Without warning, he'd lash out with the homemade whip, slicing it across the faces and backs of the prisoners, cutting flesh to ribbons.

The Chinese ensured that the Tibetans were implicated in their own suffering. Soepa was forced to beat his fellow Tibetans in *thamzins*, and he watched formerly brave resistance fighters do the same. "[They] were so full of fear and suspicion that they lost their principles," he said. He even came across an official who, decades before, had journeyed through snowstorms and up stony paths to the far-flung province of Amdo as part of the search party for the Fourteenth Dalai Lama. When Soepa saw a prisoner in ragged clothing and with filthy knotted hair, he whispered to the official, "Look, here is a model of socialism." The man looked at him in terror. "Shut up!" he hissed. Soepa, looking at this Tibetan luminary now "scared beyond his wits," became despondent. The joy of the Fourteenth's discovery all those years before now seemed almost ludicrous, with the Dalai Lama driven into exile, unable to offer them even a word of comfort.

Soepa never told his interrogators the part he had played in the escape. But, secretly, he was proud of what he had done. "Before it, nobody knew of Tibet's existence," he says. "Now this unique, peaceful culture is felt in the world."

The total number of deaths in Tibet under Chinese rule is impossible to ascertain. The figure of 1.2 million, which has been commonly accepted by aid organizations and by the Tibetan government-in-exile, is almost certainly too high. The Tibet scholar Patrick French writes that 500,000 is probably the best available estimate. With a preinvasion population of 2.5 million in Tibet and its border areas, that translates into one death for every five Tibetans.

. . .

As more and more refugees poured into India in the spring of 1959, the world waited to meet the man who would lead them forward. As did Nehru. The last time they had met, the Indian prime minister had overawed the young Tibetan. But when the two leaders met after the escape, it was clear there'd been a change in the Dalai Lama. He was respectful, but firm in his demand that Tibet be free. As he made his case for Tibetan independence, Nehru grew furious, banging the table and yelling, "How can this be?" The Dalai Lama didn't relent. "I went on in spite of the growing evidence that he could be a bit of a bully." His Holiness set out two aims: the violence in Tibet had to stop, and Tibet had to be free. At that, Nehru exploded. "'That is not possible!' he said in a voice charged with emotion. . . . His lip quivered with anger as he spoke."

His Holiness stood fast. Nehru still regarded him—indeed, all the Tibetans—as naïve, and kept him and his ministers confined to their camp at Mussoorie, unable to even contact foreign governments. But when an American journalist remarked he "hadn't expected much" from the Dalai Lama, Nehru told him he was wrong. The young man, he said, "was extraordinary." He possessed "a kind of radiance."

Many observers initially dismissed the Dalai Lama. The man from *Reader's Digest* "snorted and said belligerently" that His Holiness was "a child." *Life* magazine thought he looked like a "nice boy." No one could predict the remarkable figure he was to cut in the world, the unique spiritual influence on modern life he was to become.

The most revealing look at the monk came when a young Indian poet got an assignment from *Harper's* magazine. Arriving at the Dalai Lama's hotel in Hyderabad months after the escape, he found "grim, black-robed elder lamas" guarding the entrance to His Holiness's rooms. The Dalai Lama's minders laid out the rules for the audience, in a conversation that could have taken place in 1750 or 1850: " 'Now, there are certain other things. Do not touch His Holiness. That is sacrilege. When the audience is terminated, do not turn your back on His Holiness. Leave the room backwards. Also, kindly do not ask His Holiness rude questions.'

" 'How do you mean, rude questions?'

" 'Do not ask His Holiness if he believes he is a god.' "

It was the protocol of the ancient Lhasa court. The poet was ushered into His Holiness's rooms and found a young man with nice skin and color in his cheeks. The Dalai Lama, immediately upon meeting him, began to disregard all the rules that his minders had laid out. He shook hands before the two sat on a long couch for the interview. He ignored his interpreter's warning when certain subjects were declared off-limits. In fact, he was so effusive and warm that the horrified poet, convinced he was committing a host of sins, retreated across the couch. The Dalai Lama cheerfully followed, making his points with a gentle tap on the poet's knee.

The politics of the interview are almost beside the point. His Holiness laid out the Tibetan position in strong, clear language and appealed for international help in regaining his country. But it is in his gestures that we are introduced to the figure the world would come to know. At the end of the interview:

> The Dalai Lama dropped his arm round my shoulders in a friendly gesture. I remembered what I had been told about not turning my back. I accordingly began to sidle out backward, crab-fashion. The Dalai Lama watched me

for a moment. Then he suddenly took a few steps forward, dropped his hands to my shoulders, and turned me around so that I faced the door. He gave me a friendly push to speed me on my way.

I heard his laugh behind me, for the last time.

These simple human gestures might seem small things, but for a Dalai Lama they were almost unthinkable, especially because they involved a foreigner, someone who in previous years could have been killed for simply entering Tibet. His Holiness would follow up this change in his personal style with more-profound alterations: a Tibetan constitution in 1961, a suggestion that future Dalai Lamas be religious figures only and their political power be given over to an elected representative, even the idea that the next incarnation could be a woman. He suggested that the Tibetan people could vote the Dalai Lama out of office. It was all, from the standpoint of Tibetan tradition, unimaginable. In exile, the Fourteenth modernized Tibetan culture in ways the Thirteenth could only have dreamt of.

The Dalai Lama today would be unrecognizable to a Tibetan of 1930, or 1850. For generations of Tibetans, Chenrizi was an occult figure, hidden behind bull-shouldered monks, an object of extreme reverence. When he arrived in the West, the Fourteenth shed traditions as one steps out of a suit of clothes. He made himself as ordinary and approachable as possible. He dispelled his own mysteries. Even today, a typical way for him to open a conference is to say, as he did in 2000: "Given the significance of this event, I would like to encourage everyone, for the space of these few days, to dispense with ostentatious posing and the empty formalities of ceremony. Let us try to get to the heart of the matter."

That all came later. Hemmed in by Nehru, who didn't want the

Tibetan issue publicized, the Dalai Lama wouldn't even be allowed to leave India until 1967. There were years of political intrigue and disappointment ahead. After Mao died in 1976, the new Chinese leader Deng Xiaoping offered to negotiate with the Dalai Lama on all issues except independence, but deep mistrust and political maneuvering spoiled any chance for progress. Politics continued to baffle and elude His Holiness.

But he was on his way to becoming a larger figure in the world. And the persona that the world would come to know was all present in that gesture of taking a flummoxed poet by the shoulders and turning him around.

Today the Dalai Lama lives in a compound atop the hills of Dharamsala, India, a mountain town dotted with the last survivors of the escape. Down the road, Yonten, who as a sixteen-year-old joined the protests in front of the summer palace, sits at a desk in the security department of the Tibetan government-in-exile. He's now a neatly dressed man of sixty-six, handsome, compact, and quick to smile. Fifty years after the revolt, and forty years after he left a Chinese jail where he'd been held for a decade, 1959 is still as alive to him as the afternoon heat. When he talks of his father, who died in an obscure Chinese labor camp, his head drops suddenly into his hands, and he weeps unreservedly.

One Sera monk who became a gunrunner during the uprising spends his days in a low-roofed hut at the bottom of a hill in Dharamsala, reading scriptures. An old woman shambles into the room and begins to make tea. "Nowadays, when I recall that time, I realize that the Chinese unified Tibet," the old monk says. "They brought us awake."

The Dalai Lama passes by the survivors every so often on his way out into the world, his golden palanquin now replaced by a brown Toyota. Crowds of believers, as well as monks, dreadlocked blond backpackers, and the Kashmiri traders, all wait by the side of the dusty road that will bring him to the airport, there to jet to Copenhagen, or Santa Barbara, or Sydney. The world is quite literally his home now, and he travels it in a never-ending service to the Dharma. As he passes in the Toyota, he smiles, that sudden, beautifully spontaneous smile, and waves. He is, by all appearances, a very happy man indeed. The backpackers, seeking an appropriate gesture of reverence at the last moment, bow their heads awkwardly.

But it's in person that one discovers why this monk has become such a significant figure in modern life. Grasping your hand, he seems completely entranced by you for the moment, interested beyond all reason in questions he's probably heard a hundred times. The Dalai Lama has a charm that leads deeper. But he isn't without flaws. The old childhood anger still flares occasionally. One Tibetan remembers His Holiness becoming absolutely furious when he met a group of former monks who'd abandoned their vows in exile. "He said that the Chinese were forcing monks to remove the robe in Tibet," the man says, "but here in India nobody was forcing us to take them off." The Dalai Lama chastised the men "very strongly."

His Holiness is nothing if not honest about how the escape was fortunate for him personally. "There is a Tibetan saying," he offers. "Wherever you find happiness, that is your home. Whoever shows kindness to you, they are your parents. So, as for me, I'm a homeless person who found a happy home." He knows he'd be a different man if he'd stayed in Tibet and suffered through the terrors of the Cultural Revolution, as the Panchen Lama was forced to. After accepting the nominal leadership of Tibet after His Holiness's escape, the Panchen Lama toured the country's border areas and sent a blistering letter to Mao in 1962 detailing the abuses committed by the Chinese in Tibet: the willful destruction of monasteries, the starving of rural people ("whole families dying out"), and even the "elimination of Buddhism" itself. The Tibetans have sometimes been prone to exaggerating Chinese atrocities; for a people raised on myths and legends, hard numbers and objective reporting sometimes give way to allegory. But these were things the Panchen Lama had seen and heard for himself. The letter was a suicidally brave gesture, and it earned the Panchen nothing but anguish. His missive was deemed "The Seventy-Thousand-Character Document of Reactionaries," and the Tibetan leader was *thamzined*—beaten and humiliated in front of throngs of cheering Red Guards—and placed under detention for fifteen years. It was a fulfillment, in a way, of the rumor that had swept through the streets of Lhasa in March 1959. The Tibetans had seen what awaited His Holiness if he'd stayed in Tibet. The Panchen Lama's life proved their premonition right.

The Dalai Lama still has nightmares about his escape. They are mixed in with more pleasant dreams. "A few days ago I had a dream about my return to Lhasa, wandering about . . . ," he said in 2003. When asked what the happiest moment in his life has been, he recalls the second day out of Lhasa, when flying down the far slope of Che-La and knowing he was free from the Chinese. And the saddest? Saying good-bye to his Khampa guards at the Indian border as they turned back into Tibet.

The escape changed him. "The refugee status brings a lot of positive opportunities," the Dalai Lama says. "Meeting with various different people from different levels of life. I really feel if I remained in the Potala, on the throne, the Dalai Lama would be a more holy person. But he would have less chance for talk, less experience. I really feel personally being outside has been a good opportunity."

Becoming famous—and famous as himself, not as an anti-Communist icon or Westernized guru—has been his only real weapon against the Chinese occupation. He is a movable Tibet. He is proof against Chinese fictions.

In leaving Tibet, the Dalai Lama gained an unprecedented personal liberty. From that moment on, freedom—not a traditional Buddhist subject of contemplation—became a subject he returned to again and again. And his words were given weight by the people he'd left behind. "Brute force . . . can never subdue the basic human desire for freedom," he would write years later. "It is not enough, as communist systems assumed, to provide people with food, shelter and clothing. If we have those things but lack the precious air of liberty to sustain our deeper nature, we remain only half human."

The escape also forced the Dalai Lama to think beyond Buddhism. "His exile was huge in his life," says Paul Jeffrey Hopkins, a Tibet scholar and former interpreter for His Holiness. "Without it, it would be very difficult for him to develop a message that is applicable to the entire world. Instead of becoming someone who's trying to drive Buddhism forward, he's attempting to call to everybody in society and thus address their need for kindness and compassion. There would be no way for that to develop had he remained in Tibet."

He has not escaped the bitter truths of his faith. Every refugee arriving in Dharamsala is granted an interview with His Holiness; it's a policy unchanged since 1959. This means His Holiness has consoled thousands of men and women, bewildered, wounded people with stories of persecution and loss. One story from thousands: The father of Norbu Dhondup, who had castrated himself after being humiliated in a *thamzin*, spent twenty years in a Chinese prison before being released and allowed to travel to Lhasa. Norbu, at sixty-five, with little money and no connections, made the trip from India to see him. When he walked into the old folks' home in Lhasa where his father was staying, the two didn't recognize each other. "It had been so many years," Norbu says. "He hugged me and I cried." Norbu's father got down to practical matters, asking him, "How do you live in India? What type of house do you have? Do you have cows?" The older man's mind had clearly been affected by the decades in a Chinese prison, so that he seemed to have erased, or was unable to recall, the years spent there. And Norbu couldn't find the words to ask him.

Father and son left by bus for Nepal, where the crossing out of Tibet was easiest, to a place called Dam, near the border. The roads ahead were bad and there were no vehicles that would risk them, so Norbu was forced to carry his elderly father on his back. From Nepal they took a bus to India. Norbu's father had one wish he wanted fulfilled before he died: to see His Holiness. Faith in the Dalai Lama had sustained him in the long years in prison. Finally, after weeks of trying, a meeting was arranged. Norbu stayed outside while his father went to speak to the Dalai Lama. "When he came out," he remembers, "he was crying so much that he was speechless."

The meetings are private, but they give weight to everything His Holiness does. His encounters with suffering and death animate the Dalai Lama's message to the world: compassion is, finally, strength. "When, at some point in our lives, we meet a real tragedy," he said, "which can happen to any one of us, we can react in two ways. Obviously, we can lose hope, let ourselves slip into discouragement, into alcohol, drugs, unending sadness. Or else we can wake ourselves up, discover in ourselves an energy that was hidden there, and act with more clarity, more force."

Buddhists believe the Dalai Lama perfected his gift for compassion in the course of many incarnations. Unbelievers may question that. But he has, at least in this lifetime, exemplified the virtue.

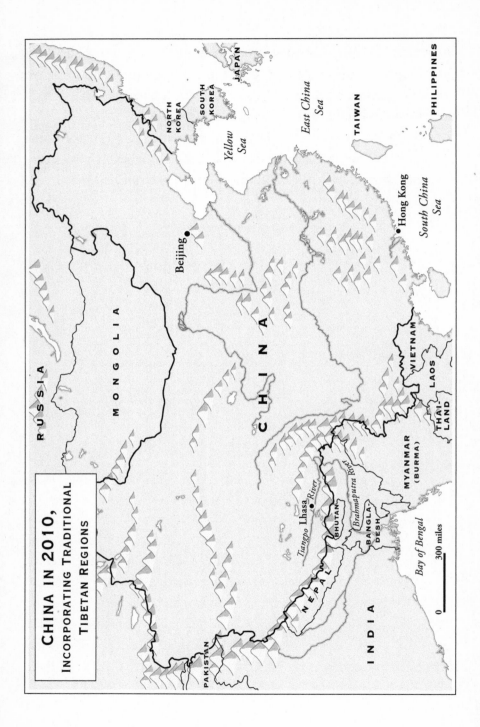

CHINA IN 2010,
INCORPORATING TRADITIONAL
TIBETAN REGIONS

RUSSIA

MONGOLIA

C H I N A

NORTH
KOREA

SOUTH
KOREA

JAPAN

Yellow
Sea

East China
Sea

TAIWAN

Beijing

Hong Kong

South China
Sea

PHILIPPINES

VIETNAM

LAOS

THAI-
LAND

MYANMAR
(BURMA)

BANGLA-
DESH

Brahmaputra River

BHUTAN

Lhasa

Tsangpo River

NEPAL

INDIA

PAKISTAN

Bay of Bengal

0        300 miles

# BONFIRES

*T*he first thing I noticed were the shotguns. Slim, blunt-nosed shotguns, being carried by patrols of PLA troops as they swaggered through the streets of Lhasa. The guns looked like deadly black eels nestled on the shoulders of the young soldiers. The weapons seemed out of place among the picturesque alleys full of traders and Buddhist pilgrims.

It was February 2009. I was in Tibet fifty years after the Dalai Lama had escaped over the Kyichu, a clear cold stream filled with snowmelt that comes up to one's knees. The city itself had changed a great deal. The landmarks of the events of 1959 were still there:

the Norbulingka, now open to tourists for a small admission fee; the Jokhang; the cobblestoned streets of the old city where Tibetan rebels had fallen. But over them had been laid a twenty-first-century metropolis, a Chinese city that now dominates the centuries-old Tibetan one. And, as the anniversary of the uprising approached, the city was under something approaching martial law.

But why *shotguns*?

In the big public squares, where the distances are greater and the firing angles more open, the PLA troops carried automatic rifles, which were almost comforting to see. In the post-9/11 world, they are everywhere: carried by American soldiers in Penn Station and British marines at Heathrow. These days, an automatic rifle in a public place isn't so much an actual gun as it is a prop in a ritual. The world's ugliest and most-capable-looking guns are paraded through city squares, so that people might feel safe. Lhasa was no different.

But what message were the Chinese sending with the shotguns, which are far less menacing, less recognizable tools to intimidate terrorists than UZIs or M16s? It took me a couple of days to realize that I was being too abstract. This was not theater. Shotguns were the best weapon for shooting Tibetans in the narrow alleys of the old city should another uprising be touched off fifty years after the last one. That was the message.

I'd spent weeks arranging the trip, while the Chinese issued a blizzard of restrictions as the anniversary drew closer. No journalists were allowed in. Two reporters were kicked out weeks before I'd arrived. (I'd listed myself as "Salesman" on my Chinese visa to avoid the same fate.) No individual travel—all visitors had to be part of a tour. No travel to the western provinces of Tibet.

The authorities were desperately trying to avoid a repeat of

2008's protests, when 239 people were killed (19 Chinese and 220 Tibetans, according to the Tibetan government-in-exile), 1,300 were injured, and nearly 7,000 were taken into custody or thrown in jail. To the Chinese, the startling thing about the wave of protests was that it was centered in the rural regions, among nomads and farmers who attacked police stations and raised the Tibetan flag. China had poured money into the regional towns that dot the Tibetan plateau and created a new native middle class. The Chinese felt they'd won hearts and minds in those places. But peasants, farmers, and monks had largely missed the influx of new money, and they deplored the laws outlawing Tibetan flags and even the most innocent displays of cultural pride. "Even the high-ranking Tibetan cadres in the Communist Party were *furious* with Beijing," says Professor Gray Tuttle. "They're strong nationalists, even though they're making Shanghai-level salaries. And the level of respect for the Dalai Lama is incredible."

The swell of anger astonished the Chinese. And the recent independence movements in places such as Ukraine and Georgia shocked the Communist Party into a newly paranoid view of nationalist sentiments.

But Lhasa would always be the focal point during the anniversary of the 1959 uprising. Anniversaries of key political events have always been important in Chinese history. Grievances spill out. In Tibet, March 2009 was the biggest anniversary of all.

I was in Chengdu when the Chinese issued another edict: no *injis* (Tibetan for "foreigners") after February 28. I'd be one of the last to get in.

The final requirement was to have an English-speaking guide. When I finally arrived in Tibet, I met Sharma, a slim, short, sad-eyed Tibetan who'd been guiding for several years. Sharma was dead silent during the hour's ride from the airport, avoiding the inane chitchat that most guides engage in to fatten their tip. It was a little unsettling.

When he dropped me at my hotel, Sharma left me with a warning.

"You can't photograph police or army in the city," he announced.

"Why not?" I asked.

His eyes widened, as if to say, *What kind of question is that?*

"It is forbidden."

I already knew it was unhealthy to talk to Tibetans—for them, not for me. The Chinese bureaucrats who ran Tibet—the United Front Department of the Chinese Communist Party—had been on edge since the 2008 protests. Any Tibetan who ran onto a Lhasa street waving the Tibetan flag would be shot on sight. (One of the tragedies of the aggressive policies coming out of Beijing since the mid-1990s is that every display of pride in Tibet is taken as a sign of dissent, which it may or may not be.) And locals who talked about the political situation with Westerners could end up in jail. I'd heard rumors that there were cameras and microphones secreted everywhere in the main tourist areas of Lhasa. "You have to pretend that you have this contagious disease," one Tibetan activist told me. "And anyone you talk to will immediately catch it."

But as I walked through the streets the first day, where the protesters had swept "two turns around" that first night in March 1959, I noticed that it was easy to fall into conversations with Tibetans. Traders called me over to their carts and tried to sell me jade necklaces at exorbitant prices. One merchant fell off his stool, and when I helped him back up, he grabbed my hands and thanked me in broken English. There were tiny gaps in the surveillance that—if I stayed away from the microphones and kept the conversations brief—could give me a chance to talk to Tibetans.

The city looked prosperous and clean, if militarized to an

almost absurd level—a mashup of Pyongyang and Shanghai. There were shops selling Nikes and flat-screen TVs, an Audi dealership next to the one peddling BMWs. Someone is getting very rich off this occupation, and some of them are Tibetans.

The Chinese have unquestionably done good things in Tibet. They've poured billions into the country, built infrastructure that could sustain growth, especially in mineral extraction and agriculture, for years. They've curbed the worst abuses of the monastic system (the monasteries survive now only by private donations). "We are helping Tibet catch up with the West," writes the Chinese scholar Ma Lihua, who's lived in Tibet and traveled there extensively. "It is not 'Hanification' but globalization. I'm not saying this because I simply accept government propaganda, but because I have seen improvements in Tibet with my own eyes." The Chinese today simply aren't the monolithic villains that some in the pro-independence movement paint them as, nor are they intent on wiping out Tibetan culture by diktat. But the policy struggle that was going on in 1950 between those who favor engaging the Tibetans and those who want to violently suppress them, is still being played out in Beijing, and there are competing cliques, each with their own personalities and bureaucrats and career considerations. For more than a decade, the hard-liners have been winning, and it shows in Lhasa. To see the capital on the fiftieth anniversary of the Dalai Lama's escape was to see the Chinese administration there at its most paranoid and hostile, so over-the-top it almost seemed a parody of a police state. It was the hard-line style in its full dark bloom: the shiny black boots of the PLA everywhere you looked, like weeds.

The visual landscape kept pulling me toward March 1959. Just as it was fifty years before, the city was filled with pilgrims, nomads, and farmers who'd come to Lhasa for the Buddhist equivalent of

doing the hajj to Mecca. The black-eyed nomads looked like they'd
arrived from the fourteenth century, with their wild-haired kids
strung around their backs and their windburned faces that spoke of
Tibet's vast, rugged interior. But there were also teenagers wearing
the latest slim jeans and trucker hats with odd slogans (my favorite being "I HEART STAGE," apparently worn by a theater lover).
Modernity—and modern vice—is here in Lhasa, if cleverly disguised.
The city has, for example, an unbelievable number of hair salons,
which makes no sense until you realize that many of them are actually
whorehouses, staffed mostly by native girls who service the thousands
of Chinese soldiers stationed in the Tibetan capital.

The first afternoon, Sharma and I walked to see the Jokhang
Temple, the place from which Narkyid, the young monk in charge
of the temple, had gazed down on the innocent-looking Chinese
soldiers before the gunfire began. As we strolled through the courtyards, Sharma walked over to talk to another guide and pulled out a
pack of cigarettes. Most of the guides were Tibetan, I noticed, which
was a very smart move on the part of the Chinese. If a Westerner
did something stupid, his guide could be penalized or even thrown
in jail. On arrival, every *inji* was given his very own hostage.

I stood at the place from which Narkyid had watched the
Chinese polish their rifles. There were six soldiers within view.

After seeing the temple's interior, I walked up to Sharma. The
other guide saw me coming and hurried off. Sharma turned to me
with a worried look on his face.

"I have news," he said. "I must stay at the hotel with you. And
you cannot leave it without me."

"What," I said, looking at him in horror, "are you talking about?" The last thing I wanted was Sharma tailing me every
minute.

"It is a new rule," he answered. "It is getting very strict."

I protested, but Sharma assured me that this was the latest order from the Chinese government. It covered all Westerners in Lhasa.

"Please do not leave the hotel without me," he repeated. "I will get in trouble."

We rushed back to the hotel, where I sent an e-mail to the fixer in Chengdu who'd arranged my trip. "I am very sorry," she wrote back. "This has never happened before."

I was stuck with Sharma full-time.

I heard chanting from outside my window. I looked out and saw that next door was an army camp, built in an old sports stadium. Recruits were running around the track carrying heavy sacks over their shoulders. They were, presumably, practicing carrying wounded colleagues to safety.

The next day, security had been notched up in the old town. Soldiers stood on the rooftops of the two-story buildings with walkie-talkies, and tear-gas guns, and rifles. Some had binoculars—I looked up and noticed one soldier looking directly at me with a bug-eyed pair.

Figuring it was too dangerous to talk to a Tibetan with Sharma around, I told him to ask one of our Chinese taxi drivers how he liked Lhasa.

"What? How does he like Lhasa?"

"Yes," I said. "Ask the driver that."

"Him?" Sharma said. "No, you don't understand. He isn't a local. They come here on ten-month contracts and then they leave."

That was interesting. I knew that many Lhasans deeply resented the Han migrants who had arrived in the city since Beijing had adopted a rapid economic development policy focused on revving up the Tibetan economy without, many Tibetans felt, investing in things such as the education of locals. But I hadn't heard that some of these entrepreneurs were here for only ten months. "Please ask him anyway," I insisted.

Sharma turned in the front passenger seat to stare at me full in the face. Then he turned around and stared out the front window. He refused to talk to me for the rest of the ride.

Not only could I not talk to Tibetans, now Chinese were out as well. We were reaching North Korean levels of irrationality. Soon silence became Sharma's way of dealing with me. If I asked an inconvenient question, he simply tuned me out.

I began to resent him. Sharma was a stooge, I decided. My guide was enforcing bans *that didn't even exist.*

Still, I had to use him to see Lhasa. The next morning, we trekked out to Drepung Monastery.

In 1959, the three monasteries that ring the perimeter of Lhasa had played a major role in the uprising. Since then, monks had been the leaders of the sporadic anti-Chinese protests that flare up in Tibet. Three days after I left Tibet, a monk from Kirti Monastery would set himself on fire—and then be shot at by Chinese troops. I wanted to see how the monks were faring as the crackdown intensified.

We took a taxi to the monastery at the foot of Mount Gephel, one of the low mountains that ring Lhasa. Drepung at one time housed as many as 10,000 monks. It was one of the great centers of Buddhist learning, the Harvard of Tibet. It should have been teeming with earnest young men.

But the place seemed deserted. A handful of Chinese tourists and Tibetan pilgrims wandered around, poking into the tiny chambers while their guides droned on.

Sharma cleared up the mystery. "Since 1959," he told me, "only five hundred monks have been allowed to stay here." Many others, perhaps hundreds, I later learned, were being kept in military detention camps in neighboring Qinghai province.

The Chinese had drained the swamp, stripping Drepung and the other monasteries of all but a token number of monks. That action was part of a religious crackdown that included a ban on practicing Buddhism in the towns, in force since the mid-1990s. The ban was decided upon at a meeting of the Chinese Communist Party on Tibet policy in which the hard-liners inside the party, who have always favored an aggressive approach of crackdowns and religious bans, reinvigorated their attacks on the Dalai Lama and on Buddhism itself.

The monasteries had been turned into sad museums. I noticed that even the chapels had been wired with surveillance cameras.

In the main chapel, I noticed something peculiar hanging on one of the red pillars.

"What's that?" I asked.

Sharma looked up. "Oh," he said, "it's a suit of armor."

It was tiny, made up of square pieces of thin metal. A shield hung next to it, with a quiver filled with arrows on one side and a bow on the other.

"After killing many enemy, warriors would come here," Sharma explained, "and ask for forgiveness for their sinfulness." Fighters came to the monks to repent for the blood they'd spilled. It was called "following the white path of peace."

The warriors' act of renunciation seemed to illustrate Tibet's dilemma. From a land of warriors, Tibet had over centuries become a huge open-air monastery. The Tibetans just didn't seem equipped for the viciousness of the world they lived in.

Sharma, at least, was skilled at psy-ops. He had me studying his every move in excruciating detail. One high point came when we were having dinner and he got a call on his cell phone. Sharma ran into the street to talk out of earshot.

"What is he doing that for?" I said to the empty seat. "I don't even speak Chinese." I began to share, in the tiniest sliver, the paranoia of a Tibetan living under Chinese rule. I wondered what I'd done to tip the military off. Was it taking notes at the Jokhang Temple? Or that e-mail I'd sent to a friend back home?

We headed back to Barkhor Square. I wanted to try getting some pictures of soldiers with my digital camera. We walked the streets, and I fell behind Sharma. As a patrol passed, I held the camera by my side and clicked off a few shots.

I looked at the screen. Pictures of legs in green wool. I'd have to find a better way.

We sat on the railings that ran the edge of the square, and I waited. I noticed a PLA squad patrolling the square. I placed the camera on my thigh and pretended to be looking at the crowd.

Out of the corner of my eye, I saw the soldiers approach. I got ready to shoot.

But just then, three young Tibetan boys came tumbling into the square, laughing uproariously. The lead boy stumbled into the middle of the patrol. In an instant, the lead soldier was on him, screaming in Chinese and pulling the terrified child by his sweater until his feet almost left the ground.

It was ugly, the occupation in miniature. The leader released the boy, and he ran off, his face twisted with fear.

I was about to turn the camera to catch the patrol reorganizing when three policemen in blue uniforms came up to Sharma and me. The oldest, with a pockmarked face, barked something to Sharma, and he instantly hopped off the railing. "We have to go," he said quietly.

Had the PLA spotters on the roofs noticed me? I decided the surveillance in Lhasa was very, very good.

In town, the army's presence had become almost claustrophobic. There were patrols on every block. Some troops now wore helmets and bulletproof vests, and I saw two gray vans converted into armored vehicles, with blue and red lights on top and three gun ports on each side. From what I could tell, they were circling the city endlessly.

As we headed back to our hotel, I slipped my camera out of my pocket and pointed it at the gray vans. One of the Chinese drivers—who I later realized must have been watching me in the rearview mirror—turned violently and nearly drove his vehicle into oncoming traffic. I slipped the camera back into my pocket.


The next day we headed to the Potala, the stunning winter palace of the Dalai Lama. Opposite it, the authorities had built a beautifully landscaped park with one of those statues one sees everywhere in China where workers and hammers and sheaves of wheat soar toward the heavens. By the park's reflecting pool, women were cleaning their hands and faces and then prostrating themselves. They clasped their hands together and then dropped to the pavement, facing the empty palace.

Sharma was distracted, having a smoke. I sidled up to a middle-aged Tibetan man in a brown coat, nodded, and asked what the women were doing.

"They're praying to the Dalai Lama," he said.

It was strangely thrilling to hear the name of the public enemy uttered in public.

"So they haven't forgotten him?" I asked.

He turned to me. "No, they haven't forgotten him." Then he moved off nervously.

Everything I saw around me confirmed what the man said. In Lhasa, young men did circuits around the Jokhang Temple, throwing themselves to the ground in devotion. Tibetans of every age thronged to the holy places, old nomad women bent double but still climbing to see where the Dalai Lama had slept. There was a palpable devotion here that's been missing from Western countries for so long that it was almost a physical shock to witness it. Footage smuggled out of Tibet by businessman-turned-documentarian Dhondup Wangchen (later arrested and now serving a six-year prison sentence) showed nomads crying at a video of His Holiness, with one telling the camera, "For the Dalai Lama to come back is my greatest wish and dream. . . . I only have to hear his name and I am filled with faith, devotion, and a deep, deep sadness."

"There's no question that his legend is tremendous inside Tibet," says Paul Jeffrey Hopkins, the Tibetan scholar. "So many of the people there have one wish: to see His Holiness before they die."

Lhasa exists around an absence. The Chinese have outlawed anything to do with the Fourteenth Dalai Lama—books, photographs, everything. But everywhere I looked, men and women were bowing and praying to him as if he had never left. The irony is that Tibet had for centuries been kept secret by the Tibetans. Now it is again off-limits, secluded in a new and more menacing way by its occupiers.

And spending more time with Sharma, I began to see him differently. Walking around Lhasa with him was, in some ways, like walking around Tuscaloosa, Alabama, with a black man in 1954. When he talked with other Tibetans, his voice was normal. He even snapped at our local driver for forgetting his driver's license—you do not, apparently, want to be a Tibetan caught on the roads without proper ID. But when he spoke to a Chinese, any Chinese person, his voice and his posture underwent a sickening transformation. His face took on a worried, almost pleading look. He seemed to shrink inside himself. His voice became hesitant and soft, question marks floating up at the end of all his sentences. The nerve endings in his face seemed to go dead, as if his unrehearsed self was too dangerous to display.

And the Chinese often treated him as if he were an unpleasant fact of living in Tibet. Businessmen cut in front of him in lines. Clerks angrily waved him away when he tried to ask a question, only to look up attentively at the next Chinese customer. Sharma took it all as meekly as a lamb. *In his own country,* I thought.

I was coming to the end of my trip, but I had to see the Norbulingka. As we drove to the site, I remembered what had happened on this road fifty years ago, sixteen-year-old Yonten and the masses of Tibetans running toward the palace and everything that followed that wild, unscripted moment. That cycle—oppression, protest, crackdown, casualties—had repeated endlessly ever since.

When he first saw the plains outside Lhasa, the landscape shocked the young Choegyal because it looked so much like Palestine, "arid and flat." And soon after the escape, Tibet was grouped with the Middle East as one of the earth's insoluble, god-forsaken messes. But what the Tibetans want—autonomy, the Dalai Lama to return, respect and support for Tibetan religion and culture—isn't particularly exotic in Chinese terms. Most of the people in Mongolia or Shanghai get much the same already, not abstract freedom but a practical one, so long as they don't challenge the Communist Party. Freedom of religion is written into the Chinese constitution; it isn't an alien concept here at all.

Tibetans tell jokes about their odd status. One goes like this: The Dalai Lama is pushing for "one country, two systems"—for Tibet to remain within China but to be governed differently—while ordinary Tibetans themselves want "one country, one system." That is, they just want what everyone else in China has. And, of course, to see His Holiness.

When we got to the Norbulingka, I was astonished to see that the open square in front of the palace where the 1959 protests had begun was now a park cut into an intricate pattern of small hillocks and ponds. The park was exquisitely crafted, but obviously a mass rally would be impossible here. What looked like a gift to the Tibetan people had the added bonus of keeping them from rioting.

We walked along the yellow-and-red walls where so many Tibetan rebels had died. As we passed through the groves of poplar and bamboo trees that shade the Norbulingka's grounds, I saw a young, thin Tibetan man walking to our left. Sharma was on the phone again. I let him walk ahead and fell in stride with the Tibetan. I couldn't see any cameras or microphones in the grove of poplars that surrounded us.

I nodded. "Hello?" the man said. "English?"

I pretended to look at the trees and ask questions about them. But we talked about the situation in Lhasa. As I walked alongside the young man, I mentioned the troops in Lhasa, the rising tension. The man nodded. "They're worried there's going to be trouble," he acknowledged. "It's worse than it's ever been."

I nodded. "What about the Dalai Lama?"

"We want the Dalai Lama to return," the man said, smiling slightly, his voice ragged with emotion. "But sometimes it seems hopeless." Many old farmers and nomads couldn't afford the visas that would let them travel to India, he told me; their last wish was to see the Dalai Lama, but they would die without looking on his face. A Westerner must imagine the spirit of Christ alive somewhere in the world, and a Christian unable to go and see and be touched by him, to really get a sense of what Tibetans feel, the almost physical pain the separation causes them. Not to see the face of their Precious Protector is like passing through life as a restless ghost.

I looked ahead of us. Sharma had pocketed his cell phone and was waiting. I nodded to the man and hurried to catch up with my guide.

That night, Sharma and I went out for Losar, the Tibetan New Year. It seemed that Lhasans were intent on ushering in the Year of the Female Earth Ox by burning their city to the ground. There was fire everywhere. Girls ran by with torches lit with thick flames, sending a brief wave of heat across our faces as they dashed down the alleys. Roman candles shot up from street corners where people, reduced to slim silhouettes in the darkness, stood by boxes packed with what looked like every firework known to man. Enormous bonfires burned in the middle of the streets, and young men ran up to them and tossed in fistfuls of fireworks, which exploded in an earsplitting roar as the men danced into and then away from the flames.

Glowing beneath the dark dome of sky, the city felt alluring, incendiary, free. The people were smiling, and hawkers were selling sweets. But this was a party, not an insurrection. The Chinese troops, some of them wearing white dust masks, ghostly in the gloom, followed behind the young men who were spiking the bonfires, dutifully putting out the flames with brooms and shovels as the clock ticked toward midnight, like conscientious parents making sure the house didn't go up in a blaze.

Tibetans, their faces happy and entranced, watched the orange flames as they licked the night air and fell back. Sharma and I walked the Barkhor, circling the darkened Jokhang. For a few hours Lhasa seemed transformed. It was for a moment no longer an occupied capital with an empty throne sitting at its heart.

Sharma and I walked in silence. There was nothing to say that could be said.

# GLOSSARY

**amban:** A representative of the Chinese emperor.

**bodhisattva:** A person who has attained complete enlightenment but postpones Nirvana in order to help others obtain liberation from suffering.

**Chenrizi:** The *bodhisattva* of Infinite Compassion, the deity whom each Dalai Lama manifests in human form.

**choe-ra:** A common area in a Tibetan monastery where teaching was often conducted.

**chuba:** A long sheepskin coat made of Tibetan wool; a common outer garment worn by Tibetans.

**Dharma:** The body of teachings expounded by Buddha; the essential doctrines and practices of Buddhism.

**dob-dob:** One of the Dalai Lama's bodyguards.

**dzo:** A Tibetan hybrid of a yak and a cow.

**geshe:** An advanced degree earned by a Tibetan monk.

**kalön:** A *Kashag* member; a cabinet minister.

**Kashag:** The Tibetan cabinet, or council of advisers.

**kata:** A white ceremonial greeting scarf.

**Khampa:** A Tibetan from the eastern region of Kham.

**kora:** A walking pilgrimage, often around a Tibetan holy site such as a temple or *stupa*.

**lama:** A Buddhist teacher.

**miser:** Depending on the context, either a Tibetan serf or a citizen of Tibet. Used here in the former sense.

**Mönlam:** Mönlam Chemmo, the Great Prayer Festival, held annually in Lhasa at the beginning of the first Tibetan lunar month.

**palanquin:** A covered sedan chair carried by teams of men.

**stupa:** A structure containing Buddhist relics or the remains of a *bodhisattva* or other revered person; a burial tomb.

**Tendra:** An enemy of the Buddhist faith.

**thamzin:** A "struggle session" orchestrated by the Chinese authorities, designed to humiliate and persecute perceived "rightists" and "splittists."

**Three Great Seats:** The three most important monasteries in Tibet—Ganden, Sera, and Drepung.

**tsampa:** The basic Tibetan staple, a dough made of parched barley flour.

# BIBLIOGRAPHY

Avedon, John F. *In Exile from the Land of Snows*. New York: Vintage, 1986.

Barber, Noel. *The Flight of the Dalai Lama*. London: Hodder & Stoughton, 1960.

———. *From the Land of Lost Content*. Boston: Houghton Mifflin, 1969.

Chang, Jung, and Jon Halliday. *Mao: The Unknown Story*. New York: Knopf, 2005.

Chhaya, Mayank. *Dalai Lama: Man, Monk, Mystic*. New York: Doubleday, 2007.

Craig, Mary. *Kundun: A Biography of the Family of the Dalai Lama*. Washington, D.C.: Counterpoint, 1997.

Dalai Lama. *Essential Writings*. Maryknoll, N.Y.: Orbis Books, 2008.

———. *Freedom in Exile*. San Francisco: HarperSanFrancisco, 1990.

———. *In My Own Words: An Introduction to My Teachings and Philosophy*. Carlsbad, Calif.: Hay House, 2008.

———. *My Land and My People*. New York: Potala Corporation, 1985.

# BIBLIOGRAPHY

Dalai Lama and Jean-Claude Carrière. *Violence and Compassion: Dialogues on Life Today.* New York: Doubleday, 1995.

Dewatshang, Kunga Samten. *Flight at the Cuckoo's Behest.* New Delhi, India: Paljor Publications, 1997.

Dunham, Mikel. *Buddha's Warriors: The Story of the CIA-Backed Tibetan Freedom Fighters, the Chinese Invasion, and the Ultimate Fall of Tibet.* New York: Jeremy P. Tarcher/Penguin, 2004.

Edwards, Ruth Dudley. *Newspapermen: Hugh Cudlipp, Cecil Harmsworth King and the Glory Days of Fleet Street.* London: Secker & Warburg, 2003.

Feigon, Lee. *Demystifying Tibet.* Chicago: Ivan R. Dee, 1996.

French, Patrick. *Tibet, Tibet: A Personal History of a Lost Land.* New York: Knopf, 2003.

Goldstein, Melvyn C. *A History of Modern Tibet.* Vol. 1: *The Demise of the Lamaist State, 1913–1951.* Vol. 2: *The Calm Before the Storm, 1951–1955.* Berkeley: University of California Press, 1989, 2009.

Goodman, Michael Harris. *The Last Dalai Lama: A Biography.* Boston: Shambhala, 1987.

Gyatso, Palden. *Fire Under the Snow.* London: Harvill Press, 1998.

Harrer, Heinrich. *Seven Years in Tibet.* New York: Jeremy P. Tarcher/Putnam, 1996.

Hopkirk, Peter. *Trespassers on the Roof of the World.* New York: Kodansha International, 1995.

Hutheesing, Raja. *Tibet Fights for Freedom.* Bombay, India: Orient Longmans, 1960.

Iyer, Pico. *The Open Road: The Global Journey of the Fourteenth Dalai Lama.* New York: Knopf, 2008.

Khetsun, Tubten. *Memories of Life in Lhasa Under Chinese Rule.* New York: Columbia University Press, 2008.

Knaus, John Kenneth. *Orphans of the Cold War: America and the Tibetan Struggle for Survival.* New York: PublicAffairs, 1999.

Laird, Thomas. *The Story of Tibet: Conversations with the Dalai Lama.* New York: Grove Press, 2006.

Levenson, Claude. *The Dalai Lama.* London: Unwin Hyman, 1988.

———. *Tenzin Gyatso: The Early Life of the Dalai Lama.* Berkeley, Calif.: North Atlantic Books, 2002.

Ling, Nai-Min. *Tibet 1950–1967.* Hong Kong: Union Research Institute, 1968.

MacFarquhar, Roderick, Eugene Wu, and Timothy Cheek, eds. *The Secret Speeches of Chairman Mao.* Cambridge, Mass.: Harvard University Asia Center, 1989.

McCarthy, Roger. *Tears of the Lotus: Accounts of Tibetan Resistance to the Chinese Invasion, 1950–1962.* Jefferson, N.C.: McFarland, 1997.

Norbu, Dawa. *China's Tibet Policy.* New York: Routledge, 2001.

———. *Red Star over Tibet.* New York: Envoy Press, 1987.

———. *Tibet: The Road Ahead.* London: Rider, 1997.

Norbu, Thubten Jigme, and Heinrich Harrer. *Tibet Is My Country.* London: Rupert Hart-Davis, 1960.

Norbu, Thubten Jigme, and Colin Turnbull. *Tibet.* New York: Simon & Schuster, 1968.

Patt, David. *A Strange Liberation: Tibetan Lives in Chinese Hands.* Ithaca, N.Y.: Snow Lion Publications, 1992.

Patterson, George. *Journey with Loshay.* New York: W. W. Norton & Company, 1954.

———. *Patterson of Tibet.* San Diego, Calif.: ProMotion Publishing, 1998.

———. *Requiem for Tibet.* London: Aurum Press, 1990.

———. *Tibet in Revolt.* London: Faber & Faber, 1960.

Peissel, Michel. *Cavaliers of Kham: The Secret War in Tibet.* London: Heinemann, 1972.

Petech, Luciano. *China and Tibet in the Early Eighteenth Century: History of the Establishment of the Chinese Protectorate in Tibet,* 2nd ed. Leiden, Neth.: Brill, 1972.

Powers, John. *Introduction to Tibetan Buddhism,* rev. ed. Ithaca, N.Y.: Snow Lion Publications, 2007.

Prados, John. *Presidents' Secret Wars.* New York: William Morrow, 1986.

Roberts, John B., II, and Elizabeth A. Roberts. *Freeing Tibet.* New York: AMACOM, 2009.

Shakya, Tsering. *The Dragon in the Land of Snows: A History of Modern Tibet Since 1947.* New York: Columbia University Press, 1999.

Smith, Warren W., Jr. *Tibetan Nation: A History of Tibetan Nationalism and Sino-Tibetan Relations.* New York: HarperCollins, 1997.

Soepa, Tenpa. *20 Years of My Life in China's Death Camp.* Bloomington, Ind.: AuthorHouse, 2008.

Strober, Deborah Hart, and Gerald S. Strober. *His Holiness the Dalai Lama: The Oral Biography.* Hoboken, N.J.: John Wiley & Sons, 2005.

Strong, Anna Louise. *Tibetan Interviews.* Peking: New World Press, 1959.

———. *When Serfs Stood Up in Tibet.* Peking: New World Press, 1965.

Taring, Rinchen Dolma. *Daughter of Tibet.* London: John Murray, 1970.

Thomas, Evan. *The Very Best Men: The Daring Early Years of the CIA.* New York: Simon & Schuster, 2006.

Thurman, Robert, A. F. *Essential Tibetan Buddhism.* San Francisco: HarperSanFrancisco, 1995.

Tsering, Diki. *Dalai Lama, My Son.* London: Penguin, 2001.

Yonten, Lobsang. *The Fire of Hell.* Kathmandu, Nepal: Pilgrim Books, 2008.

Younghusband, Sir Francis. *India and Tibet.* London: John Murray, 1910.

# NOTES

## *Introduction*

2 "dizzying, frightening blur": Dalai Lama, *Freedom*, p. 135.

2 "between two volcanoes": Dalai Lama, *My Land*, p. 172.

3 "They were almost": Dalai Lama, *Freedom*, p. 124.

3 "I feared a massive, violent reprisal": Ibid., p. 117.

3 "There was an unforgettable scent": Dalai Lama, *My Land*, p. 33.

4 "driven into barbarism": Ibid., p. 137.

4 Some 40,000 Chinese troops: Dunham, p. 264.


## *One*
## AN EXAMINATION OF PRIOR MEMORIES

7 Details of the death of the Thirteenth Dalai Lama and the search for the Fourteenth are drawn from the Dalai Lama's two memoirs, from Goodman, and from Avedon.

9 "everywhere else is to be feared": Gyatso, p. 13.

14 "In 1950": The population figures are from French, pp. 278–79.

16 "'Good,' he said": quoted in Avedon, p. 9.

16 "Clear springs": Dalai Lama, *My Land*, p. 16.

17 "I used to torture": Q&A with the Dalai Lama, University of California at Santa Barbara, February 24, 2009.

17 "I have memories": Quoted in Chhaya, p. 52.

20 "I'm packing": Quoted in Goodman, p. 13.

21 "Now that we had witnessed": Ibid., p. 14.

*Two*

## TO LHASA

24 What the Dalai Lama especially remembered: Dalai Lama, *Freedom,* p. 14.

24 "gargantuan mountains": Ibid., p. 13.

25 "as if I were in a great park": Dalai Lama, *My Land,* p. 33.

26 "huge monastery": Quoted in Hopkirk, p. 13.

26 "organized gold-bricking": *Life* magazine, April 6, 1959.

26 And one young monk: The reference is to Tashi Tsering's memoir *The Struggle for Modern Tibet.* Armonk, N.Y.: East Gate Books, 2000.

27–28 "the last temporal liberty": Dalai Lama, *Freedom,* p. 15.

28 "a solid, solemn": Quoted in Goodman, p. 64.

29 "So strong": Dalai Lama, *Freedom,* p. 19.

30 "I missed my mother": Quoted in Craig, p. 176.

31 "It was pitifully cold and ill-lit": Dalai Lama, *Freedom,* p. 21.

33 "My only interest was in playing": Q&A with the Dalai Lama, University of California at Santa Barbara, April 24, 2009.

34 "When he left after each visit": Dalai Lama, *Freedom,* p. 20.

34 "Those children": Quoted in Craig, p. 54.

34 "They unnerved me": Dalai Lama, *My Land,* p. 40.

35 "He laughed enthusiastically": Harrer, p. 250.

35 "From the first day": Dalai Lama and Carrièrre, p. 162.

37 "not yet human": Smith, p. 21.

37 "a mere puppet": Petech, p. 285.

38 "very often": Lixiong, Wang, "Reflections on Tibet." *New Left Review*, March–April 2002, p. 81.

38 "Many of them": Laird, p. 280.

## *Three*
## ACROSS THE GHOST RIVER

41–42 "[They] were held to be like butchers": Dalai Lama, *Freedom*, p. 52.

43 "liberate our compatriots": Quoted in Knaus, p. 47.

43 "What is meant": Norbu, Dawa, "The 1959 Tibetan Rebellion: An Interpretation." *China Quarterly*, no. 77 (March 1979), p. 90.

43 "The relationship": Quoted in Shakya, p. 70.

45 "When Great Heroes": Quoted in Chang, p. 14.

45 *Watch us kill*: Ibid., p. 54.

46 "The noblemen were getting truckloads": Interview with Gray Tuttle.

46 "The challenge filled me": Quoted in Levenson, *Tenzin Gyatso*, p. 78.

46 "If you don't make": Quoted in Goldstein, vol. 1, p. 705.

46 "I had to leave": Quoted in Craig, p. 78.

47 "began to realize": Ibid., p. 127.

47 "I could not believe": Dalai Lama, *Freedom*, p. 63.

49 "Some of your advisors": Quoted in Shakya, p. 81.

49 "He was isolated": Quoted in Strober, p. 107.

50 "If Tibet is to be saved": Quoted in Knaus, p. 97.

50 "Tibet will once again": Quoted in Shakya, p. 80.

51 "half convinced": Dalai Lama, *Freedom*, p. 66.

51 "Regardless of all the suspicion": Ibid., p. 67.

51 "What comes naturally": Quoted in Goldstein, vol. 2, p. 199.

51 "I had still had no theoretical training": Dalai Lama, *My Land*, p. 97.

51–52 "His Holiness is very humble": Quoted in Laird, p. 322.

52 "He thought people were so good": Interview with Tendzin Choegyal.

52 "Absolute selfishness": Chang, p. 14.

52 "Of course there are people": Ibid., p. 13.

53 "truly respect": Quoted in Goldstein, vol. 2, p. 180.

53 "When the Chinese first came": Tibet Oral History Project, testimony of Thupten Chonphel, interview #26.

53 "We had a saying": Interview with Topgay, Tibetan refugee and former security official in the Tibetan government-in-exile. Dharamsala, India, January 2009.

53 "Make every possible effort": Quoted in Shakya, p. 93.

54 "The more I looked": Dalai Lama, *Freedom*, p. 93.

54 "If you've ever been": Interview with Gray Tuttle.

54 "There is everywhere": Quoted in Shakya, p. 117.

55 "old and ruined": Dalai Lama interview with *Welt Online*, July 10, 2009.

55 "I felt": Dalai Lama, *Freedom*, p. 88.

55 "the pace of reform": Ibid., p. 89.

55 "How could he": Dalai Lama, *Freedom*, p. 99.

*Four*
## EASTERN FIRES

58 "We could not even look up": Tibet Oral History Project, testimony of Dorji Damdul (alias), interview #16.

58 "They would say": Ibid.

58 "The Chinese captured": Ibid.

58 "were brought on yaks": Ibid.

59 "most precious possession": Quoted in Feigon, p. 32.

59 "You never heard the name mentioned": Harrer, p. 93.

59 One Khampa refugee: Tibet Oral History Project.

59  As the buglers: Quoted in Dunham, p. 255.

60  "Many of our loved ones": Ibid., p. 207.

61  "Gyalo said": Athar's unpublished memoir, unpaginated.

61  "At one point": Ibid.

62  "I could see": Ibid.

62  "We pulled out": Ibid.

63  "A word from the Dalai Lama": Peissel, p. 70.

64  "When you have a piece": Quoted in Craig, p. 210.

64  "If I was recognized": Athar's unpublished memoir, unpaginated.

64  "We'd send a message": Interview with John Greaney.

65  Phala remembered: Volume 2 of an unpublished history of the Tibetan
     resistance movement by Lhamo Tsering, translated by Warren
     Smith, Jr. A rough draft of the relevent passage was published on
     mikeldunham.blogs.com.

66  "As things stand": *Indian Express*, December 15, 1958.

66  "an unguided missile": Interview with Ken Knaus.

66  "a constant source": Quoted in Craig, p. 180.

66  "My classmates were all talking": Interview with Tendzin Choegyal.

67  "What could happen?": Quoted in Goodman, p. 274.


*Five*

A RUMOR


70  This city: *Journal of the American Geographical Society of New York*,
     1905, vol. 37, p. 184.

72  "Hail to the liberation": Quoted in Dunham, p. 119.

72  "You are people who are lagging": Tibet Oral History Project, testimony
     of Sonam Dorjee, interview #86.

72  "No one could speak their mind": Quoted in Goodman, p. 274.

72  "Gradually, life in Lhasa:" Quoted in Tsering, p. 168.

73  "I would sacrifice": The quote, and details of the morning of March 10, are from an interview with Lobsang Yonten.

74  "It had been our painful experience": Dalai Lama, *My Land*, p. 165.

74  "By 1959": Interview with Narkyid.

74  "The Tibetans were out of their minds": Khetsun, p. 23.

75  "It is time": Quoted in Shakya, p. 187.

76  "Will you be responsible": Dalai Lama, *My Land*, p. 167.

77  "What are you doing?!": Quoted in Goodman, p. 295.

77  "I didn't know": Interview with Tendzin Choegyal.

78  "puffs of vapor": Gyatso, p. 49.

78  "All the people": Interview with Lobsang Yonten.

79  "I was surprised": Interview with Narkyid.

79  "Chamdo had disappeared": Gyatso, p. 50.

80  "Some in the crowd": Interview with Tenpa Soepa.

80  "Tibetans were angry": Interview with Pusang, former Tibetan army doctor and refugee. Dharmsala, India, January 2009.

81  "I remember saying": Quoted in Craig, p. 215.

82  "The Lhasan people": Dalai Lama, *My Land*, p. 173.

82  "From my window": Shan Chao, *Peking Review*, vol. 18, May 5, 1959.

82  And he secretly admired: Dalai Lama, *My Land*, p. 160.

82  The CIA agent Ken Knaus: Interview with Ken Knaus.

82–83  "I could feel the tension": Dalai Lama, *My Land*, p. 172.

84  "They are raising": Shan Chao, *Peking Review*, vol. 18, May 5, 1959.

84  "They were getting": Interview with Tendzin Choegyal.

85  His mother was growing frantic: For Diki Tsering's account of this day, see her memoir, *Dalai Lama, My Son*, pp. 168–72.

85–86  "Many officials": Shakya, p. 197.

86  "Reactionary elements": Quoted in Goodman, p. 296.

86  "You're too young": Interview with Lobsang Yonten.

87  One Tibetan doctor: Interview with Pusang.

87  "The main fear": Quoted in Patt, p. 145.

88  "She was very happy": Interview with Tendzin Choegyal.

88  "The officials kept saying": Interview with Lobsang Yonten.

90  "You're too young": Ibid.

91–92 "The loudspeakers were saying": Interview with Lobsang Norbu.

92  "I was a tough guy": Ibid.

92  "He pleaded with those": Interview with Lobsang Khunchok.

92  "My spiritual comrades": Ibid.

93  but they had essentially given up: Dunham, p. 201.

## *Six*
## FOREIGN BROTHERS

96  "I had an atlas": Dalai Lama, *My Land*, p. 57.

100  "I wanted to be like Moses": Patterson's story is taken from his memoir *Patterson of Tibet*.

102  "George," the British High Commissioner finally broke in: Ibid, p. 324.

103  Among them was: The sketch of Barber's career is drawn from his obituaries in the *Times*, the *Daily Mail*, and other London newspapers.

104  "Publicity," he notes: Interview with John Greaney.

105  "I went over": Interview with Ken Knaus.

105  "Des was very handsome": The portrait of FitzGerald is drawn largely from Thomas's *The Very Best Men*.

106  I must say: Quoted in Thomas, p. 198.

107  "The Tibetans were people fighting": Interview with Ken Knaus.

107  "They were very reverent": Ibid.

107  "the heartbeat of every Tibetan": Athar's unpublished memoir, unpaginated.

107  "Everybody wanted to be on the Task Force": Interview with John Greaney.

108  "One of the most romantic programs": Thomas, p. 276.

108  When Greaney was called: Interview with John Greaney.

109  "It was a flea biting an elephant": Thomas, p. 278.

109–10 The Khampas, who kept a photograph: From *The Shadow Circus: The CIA in Tibet*, a White Crane Films Production for BBC Television, 1998.

110  "We really felt": Athar's unpublished memoir, unpaginated.


*Seven*
## ACROSS THE KYICHU

112  "It looks as if": Shan Chao, *Peking Review*, vol. 18, May 5, 1959.

112  "The independent country": Norbu, *China's Tibet Policy*, p. 225.

114  "like a magnificent": Dalai Lama, *Freedom*, p. 214.

115  "down to the last": Ibid., p. 136.

115  "a blatant, outright fabrication": Quoted in Barber, *From the Land*, p. 110.

115  "Within the palace": Dalai Lama, *My Land*, p. 194.

116  "the odds against": Dalai Lama, *Freedom*, p. 136.

116  "I roamed all over": Interview with Tendzin Choegyal.

116  "He must have gotten it": Ibid.

116  "Everyone was anxious": Ibid.

118  "stitching bags": Ibid.

119  "I started saying good-bye": Ibid.

120  "I have no fear": Dalai Lama, *My Land*, p. 171.

122  "As I went out": Ibid., p. 198.

122  "the saddest sight": Barber, *From the Land*, p. 120.

123  "I felt like blacking out": Interview with Mingyur, by Lobsang Wangyal, Agence France-Presse, March 17, 2004.

123  "You are like ants": Quoted in Craig, p. 216.

124  "I needed to be very careful": Quoted in Laird, p. 335.

124  "I was certain": Dalai Lama, *Freedom*, p. 139.

124  "I don't know what": Interview with Tendzin Choegyal.

125 "All of a sudden": Interview with Tendzin Choegyal.

125 "He was young": Quoted in "Tibetan Officer Remembers 1959 Escape with Dalai Lama" by Matthias Williams. Reuters, March 12, 2009.

## *Eight*
## FLIGHT

127 "My feet grew numb": Interview with Tendzin Choegyal.

128 Later, he was ordered: Goodman, p. 308.

128 "It's OK": From *La Fuite du Dalaï Lama*, documentary film, France 2, 1999, directed by Marie Louville.

129 "rough and weary": Dalai Lama, *My Land*, p. 203.

129 "His saddle was slipping": Interview with Tendzin Choegyal.

129 "The ancient city": Dalai Lama, *Freedom*, p. 140.

129 "I was laughing": Interview with Tendzin Choegyal.

130 "The day after": Dalai Lama, *Freedom*, p. 99.

131 "Tendzin," he said: Quoted in Craig, p. 221.

132 "It was all new": Interview with Tendzin Choegyal.

132 "They knew beforehand": Dewatshang, p. 128.

133 "If we're going to use that bazooka": *La Fuite du Dalaï Lama*.

133 "I was surprised to see": Ibid.

134 "A great feeling": The story of Tenpa Soepa is drawn from an interview and his memoir *20 Years of My Life in China's Death Camp*.

## *Nine*
## THE NORBULINGKA

135 "I told them": Interview with Soepa.

135 "I felt that once": Ibid.

136 "The situation seemed delicate": Ibid.

137 "You don't have to ask": Shan Chao, *Peking Review*, vol. 18, May 5, 1959.

139 "I wasn't afraid": Interview with Lobsang Choenyi.

141 "A thick bunch": interview with Lobsang Yonten.

141 "Staying inside": Khetsun, p. 35.

142 "We lay there": Interview with Lobsang Yonten.

143 "Unless the Tibetans surrender": Quoted in Yonten, p. 26.

143 "I was extremely worried": Ibid., p. 25.

145 There was one man: Soepa, p. 32.

146 "The hill was very steep": Quoted in Strong, *When Serfs Stood Up*, p. 74.

147 "You must stay": Narkyid's story is drawn from an interview with the author.

151 "No account": The statement is contained in Hutheesing, unpaginated.

153 "I really can't begin": Ugyen's story is contained in Patrick French's *Tibet, Tibet*, pp. 177–85.

## Ten
## OPIM

156 "He told me": Ratuk Ngawang's story is drawn from an interview with the author.

157 "Don't play": Quoted in Goodman, p. 309.

158 "like running": John Greaney's account is drawn from an interview with the author.

160 "He particulalry wanted to see": French, p. 253.

161 "You could see": Athar's unpublished memoir, unpaginated.

## *Eleven*
## "GODLESS REDS VS. A LIVING GOD"

163 As the Dalai Lama: Patterson's account is drawn from his memoir *Patterson of Tibet* and an e-mail interview with the author.

164 "sword-swinging priests": New York *Daily News*, March 22, 1956.

165 "According to knowledgeable Tibetan sources": *Daily Telegraph*, April 15, 1959.

165 "I forgot my soup": Norbu's story is drawn from his memoir *Tibet Is My Country*, beginning on p. 259.

167 "An Inspiring Message": New York *Herald Tribune Magazine*, Late City Edition, March 22, 1959.

167 Outside the United Nations: The account of the Kalmuks is drawn from an article in the New York *Herald Tribune*, March 28, 1959.

168 "unspeakable brutalizing": Quoted in Hutheesing, unpaginated.

168 "These rebels": Ibid.

168 "The spirit of these reactionaries": Ibid.

169 "I was whisked": Barber's account is drawn from his two books on Tibet, *The Flight of the Dalai Lama* and *From the Land of Lost Content*.

169 "Very considerate of them": Barber, *The Flight of*, p. 102.

169 "It was one of the most wretched journeys": Ibid.

171 "unrest in the city": Barber, *From the Land*, p. 151.

172 "My worst fears": Dalai Lama, *Freedom*, p. 141.

172 "The Chinese would have considered": Quoted in Craig, p. 219.

172 "Why did the Chinese": Dalai Lama, *My Land*, p. 207.

## *Twelve*
## THE JOKHANG

176 "The Chinese were always ready": Narkyid's account of his escape is drawn from an interview with the author.

177 At the summer palace: Soepa's account of the battle for the Norbulingka is drawn from his memoir *20 Years in China's Death Camps* and an interview with the author.

177 "When the rebel bandits": Shan Chao, *Peking Review*, vol. 18, May 5, 1959.

178 "At dawn": Gyatso, p. 52.

179 One group of Sera monks: This account is drawn from an interview with Lobsang Norbu.

180 "Once three or four bullets": Interview with Narkyid.

181 Another young monk: *La Fuite du Dalaï Lama*.

184 "In order to encourage": Interview with Lobsang Yonten.

185 "I was hit": Interview with Pusang.

186 "I felt fulfilled": Interview with Lobsang Norbu.

186 "We had to leave her": Interview with Lobsang Yonten.

187 "As we passed": Yonten, p. 29.

189 "I remember": Quoted in Chhaya, p. 116.

189 "He performed a miracle": Interview with Lobsang Khunchok.

189 "broken beyond repair": Norbu, *Red Star*, p. 155.

## *Thirteen*
## LHUNTSE DZONG

192 "It is better to be": Quoted in Goodman, p. 310.

192 "I began": Dalai Lama, *Freedom*, p. 141.

193   The crimes of the upper-strata: From the compendium *Concerning the Question of Tibet*. Peking: Foreign Language Press, 1959.

193   "We have deep affection": Quoted in Barber, *From the Land*, p. 193.

193   "Through various intercepts": Quoted in Dunham, p. 301.

194   "It wouldn't have taken": Interview with John Greaney.

194   "We were told that we had to block": Tibet Oral History Project, testimony of Tashi (alias), interview #11.

195   "Eisenhower was delighted": Interview with Ken Knaus.

196   "So I got there": Interview with John Greaney.

198   "We were paupers": Interview with Tendzin Choegyal.

199   "We had difficulties": Dalai Lama, interview, CNN, April 2, 2009.

200   "biplane, flying low": Levenson, *Tenzin Gyatso*, p. 4.

200   "If it was Chinese": Dalai Lama, *Freedom*, p. 142.

200   "Be quiet": *La Fuite du Dalaï Lama*.

201   "The ancient city": Quoted in Barber, *From the Land*, p. 213.

*Fourteen*
## IN TIBETAN PRISONS

203   One pregnant Tibetan: Interview with Choekyi Namseling.

204   "We used to get so scared": Ibid.

204   "We were kept in a small cell": Interview with Lobsang Choenyi.

204   In one Tibetan army division: Interview with Pusang.

205   "The whole city": Ibid.

205   "When the bullet": Interview with Lobsang Norbu.

206   Some who lived: These accounts of the escape are taken from the interviews of the Tibet Oral History Project.

206   "There is no need": From the account of Ani Pachen in *Women at War*, ed. Daniela Giosefi. New York: Feminist Press at CUNY, 2nd ed., 2003.

206 "The Chinese were pursuing": Tibet Oral History Project, testimony of Thupten Chonphel, interview #26.

206 In the stony village: Tibet Oral History Project, testimony of Cho Lhamo, interview #92.

208 In southern Tibet: Tibet Oral History Project, testimony of Norbu Dhondup, interview #6.

209 As Lhasa fell: Soepa's continuing account is taken from his memoir and an interview with the author.

## Fifteen
## THE LAST BORDER

212 "There were very few houses": Interview with Tendzin Choegyal.

212 "in a daze of sickness": Quoted in Craig, p. 224.

213 "That was a powerful moment": Quoted in Strober, p. 113.

213 "We didn't have to pull": Interview with Tendzin Choegyal.

214 "It was a reality check": Ibid.

214 "He got experience": Interview with Narkyid.

214 "You discover a cynical brutality": Dalai Lama and Carrière, p. 162.

216 "It forced me": Interview with Tendzin Choegyal.

216 The race for the story: George Patterson's continuing account is drawn from his memoir *Patterson of Tibet* and an e-mail interview with the author.

217 "briefly, the news capital": *New Yorker*, December 10, 1960.

218 "Fiction is what they want": Donald S. Connery, "Waiting for the God King," *Atlantic*, March 1960, pp. 61–64.

221 "I don't think he ever covered": E-mail interview with Jeffrey Blyth.

221 "the people of India": Quoted in Craig, p. 227.

222 "I was so worried": Quoted in Hutheesing, unpaginated.

222 "He seemed": Quoted in Strober, p. 132.

222 "the Tibetans, particularly the Khampas": Quoted in Roberts, p. 61.

224  "You can't have": Quoted in Shakya, p. 153.

224  "even if": Ibid., p. 155.

224–25  "The events in Tibet": From "Memorandum of Conversation of N.S. Khrushchev and Mao Zedong." The Cold War International History Project, Virtual Archive, Woodrow Wilson International Center for Scholars.


*Sixteen*
## MEETING A POET

228  "I have heard": from Patterson, *Patterson of Tibet*, epigraph.

228  "they were a far worthier": Patterson, *Requiem for Tibet*, p. 191.

229  "suicidally down": Ibid., p. 202.

229  "We were overjoyed": Interview with John Greaney.

230  "They were incredibly disappointed": Interview with Ken Knaus.

231  "Peace, peace": Quoted in French, p. 253.

231  "I have no regret": Interview with Lobsang Norbu.

232  "I suffered": Interview with Lobsang Yonten.

232  "On the way to the toilet": Yonten, p. 41.

232  After his capture: Soepa's story is drawn from his memoir and an interview with the author.

234  A military doctor: Interview with Pusang.

236  The Tibet scholar: French, p. 282.

237  "I went on": Dalai Lama, *Freedom*, p. 147.

237  The most revealing look: Dom Moraes, "Curious Conversation with the Dalai Lama," *Harper's*, July 1960, pp. 65–68.

239  "Given the significance": The Dalai Lama's speech to the Second Gulag Conference, December 6, 2000, Dharamsala, India.

240  "Nowadays, when I": Interview with Lobsang Norbu.

241  "He said that the Chinese": Interview with Topgay.

241 "There is a Tibetan saying": Q&A with Dalai Lama, Boston, May 2, 2009.

242 "A few days ago": Interview, BBC China, February 4, 2003.

242 "The refugee status": Q&A with Dalai Lama, Boston, May 2, 2009.

243 "Brute force": Dalai Lama, *In My Own Words*, p. 174.

243 "His exile was huge": Interview with Paul Hopkins.

244 "It had been": Tibet Oral History Project, testimony of Norbu Dhondup, interview #6.

244 "When, at some point": Dalai Lama, *Essential Writings*, p. 76.


## Epilogue
## BONFIRES

249 "Even the high-ranking": Interview with Gray Tuttle.

250 Sharma: Author's note: "Sharma" is a pseudonym.

250 "You have to pretend": Interview with Robert Barnett, *Foreign Policy*, April 3, 2008.

251 "We are helping": Quoted in Laird, p. 350.

254–55 Many others, perhaps hundreds: Jane Macarthey, "Tibetan Monasteries Empty as China Jails Monks to Silence Olympic Protests," *The Times* (UK), July 7, 2008.

255 The Chinese had drained: Ibid.

# ACKNOWLEDGMENTS

For advice and access to key materials, thanks to Lisa Cathey of the "CIA in Tibet" project; Marie Louville; Marcella Adamski of the Tibet Oral History Project; the Dalai Lama's Private Office in Dharamsala; and the staff of the Library of Tibetan Works and Archives. Doma Norbu kindly allowed me to quote from the unpublished memoir of her father, Athar Norbu. Rebecca and Ronny Novick of thetibetconnection.org were unfailingly generous and helpful in my visit to Dharamsala. My tranlators Cosme J. Navarro, Phurbu Thinley, and the invaluable Chempa helped me understand the stories of the Tibetans I interviewed. My editors at Crown, Julian Pavia and Rick Horgan, honed the manuscript to a fine edge. My agent, Scott Waxman, spotted the potential in the story at the very beginning. And Jim and Mary Beth Talty provided encouragement, laughter, and nutritious meals when sorely needed.

I'd like to especially acknowledge the contribution of the many Tibetan survivors of the uprising who invited me into their homes. Their accounts were a clear window onto an often searing past.

And, as always, Mariekarl, Asher, and Delphine were the reward at the end of the day.

# INDEX

Greaney, John (*cont.*)
   the Great Fifth, political genius of, 37
Great Leader. *See* Mao Zedong
"Great Peacock," 25
Great Prayer Festival, 69
Great White Case Officer, 108
guerrillas. *See* Tibetan Task Force
Gusri Khan, 37
Gyalo Thondup (brother)
   anticipates genocide, 168
   favors rejecting Seventeen Point
      Agreement, 50
   part of CIA Tibetan Task Force, 61
   personality of, 66
Gyatso, Palden
   *Fire Under the Snow,* 231

*H*

Halliday, Jon, 52
Halpern, Frank, 109
Han migrants, 252–253
Happy Valley, *126f,* 127
Harrer, Heinrich
   declares T Lobsang Rampa a fraud, 99
   describes the Fourteenth, 36
   on Khampas, 59
   *Seven Years in Tibet,* 35
Hilton, James
   *Lost Horizon,* 98

Hopkins, Paul Jeffrey, 243, 258
horses, 133
Hoskin, Cyril Henry, 99
Hunt, E. Howard, 105

*I*

ignorance, in Buddhist philosophy, 31
"impure bones," 42
India. *See also* Nehru, Jawaharlal
   asylum requested, 195–196
   escape route to, *126*
   fails to support Tibet, 48
   journalists in, 216–218
"Instant Enthusiast," 105
intoxicating air, 13–14
"inviting the clothes" ceremony, 8
"Island of the Dead," 61

*J*

Jiang Zemin, 224
Jokhang Temple
   in 2009, 248
   attacked by PLA, 149–150, 180–181
   rebel headquarters and refugee
      station, 147

## W

Wangye, Geshe, 158–159, 160
westerners as *Tendra,* 9
women, Tibetan, 91, 181, 203–204
women's association march, 138–139

becomes a gunrunner, 142–143
becomes volunteer guard at palace,
86–87, 89
captured attempting to flee,
186–187
exile in India, 240
in Ngachen labor camp, 231–232

## Y

yeti, 98
Yonten

## Z

Zhou Enlai, 192, 224